signing

HOW TO SPEAK WITH YOUR HANDS

signing

HOW TO SPEAK WITH YOUR HANDS

ELAINE COSTELLO
Illustrated by Lois A. Lehman

BANTAM BOOKS

TORONTO • NEW YORK • LONDON • SYDNEY • AUCKLAND

SIGNING: HOW TO SPEAK WITH YOUR HANDS
A Bantam Book / April 1983

Library of Congress Cataloging in Publication Data

Costello, Elaine.
Signing: how to speak with your hands.

Includes index.
1. Sign language. I. Lehman, Lois A. II. Title.
HV2474.C67   1983   419   82-45947
ISBN 0-553-01458-7 (pbk.)

Published simultaneously in the United States and Canada

PRINTED IN THE UNITED STATES OF AMERICA
SEM   14 13 12 11 10 9 8 7 6 5

contents

acknowledgments

Deep appreciation is due to many people who helped bring this book to completion. Foremost is Gabriel Fontana, who had faith in my ability to do it and applauded as each milestone in the book's completion was passed. He made available the staff and facilities of Fontana Lithograph, Inc. and lent many personal hours in processing photographs, organizing sections, and generally lending support and aid.

Without the talent of the artist, Lois Lehman, this book would not have been completed. She gave the book credibility and beauty at the same time through her incredible skill.

The critical molding provided by consultants has insured the book's accuracy. Gerald Buisson and Margaret Buisson reviewed early illustrations and assisted in developing the sign descriptions. Harry Hoemann and Larry Berke provided the final reviews to assure that all aspects of the book were linguistically sound.

This book might well be considered a family project since it took precedence over other aspects of family life while it was being developed. My daughters, Jennifer, Maria, and Laura, cleaned house, cooked meals, and otherwise provided for themselves when Mom was engrossed in writing. They typed rough drafts, sorted illustrations, developed photographs, and even moved the typewriter and boxes of resource materials along on family vacations.

The sign models illustrated in this book provided much more than their likenesses. They served the dual role of posing for endless photographs and of providing consultation in determining the most representative signs to use. Their names are listed below in grateful recognition.

Sign Models

Karen M. Barnes

John S. Borum, Jr.

Clifford P. Bruffey

Ruth A. Bruffey

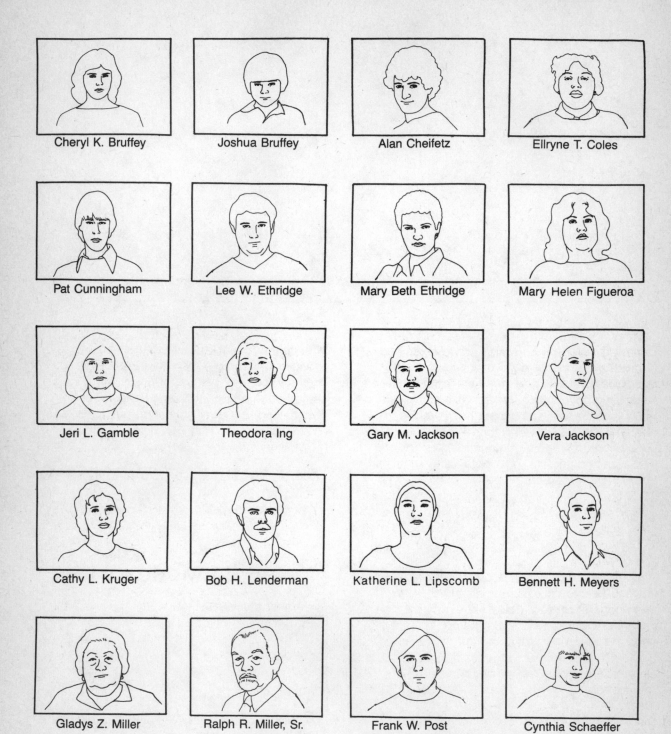

Cheryl K. Bruffey   Joshua Bruffey   Alan Cheifetz   Ellryne T. Coles

Pat Cunningham   Lee W. Ethridge   Mary Beth Ethridge   Mary Helen Figueroa

Jeri L. Gamble   Theodora Ing   Gary M. Jackson   Vera Jackson

Cathy L. Kruger   Bob H. Lenderman   Katherine L. Lipscomb   Bennett H. Meyers

Gladys Z. Miller   Ralph R. Miller, Sr.   Frank W. Post   Cynthia Schaeffer

Melinda J. Smith

introduction

In recent years sign language has shown an amazing growth in popularity. Thousands of individuals of all ages are discovering that the study of sign language can be a fascinating and rewarding adventure. *Signing: How to Speak With Your Hands* is designed to assist you in learning this vibrant, expressive language which is used by deaf people throughout North America.

This book makes sign language study easier in many ways. It presents manageable amounts of new sign vocabulary within logical topical groupings. The illustrations are large and clear, presenting the full upper torso of the body so that the new signer can accurately duplicate the sign. Even though it is difficult to isolate any sign from its context, Lois Lehman has achieved a rare degree of accuracy in rendering each sign the way it is most commonly performed.

At the beginning of each chapter, linguistic principles are described which will broaden the use of the sign vocabulary presented in the book. This information about the structure of sign language comes from recent research into its grammatical features. Incorporating these principles into your signing will help you master the language as it is used by deaf people.

This book does not contain all of the signs available in sign language. These 1,200 basic signs will provide enough vocabulary to express a vast number of ideas when coupled with the linguistic principles which are included. To use sign language fluently, you will find it necessary to practice your new skills with other signers. The more you associate with deaf people, the easier it will become for you to send and receive information through sign language.

Introduction to Deafness

In the United States it is estimated that sixteen million people have hearing losses of varying degrees of severity. Of this number, approximately two million individuals have hearing losses severe enough to be considered deaf. That is, they cannot hear or understand either speech or most of the sounds in the everyday environment, even with the help of a hearing aid. This population is comprised both of persons who have been deaf since infancy and persons who have lost their hearing later in life. Some of the causes of deafness are heredity, illness, physical abnormalities, trauma to the skull or ear, certain heavy medications, and, most common, loss of hearing acuity due to age. Hearing losses which are caused by diseases or obstructions in the outer ear can sometimes be corrected by surgery or a hearing aid. Hearing losses which result from damage to the delicate sensory cells of the inner ear or to the auditory nerve to the brain are usually not candidates for surgery, and hearing aids cannot repair the damage.

Problems in the use of the English language typically persist throughout a deaf person's life. Those who lose their hearing in infancy or at birth usually do not benefit from language stimulation from their parents and siblings during the early years when language is acquired. However, by learning sign language, deaf children can acquire the language base which will assist in the acquisition of English as a second language. People who lose their hearing after acquiring English language skills have less of an academic handicap than those with mild hearing losses.

Deaf people are employed in almost every occupational field. They drive cars, get married, buy homes, and have children, much like everyone else. Because of communication factors, many deaf people are more comfortable in association with other deaf people. They tend to marry other deaf people whom they have met at schools for the deaf or at the deaf clubs. Most deaf couples have hearing children who learn sign language early in life to communicate with their parents. Deaf people often have special electronics and telecommunication equipment in their homes. Captioning decoders may be on their televisions. Electrical hook-ups may flash lights to indicate when the baby is crying, the doorbell is ringing, or the alarm clock is going off. Modern versions of teletype equipment permit deaf people to be in contact with other deaf people through the telephone system.

When deaf people have difficulty communicating with hearing people, they will often write notes to them. Some deaf people are able to speechread, that is, to understand the mouth movements and facial expressions of a hearing person to comprehend what is said; but most deaf people have limited speechreading skill, which is said to convey at best only about 50 percent of the communicated information. In educational, medical, or legal situations, when detailed information must be understood, deaf people will often enlist the aid of a certified sign language interpreter who will translate the spoken English information into sign language and then vocalize in English what the deaf person wishes to say.

What is Sign Language?

Sign language is a visual-gestural system of communication. It is the native language of deaf people and was created by deaf people for the purpose of communicating with each other. Within the deaf community sign language is learned naturally as a first language from childhood. However, unlike most languages, sign language is more often passed on from child to child rather than from parent to child. This is because 90 percent of deaf children are born to hearing parents who do not know sign language. It has been shown that in isolated locations where there is no formal sign language, deaf people will create their own visual-gestural language to communicate. Few hearing people master sign language fluency because for them, spoken languages are learned during the formative years of language acquisition, and sign language is learned as a second language with great effort. Hearing children whose parents are deaf learn sign language naturally and often become excellent interpreters.

The term "sign language" is used to describe all forms of manual communication. In this book, however, sign language will refer to American Sign Language, the language used by approximately one-half million deaf people in the United States and Canada. Not all deaf people use American Sign Language, but those who do share a common language bond which makes them members in the "deaf community." The deaf community, like other sub-cultures, is comprised of people who share common values, experiences, and, most important, a common language, which becomes their primary identifying feature. Members of the deaf community, regardless of the severity of their hearing loss, must know and use American Sign Language in order to be included. Their language becomes the vehicle by which experiences are shared and passed on.

Nothing is known of sign language use in the United States prior to 1815. At that time, it was estimated that there were approximately 2,000 deaf people in the United States. Certainly, as demonstrated by other isolated cultures, those deaf people had established a sign language system for communicating with each other. Whether they developed it themselves or brought it from Europe is not known, but it is estimated that approximately 40 percent of American Sign Language today may be related to those early colonial signs.

In 1815, Thomas Hopkins Gallaudet went to Europe to study methods for instructing deaf individuals. His first stop was England. There he was discouraged from learning the English methods because his instructors wanted him to stay for a long period of time to work with them; he had neither the time nor the money for an extended stay. During the time he was negotiating with the English experts, Gallaudet saw a demonstration by a visiting French lecturer, Abbé Sicard. He was so impressed by Sicard's method that he traveled to France to study with him. Gallaudet returned to the United States with a new found knowledge of French signs and a deaf Frenchman, Laurent Clerc, who became the first teacher of the deaf in the United States. During his forty years of teaching, Clerc had great influence on shaping the language used by deaf Americans. American Sign Language is heavily based on French Sign Language, with approximately 60 percent of present day signs having their origins from the French.

American Sign Language is one of the most complete sign systems in the world. Most countries, however, have their own sign languages which have been refined and standardized with varying degrees of sophistication. A deaf person traveling abroad would not immediately be conversant with a deaf person in another country without studying the sign language of that country, although communication barriers between different sign languages seem to be crossed more easily than those of spoken languages.

In an attempt to encourage international sign language communication, the World Federation of the Deaf is developing an international sign language called Gestuno. The lexicon of Gestuno consists of signs chosen by an international committee. The signs are not invented, but are selected from existing sign systems. Although Gestuno is intended for

interpreting at international meetings, few deaf or hearing people know it well. Also the number of signs presently available is so limited that a great many concepts cannot be expressed. It is doubtful that Gestuno will become a full-fledged language because of the absence of grammatical rules. Each signer is permitted to use the vocabulary of Gestuno within the syntax of his or her local language. Also, since it is not used by the deaf community in any country, it will never be a living language, learned and passed on from generation to generation.

Hearing people frequently study the signs from American Sign Language without studying the grammar of the language, and then use the signs in the syntactical order of their own verbal language. This mixture of spoken and gestural language leads to the creation of "pidgin" language systems which have been formalized by some educators. Instead of signs representing concepts, as originally intended, signs are used to represent the meanings of English words. Using signs within an English syntax provides a visual way for deaf children to learn English. Also, since this language (called "Sign English") is easier for hearing people to acquire than American Sign Language, it provides a valuable communication link between hearing and deaf people. Because deaf people are familiar with the difficulty hearing people experience in trying to learn their language, they will try to accommodate by dropping many aspects of sign language's grammar and assuming the syntax of English themselves. This process is called "code-switching" and is the reason why deaf people often begin a conversation by asking whether the other person is deaf or hearing.

Signs perform a function in sign language similar to the function of words in spoken languages. Just as words are comprised of units which work together in various ways to make each word unique from other words, so also there are four units which comprise each sign to make each one unique. These four units are its (1) handshape, (2) palm orientation, (3) movement, and (4) the locations where these occur. An omission or alteration of any one of the four parts may cause the sign to become a completely different sign. In addition to these four parts which comprise the manual characteristics of a sign, there are non-manual characteristics as well. The non-manual characteristics include movements of the face, eyes, head, and body posture. As the hands execute a given sign, specific non-manual body behavior can simultaneously change the meaning or emphasis of that sign. Some simple examples of non-manual signals include the raising of an eyebrow to indicate a question and the shaking of the head to express a negative condition. A study of the linguistics of American Sign Language would reveal many more sophisticated uses of non-manual signals which can be incorporated into the meaning of a sign.

The Terminology of Sign Language

Some of the terms of sign language need clarification in order to be used correctly. First, it is correct to say that you are learning *sign language* or learning *to sign* no matter what variety of sign language is meant. It is also all right to say that you are learning manual communication, but it is not as common. Generally, it is not acceptable to refer to sign language as *hand signs* or *gestures,* since these terms do not give sign language credit for being a true language. The lexicon within sign language is referred to as *signs.* If you are specifying the native language used by deaf people in the deaf community, use *American Sign Language* or its nicknames *Ameslan* or *ASL.*

The translation of a sign is referred to linguistically as its gloss, or equivalent, in English. Often a gloss has several English words to explain the concept that the sign represents. For example, one sign which brings both extended index fingers in an arc motion from the right shoulder to pointing forward, palms up, has a three-word English gloss: "up-till-now."

In educational settings, the terms *total communication, Sign English, Manual English,* and *fingerspelling* are often used. "Total communication" is a philosophical declaration that it is the right of each deaf individual to have access to information through any and all modes available. The possible modes are aural stimulation when there is residual hearing, speechreading, written forms, gestures, facial expression, sign language, and fingerspelling. The philosophy states that neglecting to provide a deaf child with any of these avenues may prohibit the child from full language development.

"Sign English" (not to be confused with Signed English) is the use of signs from American Sign Language within an English syntactical order. It is the sign language form with which hearing people are most familiar. It is not recognized as a true language, but rather a pidgin language, a blending of two distinct languages, retaining some of the characteristics of each. Generally when using Sign English, a hearing person will speak while signing; much of the facial expression characteristic of American Sign Language is thus lost. In using Sign English, word endings, tense, articles, and plurality as we know them in English are not used. Because Sign English is not a true language, there are no established linguistic rules which govern it. It may take many forms leaning toward a heavy influence of either American Sign Language or of English, depending on the person using it. Its purpose is to facilitate communication between deaf people and hearing people.

"Manual English" is a generic classification for various sign systems which have been invented to replicate English exactly through signs. Some of the most common Manual English systems include Signed English, Seeing Essential English (SEE I), Seeing Exact English (SEE II), and Linguistics of Visual English (LOVE). All of these systems function as a visual representation of the English language. Many of the signs borrowed from American Sign Language are modified by adding the fingerspelled handshape of the first letter of the English gloss. For example, the sign for the concepts "listen," "hear," "ear," and "sound" are the same; however, in Manual English, the sign would be produced with an "l" handshape for "listen," an "h" handshape for "hear," and so forth. In this way, the sign vocabulary is increased and further clarified. Manual English is not considered a language but rather an invented code. Each Manual English system has a code, or set of rules, by which it represents the vocabulary and structure of English. The major complaint about these systems is that they change the natural function of signs to represent concepts and force them to function like English words, often violating the intent of the original signs. Invented affixes, articles, and other devices are used to specify tense, plurality, and other inflectional variations. For example, in the Signed English system a movement of the "i" handshape, palm forward, from left to right at the end of a verb sign, means that it is the "ing" form, e.g., "walk" becomes "walking." Inventors of these systems refer to them as teaching tools to be used in instructional settings and at home to increase the deaf user's knowledge of English.

"Fingerspelling," or representing each letter of each word with a specific hand configuration, is the only system for making English utterances completely visible. It has, ideally, one-to-one equivalence for sequential alphabetical symbols as found in words. It can be produced rapidly enough to keep pace with normal speaking, but it involves a high degree of concentration for both the sender and the receiver. The primary objection to the method is that it depends highly on reading skills which are not normally acquired by a young child until past the formative period of language acquisition, when language is most easily acquired with ease as a natural language. On the positive side, few aspects of English grammar are forfeited. Fingerspelling is more frequently used as a supplement to other sign systems than as a method of its own. It is usually used for those concepts which have no formal sign existing in sign language. Learning to fingerspell is more difficult than learning signs for most people, but it is worth learning first because it can greatly expand any signer's ability to communicate.

Learning to Sign

Sign language is a beautiful and expressive way of communicating. Many signs are natural gestures. Other signs are based on some characteristic of the sign's concept. For example, for

the sign "cup," one hand represents a saucer and the other hand encircles the shape of a cup. The relationship between the sign and what it represents is called its "iconicity," and it is this iconicity which makes sign language easier to learn. Research into each sign's origin would probably reveal more signs are iconically based on French than is presently thought. Because such research has not been done to date, it was not possible to include in this book the origins of many signs, though sometimes the origins are fairly easy to guess or are well known. For example, a charming nineteenth-century flavor is evident in the signs for "girl," where the thumb traces the outline of a bonnet string, and for "boy," where the fingers tip an imaginary cap. The signs for "gentleman" and "lady" include the thumb coming up and fluffing the ruffles worn on shirts and blouses in earlier days. Knowing these historical origins contributes to the fun of learning sign language.

The only way to become proficient at sign language is to use it, preferably with deaf people. If this is not possible, you should practice with other hearing people. Most hearing people learning to sign will use the signs from American Sign Language combined with an English syntax, matching each sign with an equivalent English word within the sentence. Sign language is not so very difficult to learn; in fact, a sign language student can probably express simple thoughts after only a lesson or two. However, total proficiency in American Sign Language as used by native signers will probably take years and years of study and practice.

Deaf people are usually pleased at a hearing person's attempts at sign language communication. They are patient and willing to assist. They are cognizant that hearing people use signs within an English syntax, and because they are familiar with English, they will often slow down and use signs in English order, too. You should not be hesitant to try out your limited sign language skill; you will be delighted at the encouragement you will get from deaf people for your efforts.

Here are some suggestions to help you use sign language in a natural way. Remember that a good signer incorporates facial expression and body language into what is said. Weave signs in with natural expressive gestures to be most effective. The normal signing space extends from the top of the head to the waist, extending laterally from shoulder to shoulder. Hold your hands comfortably at chest level when you are in between signs. Whether or not you are considered a good signer will be judged by a number of factors. Clarity and accuracy of producing the sign, smoothness, rhythm, and speed of production will all contribute to your skill. The only way that skill can be developed is through practice with other people. If you speak while signing, keep an even flow of speed between the vocal and manual languages.

How the Signs Were Selected for This Book

Ten years ago, it was estimated that there were between 1,500 to 2,000 formal signs which comprised all of the American Sign Language's lexicon. However, in the same way that spoken languages increase in vocabulary, sign language is a living, growing language. New signs have developed, some of which have been accepted by deaf people as part of their language, and some of which are used only by selected groups in selected environments. For example, new technology has created a need for signs to represent equipment and processes not dreamed of in earlier years. In a work environment, deaf employees may invent signs to facilitate their communication on the job. Then in describing their jobs to friends at the local deaf club, the new signs might be used and picked up by a wider circle of the deaf community. As those people take the signs home and use them, and, perhaps, use them as they travel, the signs may or may not become assimilated into the language.

The process of how new signs are developed demonstrates why sign language has variations. The variations include "home signs," that is those used within an individual family unit, local variations, as described above, and regional variations. The variations might well be thought of as dialects, not right or wrong, but simply different ways of saying the same thing—just as

there are different regional pronounciations of English words like "tomato" and "aunt."

The signs displayed in this book are those which are basic to everyday conversations. Although some arbitrary decisions were made as to which variation of a sign was included, most decisions were based on how clearly the alternatives could be illustrated and which signs the models and artist preferred to use. It is logical that because the book was developed in Washington, D.C., many of the signs reflect usage in that area. As much as possible, specific regional signs were omitted; but, sometimes it is difficult to judge whether a sign has achieved national acceptance or not.

How to Use This Book

The signs in this book have been grouped by topics for two reasons. The topics comprise a manageable number of signs which might easily be learned by a student in a single sitting. Second, signs within a category often share certain aspects of forming them that will assist the learner in remembering them. If the book is to be used as a dictionary or a resource manual, the index in the back will become an indispensable aid. The alphabetical listing of the English glosses in the index will give quick and easy access to any sign in the book.

At the beginning of each of the thirteen chapters are grammatical notes closely associated with the signs in that chapter. They will give the reader insight into many of the linguistic rules which govern American Sign Language. These notes are not meant to be definitive, but to provide basic information which will integrate the sign vocabulary into a living, expressive language known and cherished by deaf people.

It is not possible to depict signs on paper without the use of arrows and explanations. The sign illustrations in this book use multiple images along with arrows to describe the sign formation and movement as accurately as possible. In order to keep the drawings uncluttered, a simple system was used: "1" and "2" to indicate the sequence in which the parts of a compound sign are formed, and "a" and "b" to indicate a change of hand position in a sign. The written explanations further clarify the sign production. The descriptions also specify whether the sign is to be produced with a single movement, or whether it is to be repeated, which is often the factor distinguishing two signs from each other. For example, hitting the bent fingertips of the right hand into the left palm once is the sign "again"; however, hitting them twice is the sign "often."

The hints given under many of the illustrations are simply that: mnemonic clues which will help the sign language learner in recalling the sign during the learning process. Some of the hints might reflect the sign's origin, but no attempt was made to research or explain the derivation of the sign.

Most of the illustrations present the front view of the signer. This means that the illustrations are reversed from the way you would perform them yourself. For clarity's sake, some of the signs are drawn from a three-quarter view. All illustrations show a right-handed signer, and the descriptions are written for persons with a right-hand dominance. Left-handed signers should reverse the signs.

This book has deliberately avoided presenting the English gloss within a sample English sentence. Giving an English sentence may mislead the reader regarding the actual field of meaning intended by the sign. More correctly, the sign should be presented in a glossed American Sign Language sentence, but such a strategy would take more instruction than can be included in a book of this size.

Now It's Your Turn

Now you are ready to learn sign language, that wonderful, unique language that uses space and movement for the purpose of communication. It is a language that carries dignity and demands respect as the native language of the deaf community. This book is dedicated to you who are willing to make the effort to learn to communicate with deaf people. You will experience considerable satisfaction as your signing skill grows. Use every opportunity to practice your skills with deaf people and observe firsthand the fullness of the language. As your skills grow so will your appreciation of the complexity and richness of the language. May your learning of sign language be an enjoyable experience.

glossary

American Sign Language—The language system created and used by deaf people in North America. It is also known as ASL and Ameslan and has its roots in French Sign Language.

code-switching—electing to use a particular sign language variety according to the signing ability of the conversant.

deaf—a hearing loss so severe that a person cannot hear or understand speech or sounds.

deaf community—a cultural group of hearing impaired people who share a common language, values, attitude, and experiences.

fingerspelling—the spelling out of words and sentences one letter at a time on the hands using the manual alphabet.

gesture—an expressive bodily movement for the purpose of communication.

gloss—the translation of a sign into the English word or words which represent the same concept.

grammar—the structure and rules which govern a language.

hearing impaired—a generic term which describes all levels of hearing loss from very mild losses to severe.

iconicity—the characteristic of some signs which relates to the resemblance between a sign and what it represents. Those signs which resemble what they represent are said to be "iconic" or "transparent."

initialized sign—a sign that is formed with the handshape from the manual alphabet which corresponds to the first letter of the English word which has a similar meaning.

interpreting—the changing of spoken language into sign language; "reverse interpreting" is using spoken language to express what is said in sign language. "Transliteration" is also sometimes used to describe the translation process between oral and sign languages.

language—a system of arbitrary symbols and grammatical rules which are used for communication and to pass culture to future generations.

linguistics—the scientific study of a language including its acquisition by children, its grammar, and how people use it.

lexicon—the vocabulary of a language.

manual alphabet—the representation of each letter of the written alphabet with distinct handshapes.

manual communication—the generic term used to refer to any form of signing communication including sign language, fingerspelling, and the systems which use signs to represent English.

Manual English—a generic term for the various sign systems which have been invented as a visual representation of the English language using signs. The most familiar Manual English systems are Signed English, Seeing Exact English, Seeing Essential English, and the Linguistics of Visual English.

native language—the first language of a person, usually learned through assimilation from infancy through interaction with parents.

pidgin language—a language variety which shares a combination of vocabulary and grammar of two distinct languages. A pidgin language usually develops naturally when two groups of people do not share a common language but desire to communicate with each other.

sign—a unit of sign language which represents a concept. A sign is made with either one or both hands formed in distinctive handshapes. The sign also has a location, orientation, and movement which are peculiar to it.

Sign English—the use of signs from American Sign Language within an English syntactic order. Sign English is a pidgin language which may take many forms, leaning toward a heavy influence of either American Sign Language or of English, depending on the person using it.

signer—the person using sign language.

speechreading—the ability to comprehend spoken language through observation of the speaker's lip movements and facial expression. It is also known as "lipreading."

total communication—the philosophy that each deaf individual has the right to have access to information through any and all input modes, including aural stimulation, speechreading, written forms, gestures, facial expression, sign language, and fingerspelling.

variations—differences in production, vocabulary, or grammar of a language due to factors such as geographic area, racial or ethnic influences, age, sex, and education.

signing

HOW TO SPEAK WITH YOUR HANDS

one

THE BASICS

Common Phrases
Questions
Negatives
The Manual Alphabet

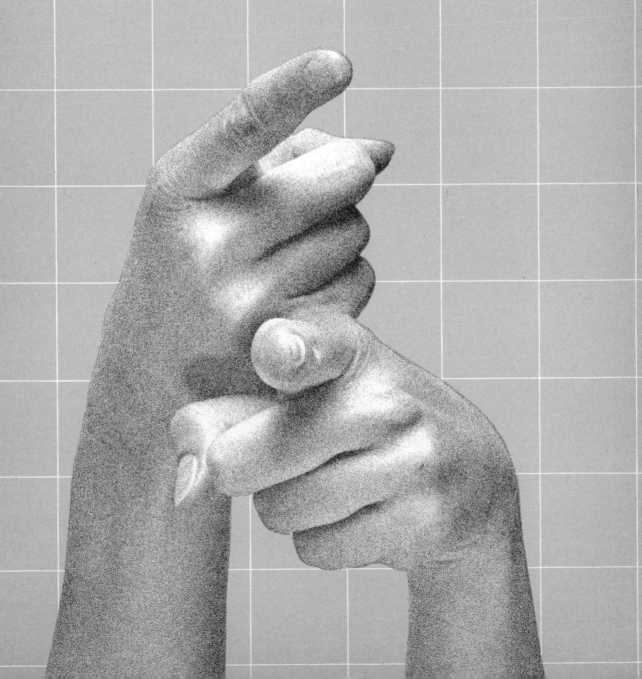

FINGERSPELLING

Fingerspelling is the spelling out of words and sentences one letter at a time on the hands using the manual alphabet. The manual alphabet has 26 distinct hand configurations to represent each letter of the alphabet. Combining them together in smooth succession makes it possible to express and receive ideas. Fingerspelling is used in sign language sentences as a supplement to express ideas for which there are no formal signs, such as proper names and technical terms. Fingerspelling is produced at a comfortable position near the chin with the palm facing out.

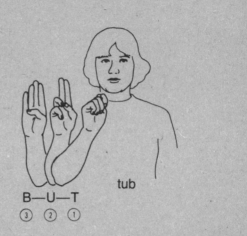

tub

B—U—T
③ ② ①

QUESTIONS

Body language is an important part of asking a question. With a quizzical facial expression, lean forward while asking the question, and hold the last sign a little longer than usual. A question mark may be added at the beginning or end of some questions.

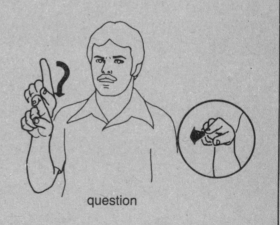

question

NEGATIVES

Some signs, such as "nothing" and "not," can be used to make a sentence negative. For example, "not" plus "honest" becomes "dishonest." Usually a negative sentence is accompanied by a side to side headshake. Other facial cues such as squeezing the eyebrows together, pinching the lips, and sucking the breath can further modify the negated sign to show sincerity, surprise, concern, anger, or other information.

Some signs become negative by a deliberate twisting outward of the wrist. Examples of these signs are "want," "like," and "know."

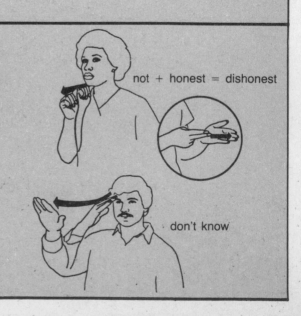

not + honest = dishonest

don't know

Common Phrases

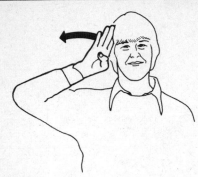

HELLO, HI
Start with the index finger of the "b" hand at the right temple, palm forward and fingers pointing up. Bring the hand outward to the right with a deliberate movement.
Hint: Saluting a greeting.

GOOD MORNING.
Bring the fingertips of the right open hand, palm facing chin, down and away from the mouth. Then bring the right hand upward from waist level, palm facing up, with the fingertips of the left open hand in the crook of the right elbow.
Hint: "Good" plus "morning."

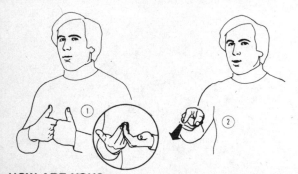

HOW ARE YOU?
With the fingertips of both bent hands touching the chest, palms facing the body and the knuckles touching each other, move the fingers up and out, ending with the right extended finger pointing outward.
Hint: "How" plus "you." It is not necessary to sign "are."

I'M FINE.
Bring the "5" hand, palm left, forward with a flick of the wrist from the middle of the chest. Note: You may leave the thumb in place in the middle of the chest and wiggle all of the other fingers to mean "super fine."
Hint: This is the sign for "fine." It is not necessary to sign "I'm."

SEE YOU LATER.
Smoothly bring the "v" hand, fingers pointing toward either eye and face toward the face, from the eyes downward, changing into an "l" handshape with a flick of the wrist.
Hint: "See" plus a modified form of "later." "You" is not necessary.

repeat movement

GOOD-BYE.
Bend the fingers of the open right hand, palm facing forward, up and down repeatedly.
Hint: Mime waving good-bye.

THANK YOU. YOU'RE WELCOME.
Bring the fingertips of the open hand, palm facing inward, down and forward from the mouth.
Hint: When meaning "You're welcome," it is almost like saying "Thank you for thanking me."

YOU'RE WELCOME.
Bring the extended arm, with an upturned palm, inward ending with the little finger near the waist.
Hint: This is the sign "welcome"; "you're" is not necessary.

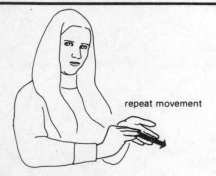

repeat movement

EXCUSE ME. FORGIVE ME.
Repeatedly brush the fingertips of the bent open right hand, palm down, across the palm and fingers of the upturned left hand.
Hint: Brushing the mistake aside.

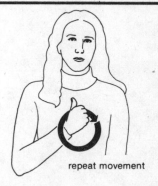

repeat movement

I'M SORRY.
Rub the "a" hand, palm facing in, over the heart in a circular motion repeatedly.
Hint: Beating the heart in sorrow.

repeat movement

PLEASE
Rub the palm of the open hand in a circular motion over the heart.
Hint: Rubbing the heart in enjoyment.

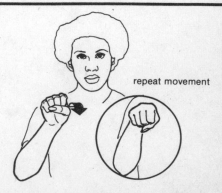

repeat movement

YES
Move the "s" hand, palm facing forward, up and down repeatedly, bending at the wrist.
Hint: Nodding the head affirmatively.

I MADE A MISTAKE.
Tap the "y" hand, palm facing in, on the chin twice. Then point the extended index finger to the middle of the chest.
Hint: "Wrong" plus "me." This sign is used almost as an apology for making a mistake.

THAT'S TRUE. REALLY.
Move the extended index finger, palm left and finger pointing upward, forward in an arc from the lips with a deliberate motion.
Hint: This is the sign for "true" which is often used for emphasis after a sentence.

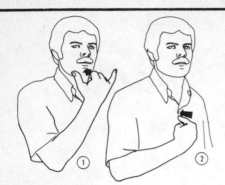

repeat movement

I SEE. I UNDERSTAND.
Gently shake the "y" hand up and down, palm down, by bending at the wrist.
Hint: This is often used as an indication of agreement with what the other person is saying.

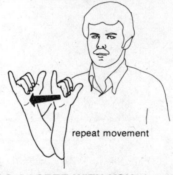

repeat movement

ME, TOO. I AGREE WITH YOU.
Move the "y" hand, palm left, from touching the thumb on the chest forward and back twice by bending the elbow.
Hint: Move the sign for "same" between yourself and the person with whom you have the same opinion.

GOOD LUCK.
With the closed hand, thumb extended upward and palm left, thrust the hand forward.
Hint: This is sometimes used as a good-bye greeting.

repeat movement

BE CAREFUL.
Strike the little finger side of the right "k" hand, palm left, on top of the index finger side of the left "k" hand, palm right, twice.

WHAT TIME IS IT?
Tap the curved extended index finger to the back of the wrist, using an inquisitive expression.
Hint: This is a natural gesture for inquiring about the time.

I DON'T CARE.
Move the extended index finger, palm toward face, outward from the nose, ending with the finger pointing outward.

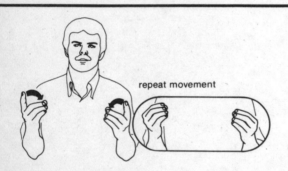

WHAT'S GOING ON?
Bring both extended index fingers of both "d" hands up and down with repeated motion, palms facing chest.
Hint: Rapidly fingerspell "d" "o." This can be translated "do-do?"

WHAT'S HAPPENING? WHAT'S UP?
Bring the bent middle fingers of both "5" hands upward and outward from the middle of the chest toward the shoulders.
Hint: This is the sign "thrill." It's used when you approach someone and you want to know what he or she is doing.

I LOVE YOU.
Hold the extended little finger, index finger, and thumb in front of chest.
Hint: This is the informal sign which is made up of the initials "i," "l," and "y."

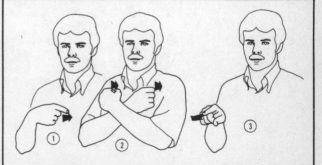

I LOVE YOU.
Place the tip of the index finger in the center of the chest, palm facing in. Cross both arms below the wrists and place the "a" hands on the chest. End with the right extended index finger pointing outward.
Hint: "I" plus "love" plus "you."

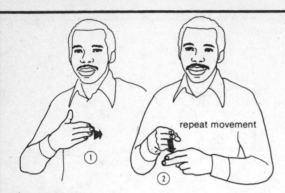

MY NAME IS . . .
Place the open palm on the center of the chest. Then tap the right "h" fingers, palm left, on the top of the left "h" fingers, palm right, twice.
Hint: "My" plus "name"; it is not necessary to sign "is." Follow by fingerspelling your name.

I DOUBT IT.
Bring the "v" fingers forward from pointing at either eye, palm toward face, crooking both extended fingers as the hand moves.
Hint: Similar to "blind"; shows you are blind to the idea.

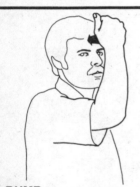

THAT'S DUMB.
Tap the palm side of the "a" hand against the center of the forehead.
Hint: This is the sign for "stupid" and should be used as a self-accusatory when you make a mistake.

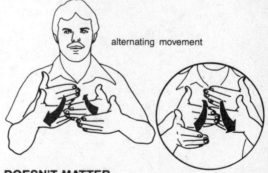

IT DOESN'T MATTER.
With both open hands facing the chest, fingers overlapping slightly, brush the fingertips of both hands back and forth with alternating movements, bending the fingertips out of the way.
Hint: Shows that your opinion can be swayed either way.

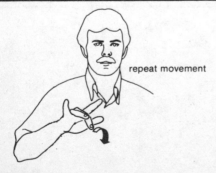

POOR THING.
With the bent middle finger of the "5" hand, palm facing outward, stroke outward toward the person or object being pitied with a double motion.
Hint: Sign "feel" in the air in sympathy for another person or thing.

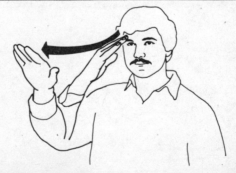

I DON'T KNOW.
Bring the fingertips of the open hand, palm down, from the right forehead outward in an arc, ending with the palm facing out.
Hint: "Know" plus the movement outward which makes it negative.

Questions

ASK
Place the open hands apart in front of the chest, palms facing each other and fingers pointing up. Bring the palms together.
Hint: Mime asking a question.

ANSWER, REPLY
Begin with the right extended index finger, palm left, in front of the lips and the left extended index finger somewhat lower and forward. Bring both fingers downward simultaneously by bending the wrists.
Hint: Words coming straight out of the mouth in reply.

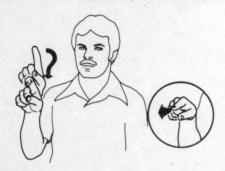

QUESTION
Move the extended index finger from pointing upward, down with a curved movement, palm forward, ending by pointing the index finger straight forward.
Hint: The finger traces the shape of a question mark in the air. This sign is used either before or after a question.

WHY?
Bring the fingertips of the bent hand from the forehead, palm toward face, down and away, changing into a "y" hand as it moves.
Hint: Taking a thought from the brain and presenting it for investigation.

FOR
Move the extended index finger from pointing at the right forehead, palm facing in, outward with a twist of the wrist, ending with the index finger and palm facing outward.

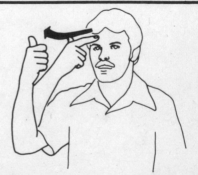

BECAUSE
Drag the index fingertip of the "l" hand, palm toward face and finger pointing left, across the forehead and outward to the right, ending with an "a" hand, thumb pointing up.

WHO?

Make a small circle around the mouth with the extended index finger, palm facing the chin.
Hint: The finger traces the shape of the mouth when you say "who."

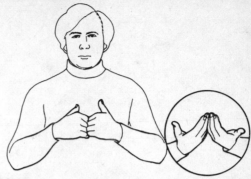

HOW?

With the fingertips of both bent hands touching the chest, palms facing the body and the knuckles touching each other, move the fingers up and out.

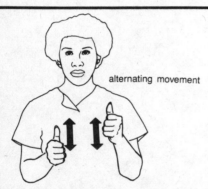

alternating movement

WHICH?

Move both "a" hands, thumbs extended upward, up and down with alternating movements.
Hint: The alternating movement indicates a sense of doubt.

WHERE?

Shake the extended index finger back and forth at the wrist, palm facing forward.
Hint: A natural sign for looking for something.

WHEN?

With the right extended index finger above the left extended index finger, palms facing each other, make a small circle with the right index finger and bring it straight down to touch the left index finger.

WHAT?

Drag the right extended fingertip, palm left, across the upturned left palm.

HOW MUCH?
With the fingertips of both bent hands touching, palms facing each other, move the fingers up and out, ending with the curved open hands apart at shoulder width, palms facing each other.
Hint: Hands encircle a vague quantity.

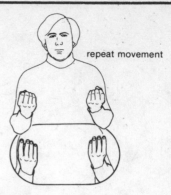

HOW MANY?
Flick the fingertips of both "o" hands, palms facing the chest, upward off the thumbs twice.
Hint: Similar to the sign for "many."

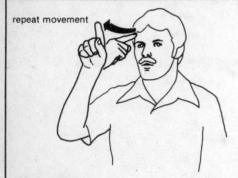

WHAT FOR?
Move the extended index finger from pointing at the right forehead, palm facing in, outward with a twist of the wrist, ending with the index finger and palm facing outward. Repeat.
Hint: "For-for."

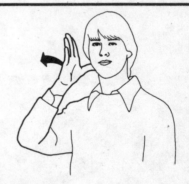

WILL? SHALL?
Bring the open hand, palm left, forward from the right cheek.
Hint: The movement forward indicates the future.

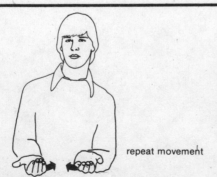

WHERE? HERE
Move both upturned hands back and forth in opposite directions in front of waist.
Hint: Something that is directly before you.

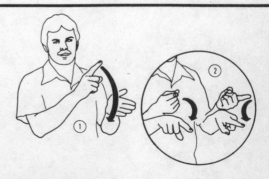

WHAT HAPPENED?
Move both extended index fingers, palms facing upward, downward a couple of times by twisting the wrists.

Negatives

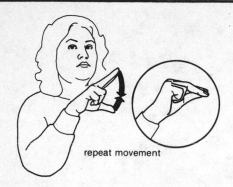

NO
Bring the extended index and middle fingers down to meet the thumb in two quick movements.
Hint: "N" and "o" produced quickly.

NOT, DON'T
Bring the thumbtip of the "a" hand from under the chin outward, palm left.

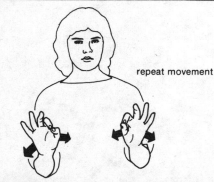

NOTHING, NONE
Shake both "9" hands, palms facing out, with short movements several inches apart in front of chest.
Hint: Shaking an imaginary emptiness.

NOTHING
Bring the "o" hand from under the chin, palm left, outward into a loose "5" hand, palm down.
Hint: Throwing "zero" away from the body.

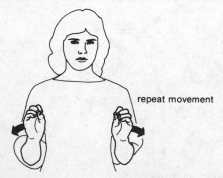

NONE, NO
Move both "o" hands, palms facing outward, back and forth in front of chest.
Hint: Two "zeros." Shows there is nothing.

DON'T, DO NOT
Bring the open hands, palms down, from crossed in front of the body outward to the sides in a deliberate movement.
Hint: Natural sign for "don't."

CAN'T, CANNOT, IMPOSSIBLE
Bring the extended right index finger downward brushing the left extended index fingertip as it passes, both palms down.

NEVER
Bring the "b" hand, palm facing left, outward from near the right cheek and then straight downward to the lower chest.
Hint: A natural sign blocking the body.

WON'T, WILL NOT, REFUSE
Bring the thumbtip of the "a" hand backward over the right shoulder, palm left.
Hint: A natural sign for refusal.

HAVE? DID? FINISH, COMPLETE
Bring both "5" hands from in front of the chest, palms facing up, downward with a twist of the wrists, ending with both palms facing down.
Hint: This sign is used at the beginning or end of a sentence to find out if an action is finished or complete.

repeat movement

LATE, NOT YET
Move the downward extended right arm, elbow out and palm back, back past the waist a few times.
Hint: Shows a past motion.

SINCE, UP TO NOW
Touch both extended index fingertips just below the right shoulder. Move fingers forward, away from body, ending with fingers pointing outward and palms up.
Hint: Indicates a passage of time from the past to another point in time.

Manual Alphabet

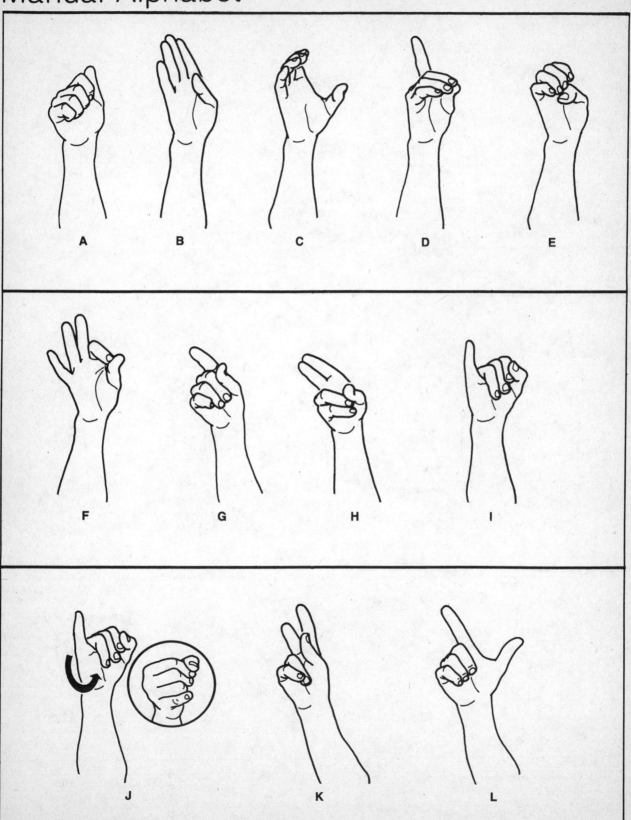

two
THINGS

Around the House
Clothing
Animals

ONE WAY TO FORM PLURALS

Plurals may be formed by adding a sign indicating quantity after the noun sign. The quantifiers that may be used include numbers or quantity signs like "horde," "many," or "all."

frog + horde = many frogs

A SECOND WAY TO FORM PLURALS

Plurals may be formed by signing the verb or noun sign several times, moving the hands sideways to a new location each time.

house—house—house = many houses

A THIRD WAY TO FORM PLURALS

Plurals may be formed by pointing the index finger at different locations where the noun sign is imagined to be, indicating that there are many objects.

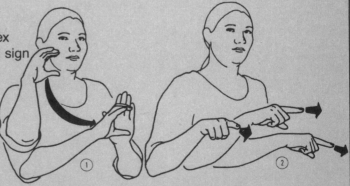

picture + there—there—there = many pictures

Around the House

HOME
With the fingertips and thumb together, touch the lower cheek and then the upper cheek.
Hint: Indicates that home is a place to eat and sleep.

HOUSE
Start with touching index fingertips of angled "b" hands at the forehead, palms down. Separate, bringing hands downward at an angle to shoulder width, then straight down, palms facing.
Hint: Trace the outline of the roof and walls of the house.

ROOF
Start with touching index fingertips of angled "b" hands at the forehead, palms down. Separate, bringing hands downward at an angle.
Hint: Trace the outline of the roof.

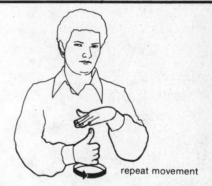

repeat movement

BASEMENT
Circle right "a" hand, thumb side up, below the open left hand, palm down.
Hint: Indicates a place below another place.

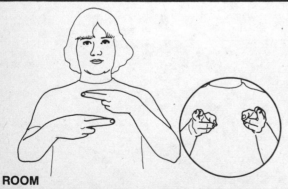

ROOM
Place the left and right "r" hands in front of body several inches apart, palms facing inward. Move hands to the sides, palms facing each other.
Hint: Initialized sign with hand forming the walls of a room.

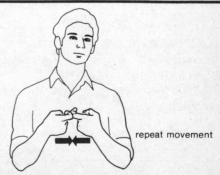

repeat movement

ELECTRICITY, ELECTRIC, BATTERY
With horizontal "x" hands, palms facing body, tap the index fingers together repeatedly.
Hint: Indicates an electrical charge.

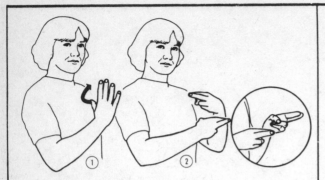

LIVING ROOM
Strike the chest with the thumb of the "5" hand, palm left, with an upward motion. Place the left and right "r" hands in front of the body several inches apart, palms facing inward. Move hands to the sides, palms facing each other.
Hint: "Polite" plus "room."

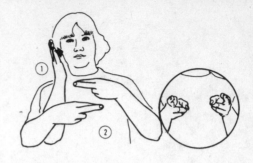

BEDROOM
Place the palm of the open hand on the side of the face. Place the left and right "r" hands in front of the body several inches apart, palms facing inward. Move hands to the sides, palms facing each other.
Hint: "Bed" plus "room."

DINING ROOM
Touch the lips with the fingertips and thumb together. Place the left and right "r" hands in front of body several inches apart, palms facing inward. Move hands to the sides, palms facing each other.
Hint: "Eat" plus "room."

KITCHEN
Place the right "k" hand, palm down, into the upturned left hand. Flip the "k" hand over ending with palm up.
Hint: Initialized sign made like the sign for "cook."

repeat movement

TOILET, BATHROOM
Shake the "t" hand, palm facing outward, in front of chest.
Hint: Initialized sign.

RESTROOM
Bounce the "r" hand, palm down, downward and then to the right.
Hint: Initialized sign.

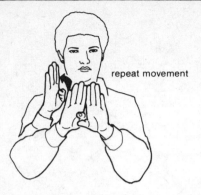

DOOR
With both "b" hands side by side, palms facing outward, swing the right "b" hand back with a circular motion twice.
Hint: Opening and closing a door.

WINDOW
Place the right "b" hand above the left "b" hand, palms facing body. Tap the lower edge of the right hand on the top of the left.
Hint: Opening and closing a window.

CEILING
Place both "b" hands above the head side by side, palms facing down. Move the right hand smoothly forward at the same level.
Hint: Indicates the flat surface of the ceiling.

FLOOR
Place both "b" hands side by side, palms facing down. Separate smoothly outward.
Hint: Indicates flat surface of the floor.

WALL
Place both "b" hands side by side, palms facing outward. Separate smoothly outward.
Hint: Indicates the flat surface of the wall.

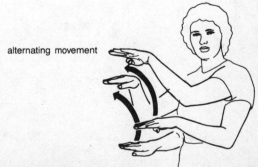

STAIRS, STEPS, STAIRWAY
Move "b" hands, palms down, in an alternating movement upward and outward.
Hint: Mime climbing stairs.

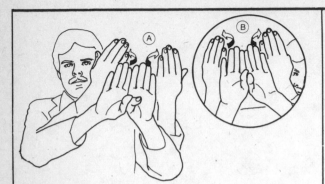

CABINET

With both "b" hands side by side at left shoulder, palms facing out, swing hands out and away from each other until palms face body. Repeat at right shoulder.
Hint: Opening of several doors.

CLOSET

Starting with the thumbtips of the "5" hands, palms down, near the armpits, sweep thumbs down chest repeatedly. With both "b" hands side by side, palms outward, swing the right "b" hand back with a circular motion.
Hint: "Clothes" plus "door."

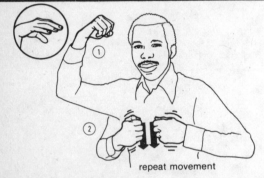

repeat movement

SHOWER, SPRINKLE

Flick open the "s" hand above the right side of head repeatedly.
Hint: Water coming from the shower head.

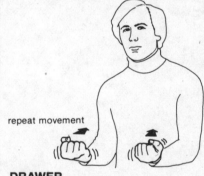

repeat movement

DRAWER

Draw extended "s" hands, palms up, toward you with a double motion. Note: Could use "c" hands, palms facing up.
Hint: Pulling open a drawer.

repeat movement

MIRROR

With finger pointing up and open palm toward face, twist hand slightly at wrist.
Hint: Seeing a reflection in a mirror.

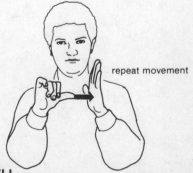

repeat movement

DOORBELL

With right "a" hand, thumb extended to the left, press the center of the open left palm twice.
Hint: Pushing the doorbell.

FURNITURE
Shake the "f" hand back and forth in front of chest.
Hint: Initialized sign.

BED
Place the open palm against the side of the face, leaning right toward hand.
Hint: Laying the head on the pillow.

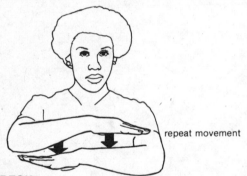

TABLE, DESK
Bring the right forearm and flat hand, palm down, down onto the top of the left arm and hand held parallel under it.
Hint: Indicates the top of the table or desk.

COUCH, SOFA
Hook the right curved "u" fingers onto the left flat "u" fingers, both palms facing down. Move "c" hands, palms down, apart from one another.
Hint: Indicates a long place to sit.

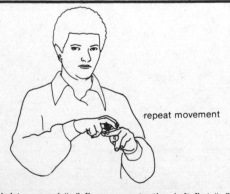

CHAIR
Hook the right curved "u" fingers onto the left flat "u" fingers twice, both palms facing down.
Hint: Two legs dangling from seat of chair.

WASTEBASKET, BASKET
Holding the left arm up near left shoulder, touch the right extended index fingertip to the bottom of the left forearm, moving in an arc to touch again at the elbow.
Hint: Carrying a basket on the arm.

RADIO
Place the "claw" hand over the right ear. Note: Can use both hands.
Hint: Headset for listening to the radio.

repeat movement

VACUUM CLEANER, VACUUM
Place right open hand bent at wrist, fingers pointing down and palm toward body, above flat open left hand, palm up. Shake right hand as it moves back and forth repeatedly.
Hint: Action of a vacuum moving across carpet.

TELEPHONE, PHONE, CALL
With the "y" hand held with the thumb near each and little finger near chin, tap the knuckles to the cheek.
Hint: Mime holding a telephone.

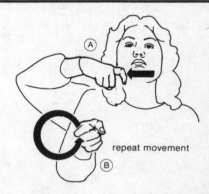

repeat movement

DRYER
Drag the bent index finger across chin, then, with the index finger pointing forward, make a clockwise circle.
Hint: "Dry" plus indicating the motion inside a dryer.

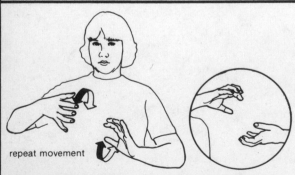

repeat movement

WASHING MACHINE
With the right "claw" hand above the left "claw" hand, palms facing each other, twist the wrists in opposite directions several times.
Hint: The movement of the washing machine agitator.

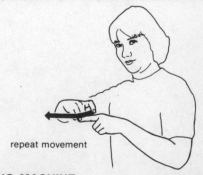

repeat movement

SEWING MACHINE
With the fingertip of the right "x" hand, make long strokes along the extended left index finger, pointing right.
Hint: Stitching along seam lines.

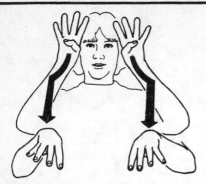

CURTAINS
With "4" hands at sides of face, palms facing out, bring fingers down and out toward shoulders before going straight down to chest level, palms down.
Hint: Indicates shape of pulled back curtains.

DRAPES
With "4" hands at sides of face, palms facing out, bring fingers down ending in front of chest, palms down.
Hint: Indicates shape of hanging drape panels.

repeat movement

TOWEL
With circular motions, rub "a" hands, palms in, on cheeks.
Hint: Drying with a towel.

BLANKET, SHEET, COVER
Bring both "b" hands, palms down, from in front of the chest up to the neck.
Hint: Covering with a blanket.

PICTURE, PHOTOGRAPH
Bring the right "c" hand, palm facing out, from the right temple down ending with the thumb side of the right "c" hand against the palm of the open left hand, palm facing right and fingers pointing up.
Hint: Taking an image and recording it on paper.

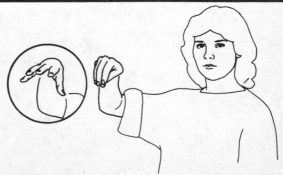

LAMP
With the fingertips and thumb together held at shoulder level, palm down, open the fingers into a bent "5," palm down.
Hint: Light radiating from a light bulb.

Clothing

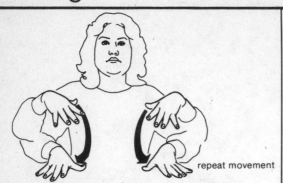

repeat movement

DRESS, CLOTHES, SUIT, WEAR, CLOTHING
Starting with the thumbtips of "5" hands, palms
toward body, near armpits, sweep thumbs downward
and outward repeatedly.
Hint: Showing location of clothing.

SKIRT
With the open hands, palms toward body and fingertips pointing down, brush from the waist downward a
couple of times.
Hint: The shape and location of a skirt.

SLACKS
With both "5" hands, fingers pointing down and
palms facing each other, move them down with a
parallel motion first down the left leg and then down
the right leg.
Hint: Hands indicate the creases in the slacks legs.

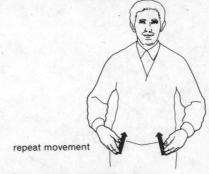

repeat movement

TROUSERS, PANTS
With loose open hands, palms facing the body, drag
the fingertips up the upper leg to the waist. Note:
This can also be used for slacks.
Hint: Showing the location pants are worn.

NECKTIE
Touch the fingertips of the "u" hand, palm toward
body and fingers pointing up, just below the neck
and then to the center of the lower chest.
Hint: Location of where a tie is worn.

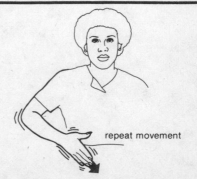

repeat movement

POCKET
Move the "5" hand, fingers pointing down and palm
toward body, up and down repeatedly on the right
hip.
Hint: Inserting hand into a pocket.

SCARF
Bring both "a" hands, palms facing each other, down from the temples to under the chin.
Hint: Mime tying a scarf under the chin.

repeat movement

HAT
Pat the open right hand on top of head, palms down.
Hint: Showing location hat is worn.

BELT
Starting at the sides, bring the "h" hands around the waist touching the fingertips in front, palms facing body.
Hint: Fingers encircle the location where a belt is worn.

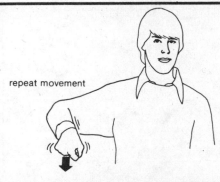

repeat movement

LUGGAGE, SUITCASE, PURSE, POCKETBOOK
Shake the "s" hand up and down, palm facing body and elbow extended at right side of body.
Hint: Mime holding a suitcase.

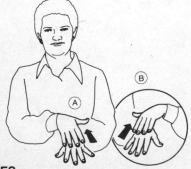

GLOVES
With both "5" hands, palms down and fingers pointing forward, stroke the right hand over the left and then the left over the right bringing the fingers upward from the fingertips toward the wrist.
Hint: Pulling on gloves.

UMBRELLA
With the right "s" hand above the left "s" hand, both palms facing the chest, raise the right "s" hand upward to face level.
Hint: Mime opening an umbrella.

SWEATER
Touch the "a" hands, palms facing body and elbows out, to the chest and then to the waist.
Hint: Mime pulling on a sweater.

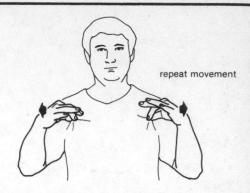

SHIRT
With both "f" hands, palms toward body, pull outward on clothes near the shoulders.
Hint: Indicates the location of a shirt.

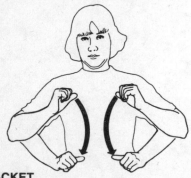

COAT, JACKET
Move the "a" hands from near the shoulders, palms facing each other, downward in an arc toward the waist.
Hint: Thumbs follow the lapels of a coat.

BLOUSE
Move the slightly curved open hands, palms angled inward and down, in a downward arc from the chest to the waist, ending with the palms facing upward.
Hint: Hands show the shape of a blouse.

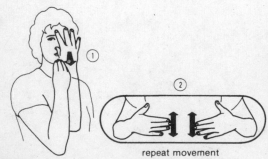

PAJAMAS
Starting with the bent "5" palm toward the face, move the hand downward closing the fingertips to the thumb. Then sweep the fingertips, pointing toward each other, up and down on the chest.
Hint: "Sleep" plus "clothes."

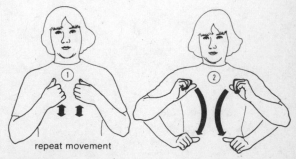

BATHROBE
Rub both "a" hands, palms facing body, on the chest. Then, with elbows out, touch the chest and the waist with the "a" hands.
Hint: "Bath" plus "clothes."

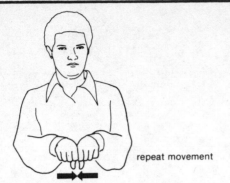

SHOES
In front of waist, hit the thumb side of both "s" hands together, palms down.
Hint: Clicking the heels of shoes together.

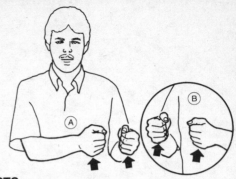

BOOTS
With both "s" hands, palms facing each other at the left hip, jerk upward. Repeat at the right hip.
Hint: Mime pulling on boots.

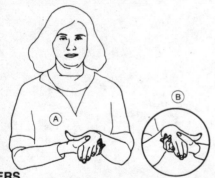

SLIPPERS
Slip the open right hand, palm down, between the thumb and index finger of the left "c" hand, palm down.
Hint: Shows slipping the foot into a slipper.

SANDALS
Draw the right index finger up and toward the body from between the index and middle fingers of the left "5" hand, palm down.
Hint: Thong between the toes.

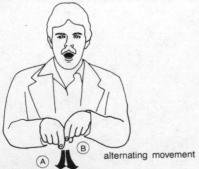

SOCKS, STOCKINGS, HOSE
With index fingers extended, side by side and palms down at waist level, rub them back and forward with an alternating movement several times.
Hint: Knitting needles making socks.

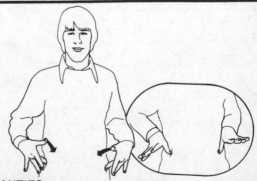

PANTIES
Touching the extended middle-finger of each "5" hand on each hip, move the fingers away from the body, ending with the thumbs on the hips.
Hint: Indicates the area of body covered by panties.

RING
Move the right index finger and thumb up and down the base of the left fourth finger, both palms down.
Hint: Putting on an imaginary ring.

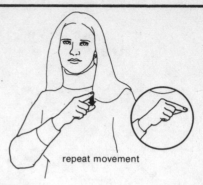

repeat movement

PIN, BROOCH
With the thumb side of the "g" hand, palm left, against the left side of the chest, close the index finger and thumb together twice.
Hint: Shows where a pin is worn.

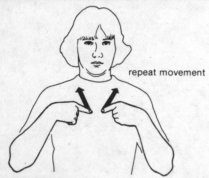

repeat movement

NECKLACE, BEADS
Point the index fingers toward each other, palms facing chest, and draw them upward away from each other toward the sides of the neck repeatedly.
Hint: Fingers outline the shape of a necklace.

COLLAR
Place the fingertips of the "g" hand at the right side of the neck and move it toward the front of the neck.
Hint: Indicates the location of a collar.

BUTTON
Place the thumb side of the "f" hand, palm left, against the center of the chest and then at the lower chest.
Hint: Fingers encircle the typical location of buttons on a shirt.

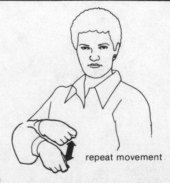

repeat movement

ZIPPER
Move the thumbtip of the "a" hand, palm facing body, up and down on the lower chest repeatedly.
Hint: Mime opening and closing a zipper.

Animals

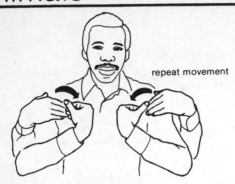

repeat movement

ANIMAL
Starting with the fingertips of the bent hands on the chest below the shoulders, palms facing in opposite directions away from each other, roll the knuckles toward each other while keeping the fingertips in place.

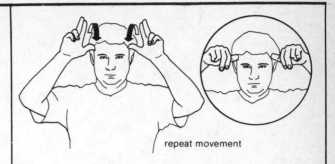

repeat movement

HORSE
With both thumbs on the temples, palms forward, bend the fingers of both "u" hands up and down with a double motion.
Hint: Shows the horse's ears.

repeat movement

DONKEY, MULE
Place the thumb side of both "b" hands at temples, palms facing forward. Bend the fingers up and down repeatedly. Note: Sign may be made with the thumb of the open hand on forehead. Sign may also be done with one hand only.
Hint: Shows the flapping of a donkey's ears.

repeat movement

COW, CATTLE
With the thumb of the "y" hand at the temple, little finger higher than the thumb and palm left, bend the wrist forward a few times.
Hint: Shows the cow's horns.

BULL
Place the thumbs of both "y" hands at the sides of the forehead, palms facing each other. Twist the hands backward.
Hint: Shows a bull's horns.

repeat movement

DOG
With the fingers pointing downward, pat the outer thigh with the palm of the open hand.
Hint: Patting the leg to get a dog's attention.

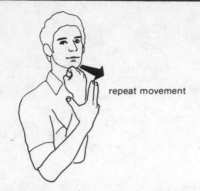

FROG

Flick the bent "u" fingers off of the thumb, palm toward body, forward from under the chin. Repeat motion a second time.
Hint: Shows the frog's throat moving when croaking.

SNAKE

Touch the index finger side of the crooked "v" hand to the chin. Circle the hand forward ending with a sharp sudden movement to the left.
Hint: Shows the fangs of a snake and its crawling movement.

TURKEY, THANKSGIVING

Move the "g" hand from under the nose, palm toward face, downward past the chin, wiggling it slightly as it moves.
Hint: Follows the shape of a turkey's wattle.

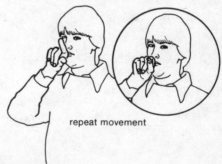

CHICKEN, BIRD

With the "g" hand at the mouth, palm forward, repeatedly open and close the thumb and index finger.
Hint: Shows how a bird's beak chirps or eats.

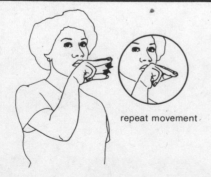

DUCK

With the "3" hand at the mouth, palm forward, repeatedly open and close the fingers to the thumb.
Hint: Shows the bill quacking.

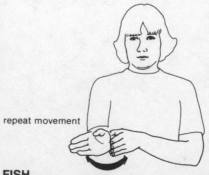

FISH

Touch the fingertips of the right "b" hand, palm facing body, to the inside wrist of the left "b" hand, palm right and fingers pointing forward. Move both hands forward in position, wiggling the left fingers as they move.
Hint: Shows a fish swimming through water.

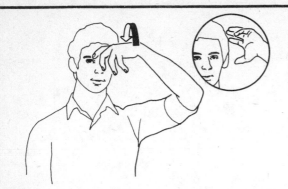

LION
Move the "claw" hand, palm down and knuckles forward, from the forehead back over the head.
Hint: Hand follows a lion's mane.

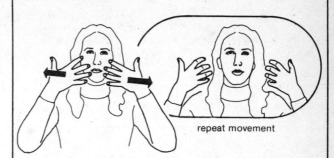

repeat movement

TIGER
Move the fingertips of the "5" hands from the cheeks, palms toward the face, outward changing into "claw" hands.
Hint: Shows the puffy cheeks of a tiger.

ELEPHANT
Starting with the bent open hand at the nose, fingers pointing forward and palm down, swoop the hand downward ending with a forward movement at chest level.
Hint: Follows the shape of an elephant's trunk.

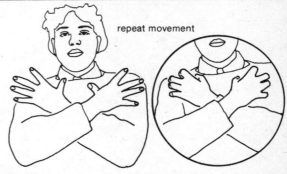

repeat movement

BEAR
Scratch the upper chest near the shoulders repeatedly with both "5" hands crossed in front of chest at the wrists.
Hint: Shows a bear hug.

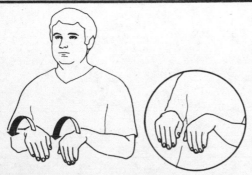

KANGAROO
Move both bent hands held side by side in front of body, palms down, from in front of the chest forward in a small arc.
Hint: Follows the hopping motion of a kangaroo.

GIRAFFE
With both palms toward the neck, move the right "c" hand from on top of the left "c" hand upward past the face.
Hint: Hands follow the shape of a giraffe's neck.

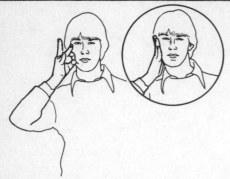

BEE
On the right cheek, touch the tips of the "f" fingers and then quickly slap the point of contact with the right palm.
Hint: Slapping a biting bee.

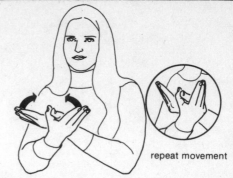

repeat movement

BUTTERFLY
With the hands crossed at the wrists, palms toward chest, and the thumbs of the open hands hooked together, bend and unbend the fingers toward the body a few times.
Hint: Shows how a butterfly's wings flutter.

repeat movement

INSECT, BUG, ANT
With the thumb of the "3" hand on the nose, palm left, crook the extended index and middle fingers.

MOSQUITO
On the back of the downturned left hand, touch the tips of the right "f" fingers and then quickly slap the point of contact with the right palm.
Hint: Slapping a biting mosquito.

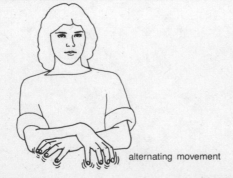

alternating movement

SPIDER
With the hands crossed at the wrists, palms down, wiggle the fingers of both "claw" hands.
Hint: Shows the spider's legs crawling.

CAT
Stroke the thumb side of both "f" hands, palms facing each other, outward from the corner of the mouth.
Hint: Shows a cat's whiskers.

RABBIT, BUNNY, HARE
With the hands crossed above the wrists, palms toward chest, curl and uncurl the fingers of both "u" hands.
Hint: Shows the movement of a rabbit's ears.

SKUNK
Move the thumb of the "k" hand from the top of the forehead, palm facing face, back over the head ending with palm facing upward.
Hint: Shows the stripe on a skunk's head.

MOUSE
Flick the extended index finger, palm left, across the tip of the nose twice.
Hint: Shows how a mouse's nose twitches.

RAT
Flick the fingers of the "r" hand, palm left, across the tip of the nose twice.
Hint: Initialized sign showing how a rat's nose twitches.

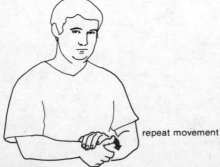

TURTLE, TORTOISE
Cup the left palm over the right "a" hand, palm left. Wiggle the tip of the right thumb.
Hint: The sign looks like the turtle's head moving under its shell.

SQUIRREL
Move the right crooked "v" hand, palm left, down from the side of the nose to tap repeatedly on the fingertips of the left crooked "v" hand, palm right.
Hint: Shows the squirrel's paws in front of chest.

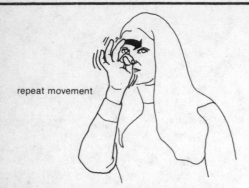

repeat movement

FOX
Twist the thumb side of the "f" hand, palm left, in front of the nose toward the left.
Hint: Initialized sign encircling the fox's pointed nose.

MOOSE
Place the thumbs of both "5" hands at the sides of the forehead, palms facing outward. Bring the hands upward and outward in a small arc.
Hint: Shows the moose's large antlers.

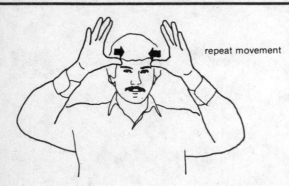

repeat movement

DEER
Place the thumbs of both "5" hands at the sides of the forehead, palms facing each other.
Hint: Shows a deer's antlers.

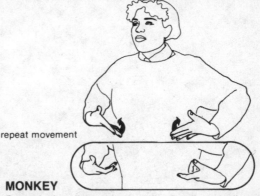

repeat movement

MONKEY
Scratch the ribs on both sides by repeatedly curling both "5" hands, palms facing body.
Hint: Mimes a scratching characteristic of monkeys.

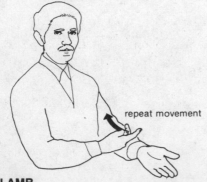

repeat movement

SHEEP, LAMB
With the left upturned hand extended, repeatedly sweep the right hand, palm up, index and middle fingers extended, up the inside of the left arm.
Hint: Shearing wool from a sheep.

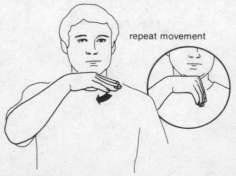

repeat movement

PIG, HOG
Move the fingers of the downturned right hand up and down several times under the chin with the fingers pointing left.
Hint: Similar to the sign for "dirty." Also shows eating too much like a pig so that you are full to the chin.

three

PEOPLE

Relationships
Careers
Other People
Pronouns

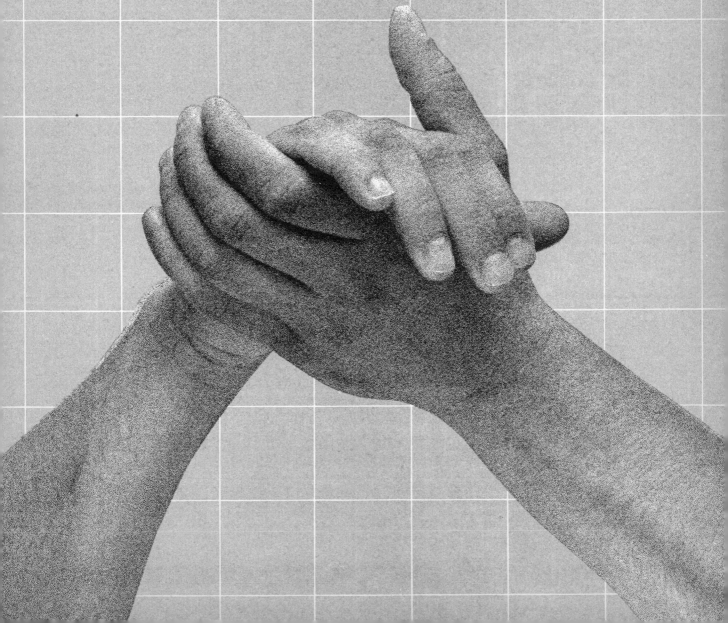

PRONOUNS

Pronouns are often indicated in sign language by establishing location where the person being discussed is imagined to be, and then pointing to that place each time the person is referred to. Using this method of establishing fixed locations for people, several people can be discussed during the same conversation by pointing to the spot for each person.

him

GENDER

The male or female gender is often incorporated into the sign by its location. Many male signs are made at the upper part of the head near the forehead. Many female signs are made near the lower cheek or chin.

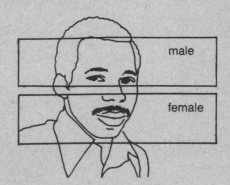

male

female

THE PERSON MARKER

Occupations and nationalities are often designated by adding an ending called a "person marker" after the sign. The marker is formed by bringing both flat hands, palms facing inward, down along the side of the body. The sign is usually related to some aspect of what the person does. For example, a cook is the verb sign "cook" plus "person marker" and a pilot is the noun sign "airplane" plus "person marker." For all nationalities, make the country's sign and follow with the person marker to designate, for example, that you are referring to an "English person" and not "England."

airplane + person marker = pilot

Relationships

FATHER, DAD
Tap the thumb of the "5" hand, palm left, on the center of the forehead. Optional: Wiggle fingers slightly.
Hint: In male position.

MOTHER, MOM
Tap the thumb of the "5" hand, palm left, on the chin. Optional: Wiggle fingers slightly.
Hint: In female position.

GRANDFATHER
With the thumb of the open right hand, palm left, on the forehead, move outward in two small arcs. The left hand follows the same motions but is held lower.
Note: The left hand is optional.
Hint: The arcs stand for generations passing.

GRANDMOTHER
With the thumb of the open right hand, palm left, on the chin, move outward in two small arcs. The left hand follows the same motions but is held lower.
Note: The left hand is optional.
Hint: The arcs stand for generations passing.

SON
Bring the "b" hand smoothly down from a saluting position on forehead to the crook of the bent left arm ending with both palms up.
Hint: Rocking a male child.

DAUGHTER
Bring the "b" hand from the right side of the chin smoothly down to the crook of the bent left arm, ending with both palms up.
Hint: Rocking a female child.

HUSBAND
Move the "c" hand from near the right side of the forehead, palm forward, smoothly down to clasp the upturned left hand held in front of body.
Hint: "Man" plus "marry"; a man who is married.

WIFE
Drag the thumb of the bent right open hand along the right side of the chin, palm left, smoothly down to clasp the left hand held in front of body.
Hint: "Woman" plus "marry"; a woman who is married.

BROTHER
Bring the "a" hand, palm left, from the right side of forehead smoothly down while extending index finger. End with the index fingers of both hands pointing outward at chest level side by side.
Hint: "Male" plus "same"; male in the same family.

SISTER
Bring the "a" hand, palm left, from the right side of chin smoothly down while extending index finger. End with the index fingers of both hands pointing outward at chest level side by side.
Hint: "Female" plus "same"; female in the same family.

FAMILY
Move touching "f" hands, palms facing each other, in a circle outward until the little fingers meet.
Hint: Initialized sign formed like "class."

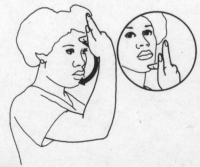

PARENTS
Touch the middle finger of the "p" hand, palm facing the face, first on the forehead, then on the chin.
Hint: Initialized sign in the male and then the female positions.

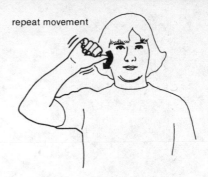

UNCLE
With "u" hand, make a small circular movement near the right temple.
Hint: Initialized sign in male position.

AUNT
With "a" hand, make a small circular movement near the right jaw.
Hint: Initialized sign in female position.

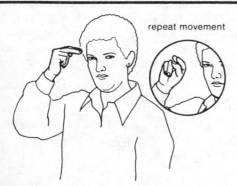

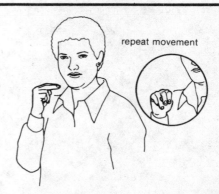

NEPHEW
Twist the wrist of "n" hand, palm facing the right temple, outward twice.
Hint: Initialized sign in male position.

NIECE
Twist the wrist of "n" hand, palm facing the right cheek, outward twice.
Hint: Initialized sign in female position.

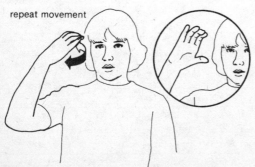

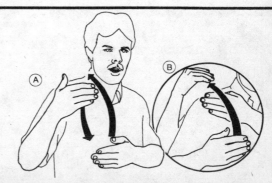

COUSIN
With the "c" hand, palm facing the cheek, twist the wrist outward twice. Note: The sign may be made near the forehead for a male cousin or near the chin for a female cousin.
Hint: Initialized sign.

ANCESTORS, DESCENDENTS, GENERATION
Move the right and left open hands over each other backward from in front of the right shoulder ending behind it. Note: Sign can roll forward from the shoulder instead.
Hint: "Born" signed repeatedly as generations pass.

repeat movement

SWEETHEART
With the knuckles of both "a" hands together and interlocked little fingers, wiggle the thumbs toward each other.
Hint: Two heads close together.

ENGAGEMENT, ENGAGED
Bring the right "e" hand downward to touch the ring finger of the left flat hand, both palms down.
Hint: Initialized sign indicating location of engagement ring.

MARRY
Bring both slightly curved open hands, palms facing each other at an angle, together and clasp.
Hint: Joining of hands in marriage.

WEDDING
With the "5" hands hanging down from bent wrists, swing toward each other and grasp the fingers of the left hand with the right fingers.
Hint: Bringing together the hands during the wedding ceremony.

repeat movement

RELATIONSHIP
Hook the right "9" hand into the left "9" hand between the thumbs and index fingers. Move the hands in and out from the body in this position several times.
Hint: The sign "join" moving back and forth to indicate the relationship between two things.

DIVORCE
Begin with both "d" hands touching and facing each other. Then twist the wrists outward jerking the "d's" apart.
Hint: Initialized sign showing an abrupt parting.

Careers

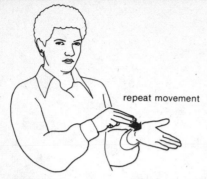

DOCTOR, MEDICAL
Touch the fingertips of the "m" hand on the wrist of the upturned left hand a couple of times. Note: This can be done with a "d" hand instead.
Hint: Initialized sign where doctors feel the pulse.

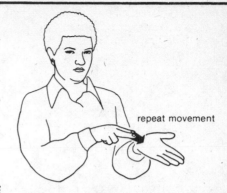

NURSE
Touch the fingertips of the "n" hand on the wrist of the upturned left hand a couple of times.
Hint: Initialized sign where nurses feel the pulse.

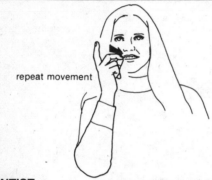

DENTIST
Tap the teeth with the index finger and thumb of the "d" hand, palm facing face.
Hint: Initialized sign pointing to what a dentist does.

PILOT
At shoulder level, move the right hand with the thumb, index, and little fingers extended, palm down, forward once. Add the person marker.
Hint: "Fly" plus "person marker"; a person who flies.

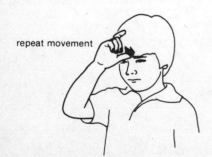

FIRE FIGHTER, FIREMAN
Move the extended and curved index finger and thumb at the center of the forehead with a quick, double motion.
Hint: Fingers encircle the badge on the fire fighter's hat.

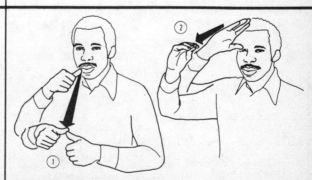

LETTER CARRIER, MAILMAN
Bring the thumb of the "a" hand, palm left, from the mouth downward to the thumb of the "a" left hand, palm right. Then move the right flattened "c" hand, palm down, from the forehead, outward as the thumb and fingertips come together.
Hint: "Mail" plus "man."

POLICE OFFICER, POLICE, COP
Place the "c" hand, palm left, above the heart.
Hint: Hand encircles police badge.

LAWYER, ATTORNEY
Place the palm of the "l" hand on the fingers and
then the heel of the open left palm facing right.
Hint: Initialized sign for "law" plus "person marker."

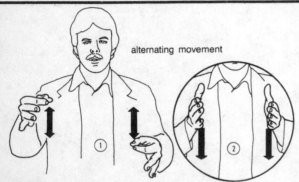

JUDGE
With "9" hands apart but facing each other, fingers
pointing outward, move with an alternating movement
up and down in front of chest. Add the person
marker.
Hint: Weigh a decision on a balance.

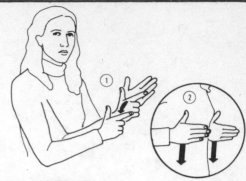

THIEF, ROBBER, BANDIT
With horizontal "h" hands, palms facing down and
fingertips touching under the nose, move the hands
apart toward the shoulders.
Hint: A mustachioed bandit.

ARTIST
With the right "i" hand, draw a squiggly line down the
palm of the open left hand, palm facing right. Add the
person marker.
Hint: A person who draws lines on paper.

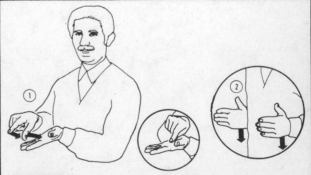

PRINTER
Bring the "g" right hand, palm down, from the
fingertips to the heel of the left upturned hand,
closing the finger and thumb together as the right
hand moves. Add the person marker.
Hint: Setting type for printing.

SECRETARY

Bring the two fingers of the "h" hand from the mouth down onto the heel of the open upturned left hand, forward off the left fingertips.

Hint: A person who records what is said.

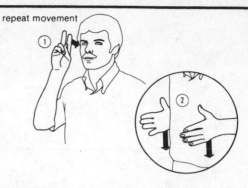

repeat movement

BARBER

Move the index and middle fingers of the "v" hand together repeatedly, moving up near the right temple. Add the person marker.

Hint: Mime cutting hair with scissors.

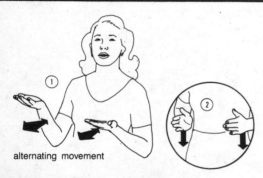

alternating movement

WAITER, WAITRESS, SERVANT

Move both open hands, palms up at chest height, outward with an alternating back and forth movement. Add the person marker.

Hint: Carrying a tray while serving.

FARMER

With the "5" hand, palm left, drag the thumb from the right side of the chin to the left side. Add the person marker.

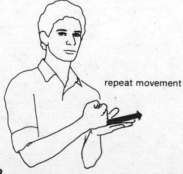

repeat movement

CARPENTER

Move the right "s" hand, palm left, outward, starting at the heel across the upturned open left palm. Add the person marker.

Hint: Using a plane on a piece of wood.

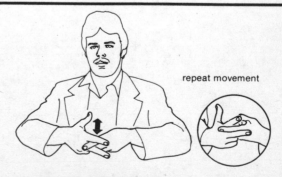

repeat movement

PLUMBER, MECHANIC

With the left extended index finger in the crook between the index and middle fingers of the "3" hand, twist the right wrist up and down repeatedly.

Hint: Twisting a wrench or a pipe.

TEACHER
With the thumb touching the flattened fingers of each hand, move the hands forward several times from the temples. Add the person marker.
Hint: Taking information from the head and giving it to another person.

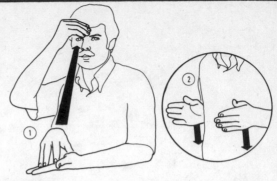

STUDENT
Bring the fingers of the open right hand, palm down, from the left open upturned palm, upward to the forehead, closing the fingertips to the thumb as it moves.
Hint: "Learn" plus "person marker."

PRINCIPAL
Circle the right "p" hand down until the middle finger touches the back of the left flat hand, palm down.
Hint: Initialized sign in "above" position; a principal is above the students.

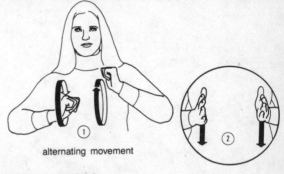

alternating movement

ACTOR, ACTRESS
Alternately circle the thumbs of both "a" hands toward the chest, palms facing each other. Add the person marker.
Hint: "Drama" plus "person marker."

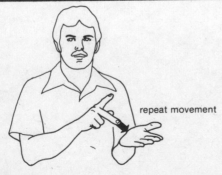

repeat movement

PSYCHIATRIST
With the open left hand in front of you, palm up, tap the middle finger of the "p" hand on the wrist of the upturned left hand.
Hint: Initialized sign in the "medical" position.

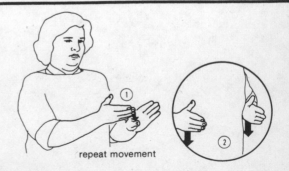

repeat movement

PSYCHOLOGIST
Tap the little finger of the open right hand, palm left, in the crook between the thumb and index finger of the open left hand, palm right.

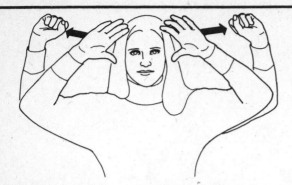

PRESIDENT, SUPERINTENDENT
Beginning with both "c" hands at temples, palms facing outward, gradually close the fingers into "s" shapes as the hands move outward to either side.
Hint: The hands follow the "horns of authority."

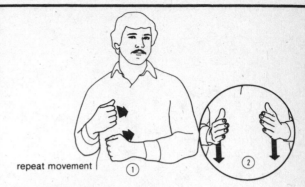

repeat movement

SOLDIER, ARMY
With the right "a" hand above the left "a" hand, palms in, hit against the right side of the chest twice. Add the person marker.
Hint: Carrying a gun military style.

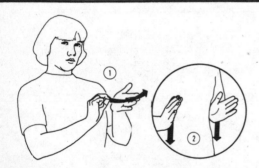

REPORTER
With the right thumb and index fingertips together, move the right hand smoothly outward starting at the heel across the upturned open left hand twice.
Hint: "Write" plus "person marker"; a person who records events on paper.

PHOTOGRAPHER
Bring the right "c" hand, palm facing out, down from the right temple ending with the thumb side of the right "c" hand against the palm of the open left hand, palm facing right and fingers pointing up. Add the person marker.
Hint: "Picture" plus "person marker."

KING
Move the "k" hand, palm toward body, from the left shoulder down to the right hip.
Hint: Initialized sign showing the location of a royal sash.

QUEEN
Move the "q" hand, palm down, from the left shoulder down to the right hip.
Hint: Initialized sign showing the location of a royal sash.

Other People

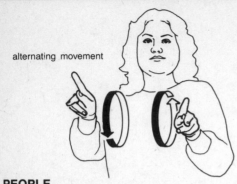

alternating movement

PEOPLE
Using both "p" hands, circle outward with alternating movement. Note: Circles may move inward instead.
Hint: Initialized sign; looks like people walking.

PERSON
Bring both "p" hands downward along the body in a parallel movement.
Hint: Initialized sign following contour of body.

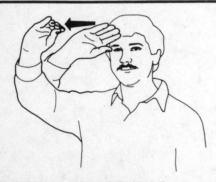

MAN, HUMAN, MANKIND, MALE
With the index finger against the right forehead, draw a flattened "c" hand away, bringing the thumb and index finger together.
Hint: Tipping a man's hat.

WOMAN, FEMALE
Form a right "5" hand palm facing left; drag tip of thumb down the cheek along jawline smoothly to an open hand with thumb on chest.
Hint: "Girl" plus "fine"; a woman with a fancy ruffle on dress.

GENTLEMAN
Place the thumb of the "a" hand on the forehead; bring the hand down smoothly to an open hand with thumb on chest.
Hint: "Man" plus "fine"; originally a man with a ruffle on his shirt.

LADY
Form a right "a" hand palm facing left; drag tip of thumb down the cheek along jawline smoothly to an open hand with thumb on chest.
Hint: "Girl" plus "fine"; a woman with a fancy ruffle on dress.

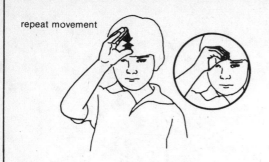

BOY

With the index finger of a flattened "c" right hand near the right side of forehead, repeatedly close the fingers and thumb together.
Hint: Tipping of a boy's hat.

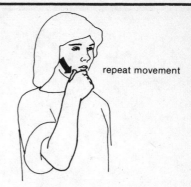

GIRL

Form a right "a" hand palm facing left; drag tip of thumb down the cheek along jawline.
Hint: Indicates a girl's bonnet strings.

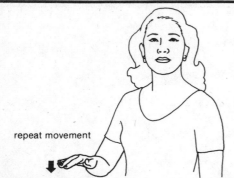

CHILD

Make a couple of short downward movements with the open hand, palm at waist level.
Hint: Patting a child on the head.

CHILDREN

Move parallel hands, palms down, from in front of waist apart from each other using a slight bouncing motion.
Hint: Patting several children on the head.

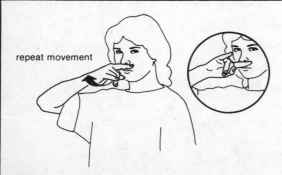

KID

Extend the index and little fingers of the right hand palm down. With index finger touching above upper lip, twist up and down slightly.
Hint: Wiping a child's nose.

TWINS

With palm facing left, touch right "t" hand on the right side of the chin and then on the left side.
Hint: Initialized sign.

ADULT

Start with "c" right hand near chin; bring down slightly, then raise both bent open hands near the temples.
Hint: "Old" plus indication of adult person's height.

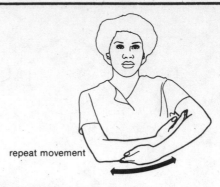

repeat movement

BABY, INFANT

Place the fingertips of the open right hand in the crook of the left elbow. The left arm cradles the right arm rocking back and forth.
Hint: Rocking a baby.

FRIEND

Hook right index finger down over the upturned left bent index finger. Repeat the action in reverse.
Hint: A close relationship.

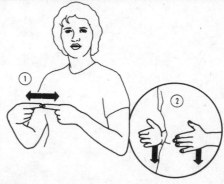

ENEMY

Touch tips of horizontal index fingers; jerk apart. Add person marker.
Hint: "Opposite" plus "person"; a person with opposite opinions.

repeat movement

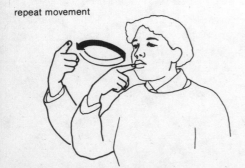

PUBLIC, HEARING PEOPLE

Start with index finger in front of mouth pointing left. Move outward in a circular motion.
Hint: Originally the sign was used to indicate that hearing (speaking) children went to public schools.

AUDIENCE

Move "claw" hands, palms down, from in front of the waist upward and inward toward the chest. Note: The movement can be downward and outward instead.
Hint: Rows of people.

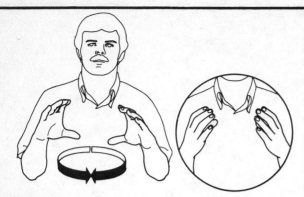

CLASS
Move both "c" hands, palms facing each other, in a circle outward until the little fingers meet.
Hint: Initialized sign.

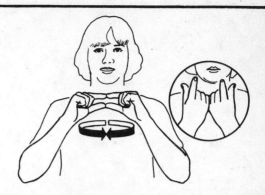

GROUP
Move touching "g" hands, palms facing each other, in a circle outward until the little fingers meet.
Hint: Initialized sign formed like "class."

NEIGHBOR, NEXT DOOR
With both palms facing body, move the right open hand outward from the back of the left hand.
Hint: The next place.

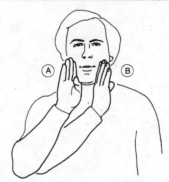

BACHELOR
Move the "b" hand, palm left and fingers pointing up, from the right cheek to the left cheek.
Hint: Initialized sign.

INDIVIDUAL
Bring both "i" hands, palms facing each other, down from the chest to the waist along either side of the body.
Hint: Initialized sign formed like "person."

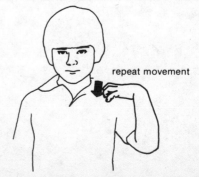

repeat movement

CAPTAIN, CHIEF, BOSS, CHAIRMAN, OFFICER, GENERAL
Tap the top of the right shoulder with the fingertips of the "claw" right hand a few times.
Hint: Indicates position of insignia on an officer's shoulder.

Pronouns

HE, HIM, SHE, HER, IT
Point the index finger outward, slightly down and a little to the right.

YOU (singular)
Point the index finger straight forward.

I, ME
Point the index finger to the center of the chest.

I
Bring the "i" hand to the center of the chest.
Hint: Initialized sign.

THEY, THEM
Move the index finger from pointing forward slightly to the right.

WE, US
Bring the extended index finger in a circular motion from the right shoulder to the left shoulder, palm toward body.

YOU (plural)
Point the index finger outward, moving it from right to left in front of the body.

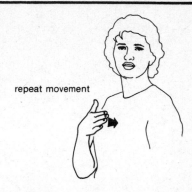

MY, MINE
Place the palm of the open hand on the chest.

YOUR, YOURS (singular)
Face the open hand straight forward.

HIS, HER, HERS, ITS
Face the open hand forward but slightly to the right.

THIS
Touch the extended right index finger into the center of the left upturned open palm.

THAT
Bring the right "y" hand down into the upturned left palm.

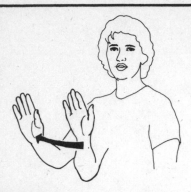

THEIR, THEIRS
Starting with the open hand facing forward, swing it slightly to the right.

OUR, OURS
With the thumb side of the open hand, palm left, at the right shoulder, make a circular movement around ending with the little finger side at the left shoulder.

YOUR, YOURS (plural)
Swing the open hand, palm outward, from the right side to the left in front of the body.

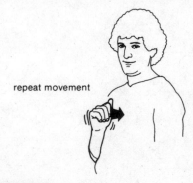

repeat movement

MYSELF
Tap the thumb side of the "a" hand to the center of the chest.

repeat movement

HIMSELF, HERSELF, ITSELF
With the thumb of the "a" hand pointing forward, palm left, move the hand forward and slightly to the left with two short strokes.

repeat movement

YOURSELF
With the thumb of the "a" hand pointing forward, palm left, move the hand outward with two short strokes.

THEMSELVES
Move the thumb of the "a" hand, palm left, from pointing forward slightly to the right.

OURSELVES
Move the thumb of the "a" hand, palm left, from the right shoulder in a circular movement ending with the thumb at the left shoulder.

YOURSELVES
Move the "a" hand, palm left and thumb facing outward, in a forward arc from left to right.

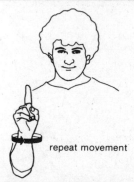

repeat movement

SOMEONE, SOMEBODY, SOMETHING
With the extended index finger pointing upward, palm facing out, make a small circle in the air with the whole arm and repeated movement.
Hint: The finger symbolizes an unknown person you are trying to identify.

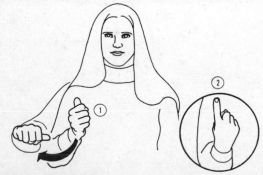

ANYONE, ANYBODY
Starting with the "a" hand in front of the body, palm left, twist the wrist down and to the left ending with palm down. Then extend the index finger upward, palm toward body.
Hint: "Any" plus "one."

EACH OTHER, ONE ANOTHER, SOCIALIZE
Circle the right "a" thumb pointing downward over the left "a" thumb pointing upward.

ANY
Bring the thumb of the right "a" hand, palm left, downward in an arc to the left ending with the palm facing downward.
Hint: A vague pointing up and down as if searching for "any."

OTHER, ANOTHER, ELSE
Bring the thumb of the right "a" hand, palm down, upward and outward in an arch by twisting the wrist, ending with palm facing up.
Hint: Pointing outward to something else.

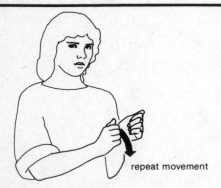

repeat movement

EVERY, EACH
Drag the thumb of the right "a" hand, palm left, down the thumb of the left "a" hand, palm right, by twisting the right wrist downward.

SOMETHING
Pull the little finger edge of the right hand, palm left, toward the body across the upturned left palm. Move the right upturned open hand outward to the right.
Hint: "Some" plus " thing."

EVERYONE, EVERYBODY
Drag the thumb of the right "a" hand, palm left, down the thumb of the left "a" hand, palm right, by turning the right wrist downward. Then extend the right index finger upward, palm facing body.
Hint: "Every" plus "one."

HORDE, CROWD
Move "claw" hands palms from in front of chest outward.
Hint: Rows of people.

four
FOODS AND EATING

Meals
Drinks
Desserts and Flavors
Fruits and Vegetables
Containers and Utensils

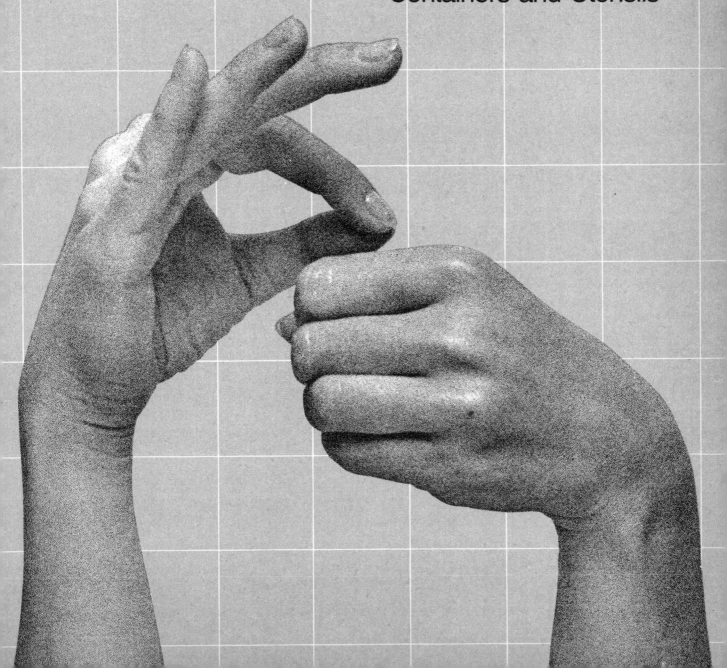

THE SIGNING SPACE

Signs are formed most frequently within an imaginary square area which extends from the top of the head to the waist, bordered on either side by the shoulder width. Signs which in the past were formed outside this area have been brought inward over time, probably because of ease in signing and greater visual clarity to the observer. Seventy-five percent of all signs are formed near the head, face, or neck, where the observer can see them most clearly.

signing space

SYMMETRY

Many signs use both hands moving independently of each other. Some examples of these signs are "let," "horse," and "place." These signs almost always have the same handshape, location, and type of movement. Sometimes the movement is an alternating movement, with the hands moving in a similar fashion but in opposite directions.

COW

THE DOMINANT HAND

Sometimes signs are formed with a different handshape for each hand. In those signs, the dominant hand moves while the other hand is held still. For a right-handed person, the dominant hand is the right hand; for a left-handed person, it is the left. Examples of these signs are "tea," "dollar," and "day."

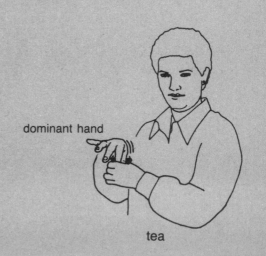

dominant hand

tea

Meals

BREAKFAST
With the right fingertips and thumb together, touch the lips. With the left fingertips in the crook of the bent extended right arm, move the right palm toward the face.
Hint: "Eat" plus "morning."

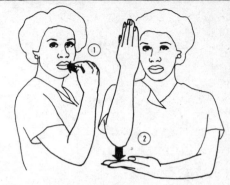

LUNCH
With the right fingertips and thumb together, touch the lips. Place the elbow of the right arm, hand extended straight up, on the left hand extended right.
Hint: "Eat" plus "noon."

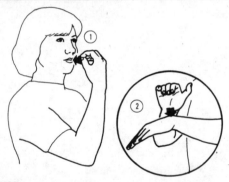

DINNER
With the right fingertips and thumb together, touch the lips. Tap the bottom of the wrist of the bent open right hand to the top of the left wrist, hand extended to the right.
Hint: "Eat" plus "night."

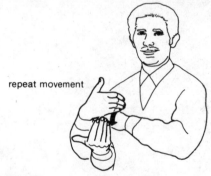

BREAD
With the left bent open hand facing the body, roll the little finger edge of the bent right hand down over the back of the left hand several times.
Hint: Slicing a loaf of bread.

SANDWICH
With the palm of the open left "5" hand facing the body, slide the right "b" hand, palm down, between the left index and middle fingers. Note: Sign may be made with the palm up.
Hint: Putting food between slices of bread.

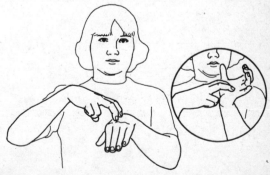

TOAST
Touch the fingertips of the crooked "v" right hand to the back of the left hand. Turn the left hand back at wrist and touch the same fingertips to the left palm.
Hint: Holding bread with a fork to toast both sides.

repeat movement

MEAT
Grasp the left hand between the base of the thumb and index finger with the thumb and index finger of the right hand.
Hint: Indicates the fleshy or meaty part of the hand.

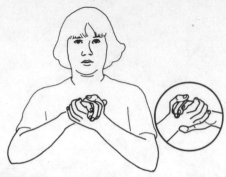

HAMBURGER
Lightly clasp hands, right over left and then left over right.
Hint: Making a hamburger patty.

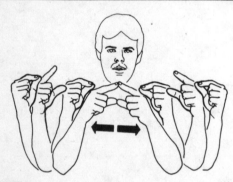

HOT DOG
Starting with the touching fingertips of facing "g" hands, pull the hands apart while opening and closing fingertips.
Hint: Fingers follow the shape of hot dogs linked together.

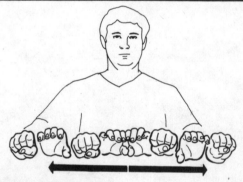

SAUSAGE, BOLOGNA
Starting with "s" hands side by side, palms down, pull hands apart while opening and closing them.
Hint: Initialized sign following the shape of links of sausage.

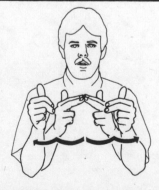

BACON
Starting with "h" fingertips touching each other, separate hands while opening and closing the "h's".
Hint: Follows the shape of bacon frying.

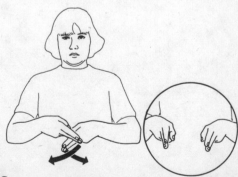

EGG
Strike the right "h" fingers across the left "h" fingers, dropping them down and away from each other.
Hint: Breaking an egg into a bowl.

PANCAKE
Place the fingers of the open right palm on the upturned left palm. Flip the right hand ending with the back of right hand on the left palm.
Hint: Flipping pancakes while cooking.

SYRUP
Pull the extended index finger pointing left under the nose to the right.
Hint: Wiping syrup from the lips.

repeat movement

GRAVY, GREASE, GREASY, OIL
Grab the open left hand, palm facing body, from underneath with the thumb and middle finger of the right hand. Drag the right hand downward, bring the thumb and middle finger together. Repeat.
Hint: Grease dripping off some meat.

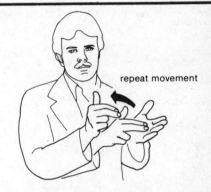

repeat movement

BUTTER
Flick the right "u" fingertips over the heel of the upturned left palm twice.
Hint: Spreading butter on bread.

FRENCH FRIES
Make an "f" twice in front of body, moving hand slightly right.
Hint: Initialized sign for both words.

repeat movement

SOUP
With the slightly curved left hand, palm up, in front of chest, use the right "h" fingers pointing left to make a circular motion from left hand toward mouth.
Hint: Eating soup from a held bowl.

SPAGHETTI
Starting with the "i" fingertips touching each other, palms toward body, separate hands with a wavy motion.
Hint: Shows the shape and size of spaghetti.

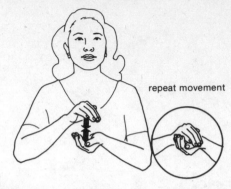

repeat movement

RICE
Bring the palms of the cupped hands together, left hand under right hand.
Hint: Indicates a portion of rice.

repeat movement

CRACKER
Tap the palm side of the right "a" hand above the elbow of the raised left arm.

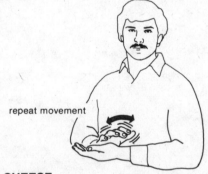

repeat movement

CHEESE
Rub the heel of the curved right "5" hand, palm down, on the upturned heel of the left hand with a twisting motion.
Hint: Pressing cheese into shape.

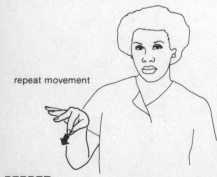

repeat movement

PEPPER
Move the "9" hand, palm down, slightly downward twice by bending the wrist.
Hint: Shaking pepper on food.

alternating movement

SALT
With the right "v" fingers crossed over the left "u" fingers, both palms down, alternately tap the index and middle fingers with an up and down motion.
Hint: Tapping salt off of a salt knife.

Drinks

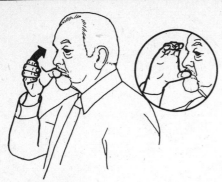

DRINK, BEVERAGE
Hold a "c" hand in front of the mouth, palm facing body and thumb touching the bottom lip. Keeping the thumb in place, twist fingers upward toward the nose.
Hint: Mime taking a drink.

repeat movement

WATER
Tap the index finger of the "w" hand, palm left, to the chin.
Hint: Initialized sign in "drink" position.

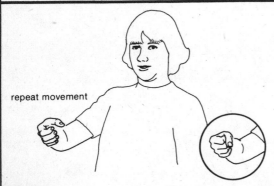

repeat movement

MILK
With the "c" hand in front of the body, palm left and fingers forward, close the hand into an "s" shape, repeatedly.
Hint: Milking a cow.

CREAM
Place the curved open hand, palm toward body, on the fingertips of the upturned left hand. Draw the right hand in toward the body.
Hint: Skimming cream from the top of milk.

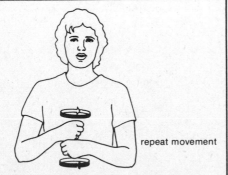

repeat movement

COFFEE
With the right "s" hand above the left "s" hand, palms facing the body, rub together in small alternating circles.
Hint: Grinding coffee beans.

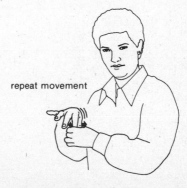

repeat movement

TEA
Place the fingertips of the index finger and thumb of the right "9" hand inside the left "o" hand held in front of the body, palm right.
Hint: Dipping a tea bag in a cup.

POP, SODA, CHAMPAGNE

With the right "5" hand, palm down, insert the middle finger bent downward into the top of the left "s" hand, palm right. Follow quickly by slapping the palm of the right "5" hand on the top of the left "s" hand.
Hint: Putting a cork in a bottle and shoving it down.

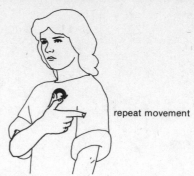

repeat movement

COKE, COCA-COLA

Jab the index finger of the "I" hand into the upper left arm, bending the thumb a few times.
Hint: Related to shooting cocaine.

repeat movement

JUICE

Make a "j" twice at shoulder level.
Hint: Initialized sign.

repeat movement

BEER

Stroke the side of the index finger of the "b" hand down the lower right cheek repeatedly.
Hint: Initialized sign.

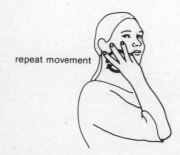

repeat movement

WINE

Stroke the side of the index finger of the "w" hand in small circles on the right cheek.
Hint: Initialized sign.

repeat movement

WHISKEY, LIQUOR

Strike the right hand, index and little fingers extended outward, to the back of the left "s" hand, palm down, twice. Note: The left hand may have fingers extended similar to the right hand.
Hint: The extended fingers indicate the size of a jigger.

Desserts and Flavors

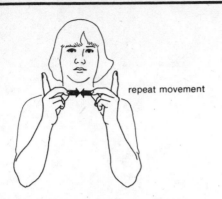

DESSERT
Tap the two facing "d" hands together at the middle fingers several times.
Hint: Initialized sign.

SUGAR, SWEET
Brush the fingertips of the open hand, palm toward face, downward and outward on the chin several times.

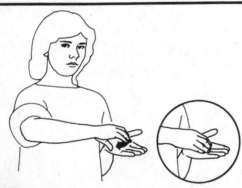

CAKE
Place the fingertips of the right "c" hand on the upturned left palm. Turn the right hand clockwise and touch the left palm again.
Hint: Initialized sign.

PIE
Slide the little finger side of the open right hand, palm left, across the upturned left hand. Repeat several times at slightly different angles on the left palm.
Hint: Slicing a pie into pieces.

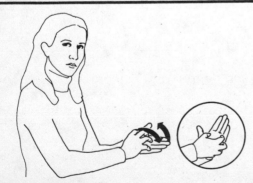

COOKIE, BISCUIT
Touch the fingertips of the right "claw" hand on the upturned left palm. Twist both hands in opposite directions and repeat.
Hint: Cutting cookies with a cookie cutter.

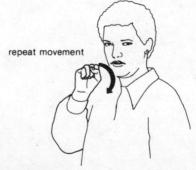

ICE CREAM
Repeatedly move the "s" hand, palm left, down with an inward arc in front of the mouth.
Hint: Licking an ice cream cone.

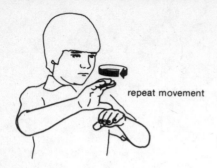

CHOCOLATE
Circle the right "c" hand on the back of the left hand, palm down.
Hint: Initialized sign.

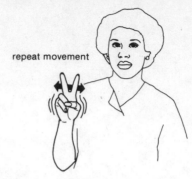

VANILLA
Wiggle the "v" hand back and forth in front of the body.
Hint: Initialized sign.

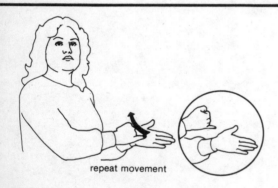

JELLY, JAM
Flick the right little fingertip on the upturned left palm with an upward "j" motion several times.
Hint: Initialized sign; spreading jelly on bread.

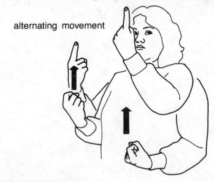

POPCORN
Alternately raise each hand, flicking the index fingers straight up, palms toward the body.
Hint: Mime popping kernels of popcorn.

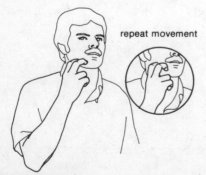

CHEWING GUM, GUM
With the fingertips of the crooked "v" hand on the right cheek, move the hand up and down, leaving the fingertips in place.
Hint: Indicates the jaw movement when chewing gum.

CANDY
With the "u" hand, brush downward on the chin repeatedly by bending the two fingers up and down.
Hint: Licking a lollipop.

Fruits and Vegetables

VEGETABLE
With the side of "v" index finger on the right side of the chin, turn the wrist slightly back and forth.
Hint: Initialized sign.

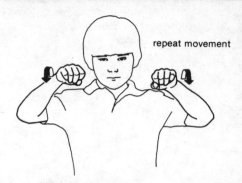

CORN, CORN-ON-THE-COB
Place the "a" hands, knuckles forward, at the sides of the chin, elbows out. Turn hands forward by twisting the wrists.
Hint: Eating corn-on-the-cob.

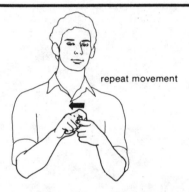

PEAS
Use the fingertip of the "x" to make short outward strokes along the extended left index finger.
Hint: Pointing to individual peas in the pod.

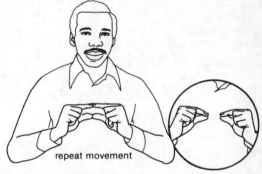

BEANS
Touch tips of extended index fingers of "g" hands, palms facing each other, to thumbs twice while drawing hands apart.
Hint: Fingers follow the shape of a bean.

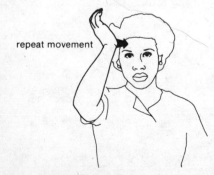

CABBAGE, LETTUCE
Tap the heel of the curved open hand, palm right, above the right temple.
Hint: Indicating a head of cabbage or lettuce.

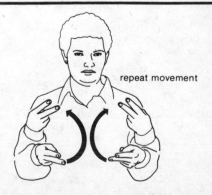

SALAD
Move both "v" hands, palms up and angled in, up with an inward arc a few times. Optional: Use upturned "claw" hands instead.
Hint: Initialized sign for "vegetable"; mime tossing a salad.

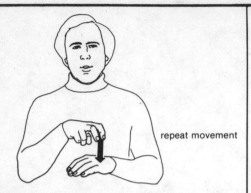

POTATO

Tap the fingertips of the crooked "v" hand to the back of the curved, open left hand, palm down, twice.
Hint: Testing a potato with a fork to see if it is cooked.

CARROT

Place the "s" hand near the right side of the mouth. Move it slowly inward toward the mouth. Note: Sign this with a quick clicking of the teeth as if biting or chewing on the carrot.
Hint: Eating a carrot.

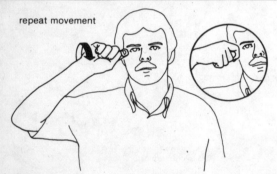

ONION

With the knuckle of the slightly curved index finger near the corner of the right eye, palm out, twist downward twice.
Hint: Wiping a tear from the eye caused by peeling onions.

TOMATO

Place the sideways left "s" hand, palm right, in front of body. Move the right "1" hand from the mouth down touching the index finger as it passes. Note: The left hand could have all fingertips touching the thumb and pointing right.
Hint: Slicing a tomato.

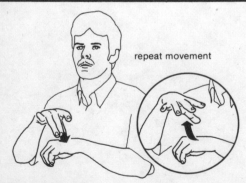

PUMPKIN, MELON

Use the thumb to flick the right middle finger onto the back of the left hand.
Hint: Thumping a melon to see if it is ripe.

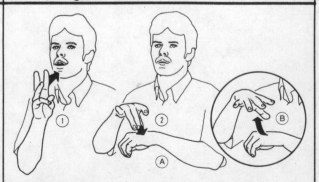

WATERMELON

Touch the index finger of the "w" hand, palm left, to the chin. Use the thumb to flick the right middle finger onto the back of the left hand.
Hint: Sign "water" plus "melon."

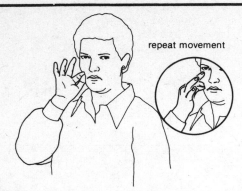

FRUIT
With the tip of the index finger and thumb of the "f" hand on the right cheek, twist forward repeatedly.
Hint: Initialized sign.

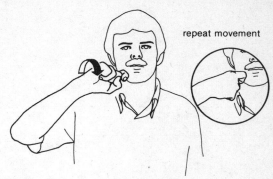

APPLE
With the knuckle of the tightly curled index finger on the right cheek, palm out, twist downward twice.
Hint: Chewing an apple in the cheek.

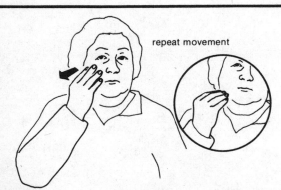

PEACH
With the palm facing it, lightly stroke the spread fingertips down the right cheek, ending with the fingertips touching the thumbtip. Repeat.
Hint: Feeling peach fuzz.

LEMON
Place the thumbtip of the "l" hand, palm left, on the chin.
Hint: Initialized sign in the same position as "sour."

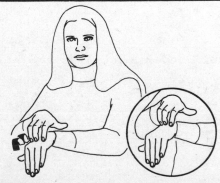

GRAPES
Draw the right "claw" hand, palm down, over the knuckles and back of the left bent hand, palm down.
Hint: Shows a bunch of grapes.

BANANA
Move the closed fingertips of the right hand, palm facing outward, down the extended left index finger, palm facing right.
Hint: Mime peeling a banana.

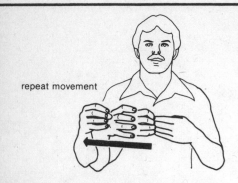

PEAR
Hold the left hand, fingertips touching the thumb and pointing right, palm toward body. Place the right fingers, pointing left, over the left fingers and pull right, ending with right fingertips touching the thumb. Repeat.
Hint: Shows the shape of a pear.

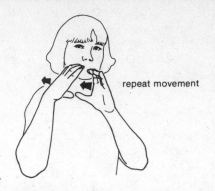

COCONUT
Shake both "claw" hands, palms facing, simultaneously near the ear.
Hint: Mime shaking a coconut to hear the milk inside.

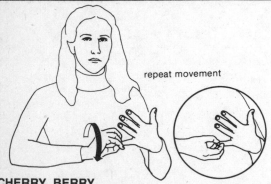

CHERRY, BERRY
Surround the little fingertip of the left "5" hand, palm toward body, with the right fingertips, thumb at bottom. Twist right hand away from body several times. Optional: The color of the berry may be added to specify which berry is meant, for example, "blue" plus "berry" for "blueberry."

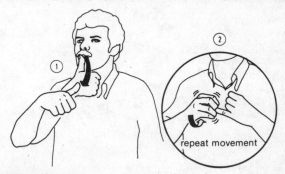

STRAWBERRY
Bring the extended thumb of the right "a" hand, palm toward body, downward and outward from on the lips in an arc. Then twist the fingertips of the right "o" hand around the left extended little fingertip, both palms toward body.
Hint: A modified sign for "red" plus "berry."

PEANUT, NUT
Flick the thumb of the "a" hand off the tips of the front teeth.
Hint: Cracking nuts with the teeth.

PINEAPPLE
Move the "5" right hand, angled forward to the left, downward past the fingertips of the "b" left hand, angled forward to the right.
Hint: Slicing a pineapple.

Containers and Utensils

BOWL
Start with the cupped hands side by side in front of the body. Then draw them apart into "c" hands, palms facing each other.
Hint: Hands form the shape of a bowl.

PLATE
Hold the curved "l" hands, palms facing each other, several inches apart.
Hint: Fingers form the side borders of a plate.

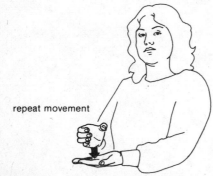

repeat movement

CUP, CAN
Move the right "c" hand, palm left, down onto the upturned left palm.
Hint: Hands show the shape of a cup on a saucer.

GLASS
Move the right "c" hand, palm left, upward a few inches from the upturned left palm.
Hint: Hand follows the height and shape of a glass.

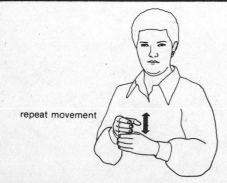

repeat movement

BOTTLE
Move the right "c" hand, palm left, up and down on the left "c" hand, palm right.
Hint: Hands form the shape and height of a bottle.

BOX, ROOM
Place both open hands in front of the body several inches apart, palms facing inward. Move the hands to the sides, palms facing each other.
Hint: Hands form the shape of a box.

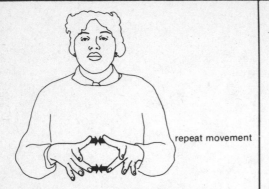

DISH
Touch the tips of the curved thumbs and middle fingers to each other twice, palms facing each other and all other fingers extended.
Hint: Indicates the shape of a dish.

FORK
Tap the fingertips of the right "w" hand against the palm of the open left hand, palm right.
Hint: Indicates the tines of a fork.

SPOON
With the right "u" hand, palm up, make an upward scooping motion in the palm of the slightly curved upturned left hand.
Hint: Eating food with a spoon.

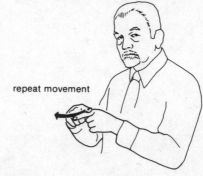

KNIFE
Slide the right extended index finger, pointing left, down the length of the left extended index finger several times.
Hint: Sharpening a knife on a honing blade.

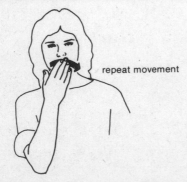

NAPKIN
Move the fingertips of the flat open hand, palm in and fingertips facing upward, across the lips from right to left.
Hint: Wiping the mouth with a napkin.

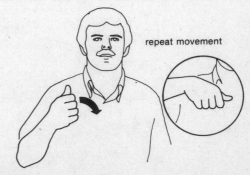

PITCHER
Starting with the "a" hand, thumb side up, tip the thumb side of hand downward toward the left.
Hint: Mime pouring with a pitcher.

five

DESCRIPTIONS

Opposites
Other Descriptions
Colors

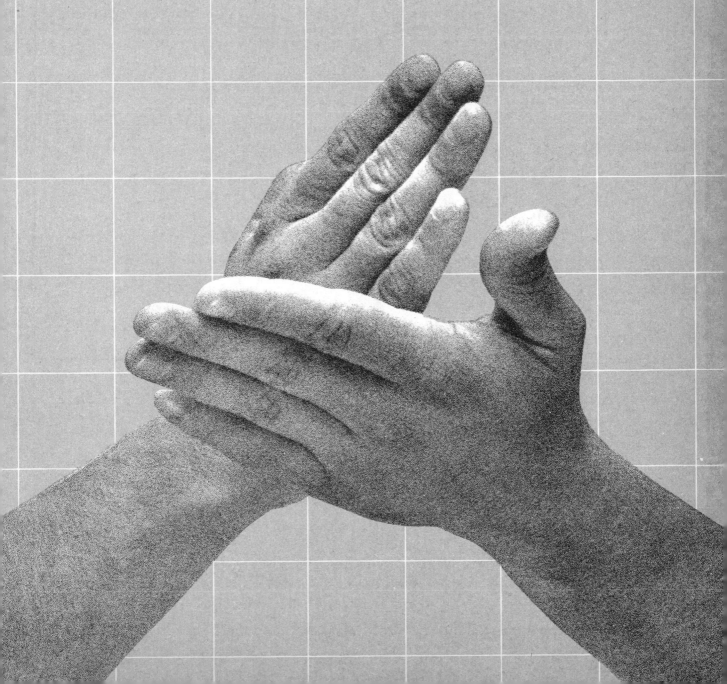

THE ORDER OF NOUNS AND ADJECTIVES

Whether the adjective or noun comes first is not a fixed rule in sign language. If the adjective is necessary to distinguish the noun from other similar nouns, the adjective usually comes last for emphasis. If a noun is used as an adjective, it always precedes the noun it modifies. For example, "baseball bat," "baby doll," and "bird cage."

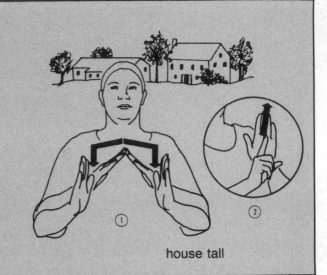

house tall

ADJECTIVES AND ADVERBS

Signs indicating size, shape, and other descriptive qualities can be incorporated into noun signs and into adjective signs. For example, if "famous" is signed with large sweeping movements, it becomes "very famous." If "green" is signed with a very small light turning motion, it becomes "light green." "Fish," signed far from the body with a distasteful facial expression, expresses much more than can be described by an English adjective.

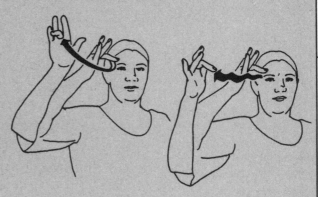

smart   brilliant or genius

OPPOSITES

There are some pairs of signs which use exactly the same handshape, but with reversed movements. Some of these signs are used as prepositions and some as verbs. The pairs of signs are usually opposites of each other. Some examples are "on" and "off"; "in" and "out"; "open" and "close"; and "come" and "go."

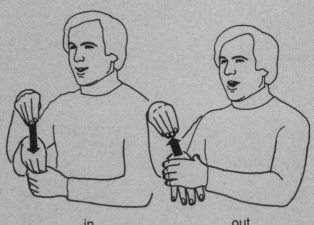

in   out

Opposites

GOOD, WELL
Starting with fingertips of the open hand on the lips, move the hand away and down from the mouth.
Optional: As the hand moves away, the back of the hand lands in the upturned left palm.
Hint: Something is tasted and presented as tasting good.

BAD
Starting with the fingertips of the open hand on the lips, turn wrist and move hand away and down from the mouth.
Hint: Something is tasted and thrown away as distasteful.

DIRTY, FILTHY, SOILED
With the knuckles of the "5" hand, under the chin, palm down fingers left, wiggle the fingers.

CLEAN, NICE
Slide the open right hand, palm down, across the upturned left hand moving from the heel to the fingertips.
Hint: Wiping something clean.

SLOW, SLOWLY
Drag the fingers of the right open hand back toward the body over the left open hand, both palms down and fingers forward.
Hint: Demonstrates a slow moving motion.

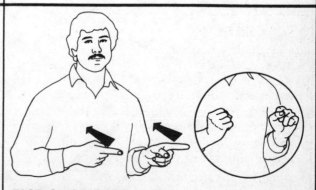

FAST, QUICK, RAPID
Point both index fingers forward, left ahead of right. Jerk hands up toward body, ending with "s" hands.
Hint: Shows a fast motion.

LARGE, GREAT, BIG, HUGE
Starting with both "l" hands with palms toward chest, twist the wrist outward moving the hands apart past shoulders.
Hint: Initialized sign; demonstrates a large area in space.

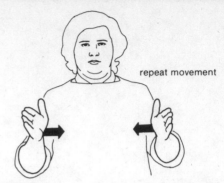

repeat movement

SMALL, LITTLE
With both open hands held palms facing each other, fingers forward, at either side of body, move hands a short distance toward each other stopping abruptly.
Hint: Demonstrates a small size.

TALL
Move the side of the extended index finger up the left open palm facing forward, fingers pointing up.
Hint: Points direction of height.

SHORT, LITTLE, SMALL
Move the bent open hand, palm down, from below shoulder level downward a short distance.
Hint: Demonstrates a short height.

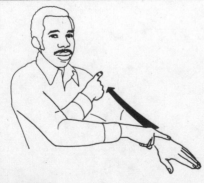

LONG, LENGTH
Move the right extended index finger up the extended left arm which is angled downward.
Hint: Demonstrates length on arm.

repeat movement

SHORT, SOON, BRIEF
Move the right "h" fingers back and forth in short strokes on the left "h" fingers. Note: This "short" is used for a short period of time or short length.
Hint: Demonstrates a short distance on fingers.

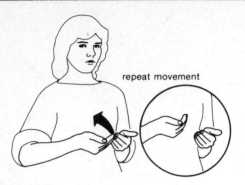

repeat movement

EASY, SIMPLE

Brush the back of the fingers of the left bent open hand with the fingers of the right open hand, both palms up, with long strokes.
Hint: The smooth movement shows ease.

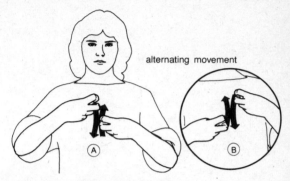

alternating movement

DIFFICULT, HARD, PROBLEM

Strike the knuckles of both bent "v" hands, palms toward body, as they pass each other in alternating up and down movements.
Hint: Shows two hard things hitting each other.

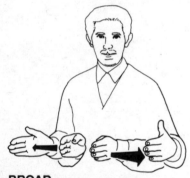

WIDE, BROAD

With both open hands held palms facing each other, fingers forward, close together in front of body, move hands apart toward sides of body.
Hint: Demonstrates something that is wide.

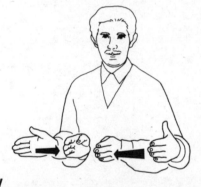

NARROW

With both open hands held palms facing each other, fingers forward, at either side of body, move palms close together.
Hint: Demonstrates something that is narrow.

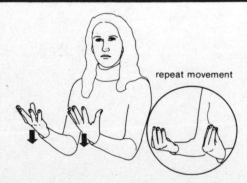

repeat movement

SOFT

Starting with both bent "5" hands, palms up, in front of body, drop hands downward closing fingertips to thumbs repeatedly.
Hint: Feeling something soft with the fingers.

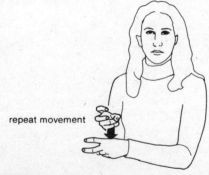

repeat movement

HARD

Strike the side of the middle finger of the right bent "v" hand on the index finger side of the left bent "v" hand, both palms toward body. Note: Left hand may be held in an "s" shape, palm down.
Hint: Left hand represents a hard rock.

WET, DEW
Starting with right "5" hand on the mouth and the left "5" hand slightly forward from face, both palms toward face, bring both hands down closing fingertips to thumbs.
Hint: Feeling something wet with the fingers.

DRY
Draw the "x" index finger, palm down, across chin from left to right.
Hint: Extracting moisture.

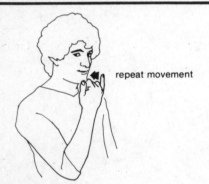

repeat movement

WRONG, MISTAKE, ERROR
Tap the chin with the middle fingers of the "y" hand, palm facing body.

repeat movement

RIGHT, CORRECT, PROPER, APPROPRIATE
With both extended index fingers pointing outward, strike the little finger edge of the right hand to the top of the index finger edge of the left hand.

repeat movement

POOR
Place the thumb and fingertips of the right bent "5" hand on the left elbow. Bring right hand downward twice, closing fingertips and thumb.
Hint: The ragged sleeves on poor people.

RICH, WEALTHY
Starting with the little finger of the right "s" hand on the upturned left palm, raise the right hand ending with a "claw" hand, palm down.
Hint: Mime holding a pile of money.

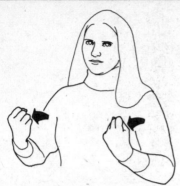

STRONG, POWERFUL
Move the "s" hands, palms facing body, outward from shoulders with force.
Hint: A natural gesture for strength.

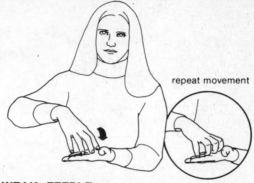

repeat movement

WEAK, FEEBLE
Place the fingertips of the lightly curved right "5" hand on the upturned left palm. Move the right hand forward and back, keeping the fingers in place but bending.
Hint: Fingers demonstrate weakness.

OLD, AGE
Bring the "c" hand, palm facing left, down from the chin changing into an "s" handshape.
Hint: Stroking a beard.

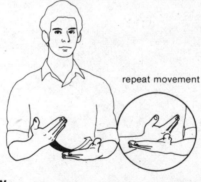

repeat movement

NEW
Sweep the back of the right bent open hand, palm up, upward across the heel of the upturned left hand. Repeat.

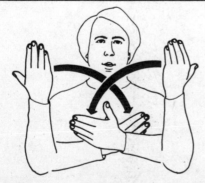

DARK, DIM
Starting with both "5" hands in front of shoulders, palms toward body, move them downward and inward crossing in front of face and ending crossed in front of chest.
Hint: Closing the light from the eyes.

LIGHT, BRIGHT, CLEAR, OBVIOUS
Starting with the fingertips touching the thumbs, palms down and near each other, move hands upward and apart opening into "5" hands, palms forward.
Hint: Wiping away a haze in front of the eyes.

WARM
With fingers loosely curled in front of mouth, palm toward the face, unfold fingers as the hand draws away.
Hint: Warming fingers from heat from the mouth.

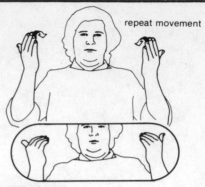

COOL, PLEASANT
With open hands, palms facing either side of the face, bend all the fingers toward the face repeatedly.
Hint: Fanning cool air toward face.

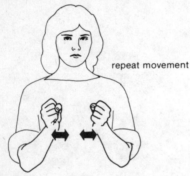

COLD, CHILLY
Shake both "s" hands toward each other, palms facing.
Hint: Shivering motion from being cold.

HOT, HEAT
Move the loosely bent "5" hand from near the mouth, palm in, quickly outward with a twist of the wrist.
Hint: Throwing something hot out of the mouth.

TRUE, REAL, REALLY, SURE
Move the side of the extended index finger up against the lips and outward in an arc.
Hint: Speaking straight from the mouth.

FALSE, ARTIFICIAL, FAKE
Place the extended index finger, palm left, against the side of the nose. Move it outward to the left, striking the nose as it passes.
Hint: Pushing the truth aside.

alternating movement

FAT, CHUBBY
Rock the middle fingers of the "y" hand, palm down, from side to side on the upturned left palm.
Hint: The right hand represents a fat person waddling.

THIN, SKINNY, SLENDER, LEAN
Starting wih the right "i" hand touching and above the left "i" hand, both palms toward body, draw hands upward and downward away from each other.
Hint: Fingers indicate thinness.

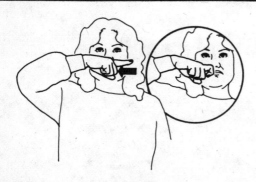

UGLY
Starting with the extended index finger across the top lip pointing left, move the hand slightly right drawing the finger into an "x" handshape.
Hint: Pulling the face into a distortion.

PRETTY, BEAUTIFUL, LOVELY
Move the "5" palm in a circular motion in front of face drawing the fingertips to the thumb near the chin.
Hint: Showing a pretty face.

LIGHT
Move both "5" hands, middle fingers bent and palms down, from in front of chest upward, flicking the palms upward.
Hint: Hands move delicately and lightly.

HEAVY
Place both slightly bent open hands below chest level, palms up. Drop hands slightly.
Hint: Mime holding something heavy.

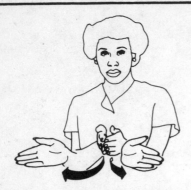

GENERAL
Start with the palms of both open hands facing each other and the fingertips touching. Move hands apart and outward.
Hint: Demonstrates a broad direction.

SPECIFIC, POINT
Move the right extended index finger, palm down, outward from the shoulder directly to the extended left index finger.
Hint: Pinpointing a specific point.

SAME, ALIKE, SIMILAR, LIKE
Begin with both extended index fingers pointing forward, palms down, apart from each other. Bring together side by side.
Hint: Bringing together things that are the same.

DIFFERENT, DIFFER
Start with both extended fingers across each other and pointing forward, palms down. Swing hands apart and outward.
Hint: Separating things that are not the same.

PARALLEL
Move both extended index fingers, palms down, forward simultaneously.
Hint: Demonstrates things parallel to each other.

OPPOSITE, OPPOSE, CONTRARY
Start with both extended index fingers touching each other, palms toward body. Pull apart in a small arc.
Hint: Pulling apart things that are not alike.

QUIET, CALM, PEACEFUL
Cross the left "b" hand in front of right "b" hand at the mouth, palms facing each other and fingertips pointing up. Smoothly move hands downward and apart, ending with palms down.
Hint: Silencing what is spoken.

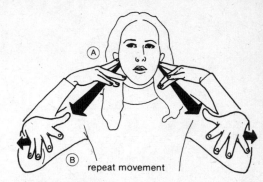

repeat movement

NOISY, SOUND, LOUD
Place the index fingertips of both "5" hands, palms down, in the ears. Pull both hands down and forward, ending with shaking hands up and down in front of shoulders.
Hint: Blocking out loud noise.

repeat movement

EXCITE, EXCITING, THRILL, THRILLING
Alternately strike the chest with the fingertips of both bent middle fingers of "5" hands, palms toward body, with an upward circular motion.
Hint: Stimulation flowing through the body.

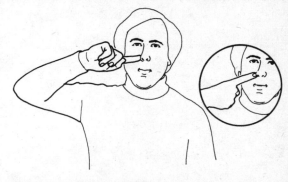

BORING, BORED, DULL
Begin with the extended index finger touching the right side of the nose, palm facing out; leaving finger in place, twist wrist ending with palm facing in.
Hint: Keeping the nose to the grindstone.

repeat movement

ROUGH, SCRATCH
Push the fingertips of the right "claw" hand, palm down, forward from the heel to the fingertips of the left upturned palm.
Hint: Showing a rough surface.

SMOOTH, FLAT
Slide the right open hand, palm down, across the left upturned palm with a slow, smooth motion.
Hint: Showing a smooth surface.

Other Descriptions

PERFECT
Circle right "p" hand down to left "p" hand, palms facing, ending with both middle fingertips touching.
Hint: Initialized sign similar to "exact."

EXACT, PRECISE, FIT
With the thumbs touching the index fingertips of both "x" hands, circle the right hand down to the left, palms facing each other.
Hint: Hitting a nail on the head.

SPECIAL, EXCEPTIONAL, EXCEPT
With the right thumb and index finger, pull upward on the fingertip of the upturned extended left index finger.
Hint: Pulling one thing into view for special attention.

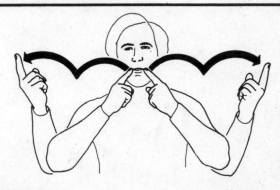

FAMOUS
Starting with both extended index fingers pointing to the corners of the mouth, move outward and forward in two arcs.
Hint: Announcing information for all to know.

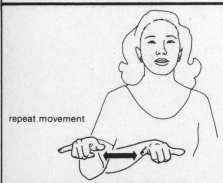

repeat movement

SAME, THE SAME AS, SIMILAR
Move the "y" hand, palm down, laterally back and forth.
Hint: Hand pulls together the similarity between two things.

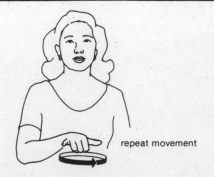

repeat movement

STANDARD, UNIFORM, COMMON
Move the "y" hand, palm down, in a large circle from left to right in front of the waist.
Hint: The sign for "same" moving around to show everything is similar.

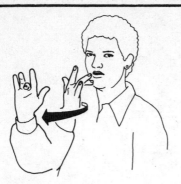

LUCKY
Touch the bent middle finger of the "5" hand to the chin, then move outward with a turn of the wrist.
Optional: Wiggle hand as it moves out.

repeat movement

FAVORITE
Touch the bent middle finger of the "5" hand a couple of times to the chin.
Hint: The "feeling" middle finger is near the taste buds.

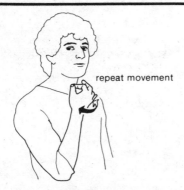

repeat movement

CURIOUS
Pinch a little skin of the neck with the thumb and index finger. Wiggle back and forth slightly.
Hint: Straining the neck from curiosity.

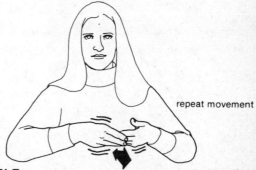

repeat movement

FLEXIBLE
Grasp the limp fingers of the left hand with thumb and fingers of the right hand, both palms toward body, and wiggle in and out.
Hint: Demonstrates flexible fingers.

SILVER
Touch the bent middle finger of the "5" hand near the right ear. Move it away with a wiggly motion.
Hint: Pointing to a silver earring.

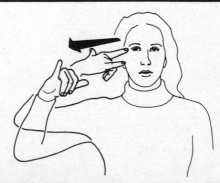

GOLD, GOLDEN
With the thumb, index finger, and little fingers extended, touch the index finger near the right ear, palm down, then move outward with a turn of the wrist while changing to a "y" hand.
Hint: Pointing to a gold earring.

SHINY, SHINING
Touch the bent middle finger of the right "5" hand to the back of the left "5" hand, both palms down. Bring the right hand up with a wiggly motion.
Hint: Indicates a shiny, reflective surface.

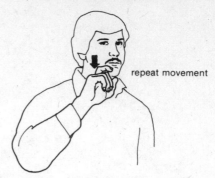

repeat movement

RUBBER
Rub the side of the index finger of the "x" hand, palm out, down the right side of chin.

repeat movement

PAPER
Sweep the heel of the right "5" hand, palm down, back against the heel of the upturned left "5" hand with an upward motion.

repeat movement

CLOTH
Brush the fingertips of the "5" hand, palm toward body, up and down on the right side of the chest.
Hint: Feeling the cloth.

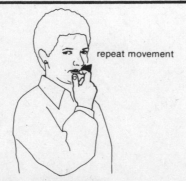

repeat movement

GLASS, CHINA, PORCELAIN
Tap the index fingertip of the "x" hand against the teeth.
Hint: Hard like enamel on teeth.

repeat movement

WOOD, WOODEN
Move the little finger side of the right "b" hand back and forth on the back of the downturned left hand.
Hint: Sawing wood.

CAREFUL
Strike the right "v" hand, palm facing left, and the left "v" hand, palm facing right, together several times.
Hint: Represents a combination of the signs "watch" and "warn."

CUTE
Brush the fingertips of the "u" hand downward on the chin changing into an "a" hand, palm toward body.

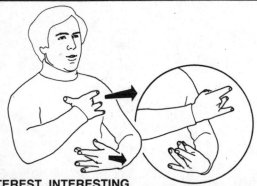

INTEREST, INTERESTING
Begin with the bent middle finger and thumb of the right "5" hand on the chest above the bent middle finger and thumb of the left "5" hand. Pull both hands outward drawing the thumbs and middle fingers together into "8" hands.
Hint: Taking feelings from the body.

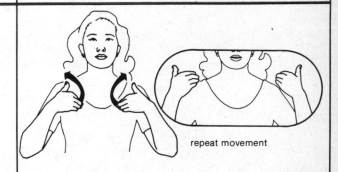

YOUNG, YOUTH
Brush the fingertips of the bent open hands against the front of the shoulders with an upward motion.
Hint: Indicating vitality in the body.

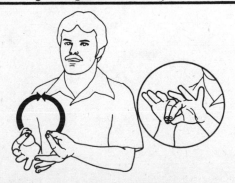

VALUABLE, IMPORTANT, WORTH
Begin with both "9" hands in front of the waist, little fingers touching and palms up. Bring the hands upward and outward in two arcs, ending with the thumbs touching and palms facing down.

FANCY, FORMAL, ELEGANT
Bring the thumb of the "5" hand, palm left, upward and outward in an arc on the chest.
Hint: Similar to the sign for "fine," but with an upward motion.

SHARP
Sweep the bent middle fingertip of the "5" hand palm down, on the back of the left downturned "s" hand forward in a small arc.
Hint: Feeling a sharp knife blade.

EXPERT, SKILL, COMPETENT, ABILITY
Grasp the little finger edge of the open left hand, palm right, with the right hand, pull the right hand down and outward in an arc.

POLITE, COURTEOUS
Tap the thumb of the "5" hand, palm left, against the center of the chest.
Hint: Similar to the sign for "fine," but with a double movement inward.

repeat movement

CONFUSED, MIXED UP, CONFUSION
Move the right downturned "claw" hand in a circular movement above the left upturned "claw" hand. Move the left hand in a circle in the opposite direction.
Hint: Mixing something up.

repeat movement

SECRET, PRIVATE, CONFIDENTIAL
Tap the thumbnail of the "a" hand against the lips with a double movement.
Hint: Sealing the lips.

ODD, STRANGE, QUEER
Starting with the "c" hand near the right side of the face, palm left, move it in a downward arc in front of face.

Colors

COLOR
Wiggle the fingertips of the "5" hand, palm facing the chin.

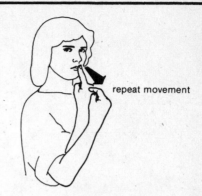

RED
Stroke downward on the lips with the extended index finger a couple of times, palm toward face.
Hint: The lips are red.

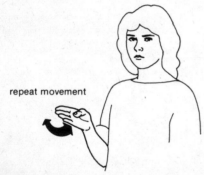

BLUE
Wave the "b" hand in front of chest, fingers forward and palm left, by twisting the wrist back and forth.
Hint: Initialized sign.

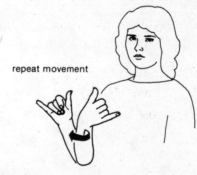

YELLOW
Wave the "y" hand in front of chest by twisting the wrist a few times.
Hint: Initialized sign.

WHITE
Starting with the thumb and fingertips of the "5" hand on the chest, draw outward pulling the thumb and fingertips together.
Hint: Shows a white shirt.

BLACK
Drag the extended index finger, pointing left, palm down, across the forehead to the right.

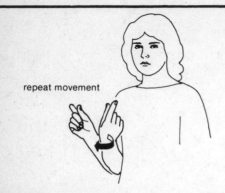

repeat movement

GREEN
Wave the "g" hand in front of chest by twisting the wrist a few times.
Hint: Initialized sign.

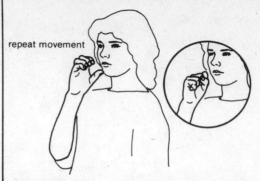

repeat movement

ORANGE
Place the "c" hand in front of the mouth and change into a "s" hand by repeatedly opening and closing the hand. Note: Use this sign for both the color and the fruit.
Hint: Squeezing oranges.

repeat movement

PINK
Stroke downward on the lips with the middle finger of the "p" hand a couple of times, palm toward face.
Hint: Initialized sign in the "red" position.

repeat movement

PURPLE
Wave the "p" hand in front of chest by twisting the wrist in and out.
Hint: Initialized sign.

TAN
Stroke the index finger of the "t" hand down the cheek, palm facing outward.
Hint: Initialized sign formed like "brown."

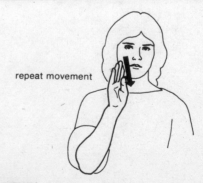

repeat movement

BROWN
Stroke the index finger of the "b" hand down the cheek, palm facing outward.
Hint: Initialized sign.

six

NUMBERS, MONEY, AND MATH

Numbers
Quantity
Money and Math

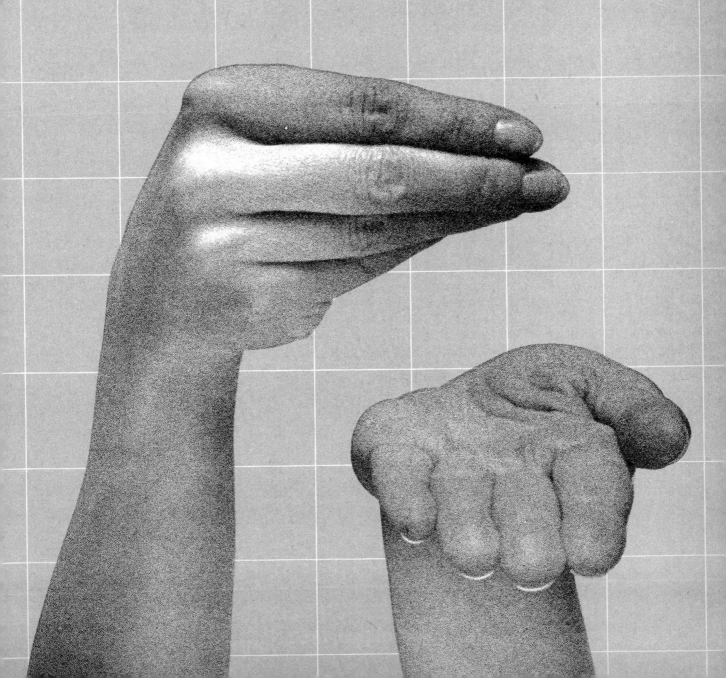

YEARS, HOUSE NUMBERS, AND MONEY

Years, house numbers, and money amounts are usually signed like they are spoken in English. For example, "1982" is signed "19" and then "82." Even money amounts less than $11.00 can be expressed by signing the numeral and twisting the palm sharply inward. Monetary amounts greater than $11.00 must be followed by the sign for "dollar." Uneven amounts of money of any size are signed as they are spoken. For example, $67.52 is signed "67" "dollar" "52" "cents."

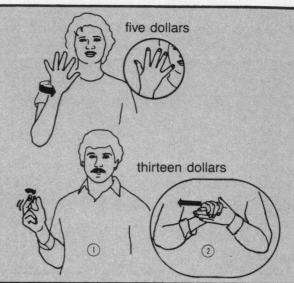

five dollars

thirteen dollars

THE TEENS

The signs for the numerals sixteen, seventeen, and eighteen may be made as demonstrated in this chapter, or they may be formed by rubbing the thumb along the inside edge of the little finger for sixteen, the inside edge of the fourth finger for seventeen, and the inside edge of the middle finger for eighteen, while holding the other fingers extended in each case. The rubbing movement is the only thing that distinguishes six from sixteen, seven from seventeen, and eight from eighteen.

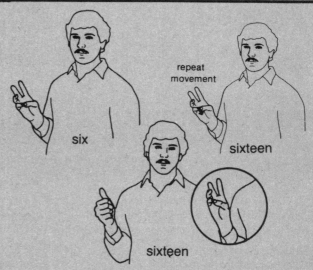

six

repeat movement

sixteen

sixteen

FIRST, SECOND, THIRD . . .

Ordinals may be signed three different ways. The signs illustrated in this chapter use the fingers of the left hand as the primary source of information as they are struck by the index finger of the right hand. Another way of expressing ordinal numerals is to sign a numeral twisting the palm sharply toward the right shoulder. In that way "one" becomes "first," "two" becomes "second," and so forth. Ordinals formed by twisting the wrist are usually used as nouns, while the two-handed ordinals are used as adjectives. The third way to sign ordinals is to move a horizontally held numeral sign across the chest from left to right.

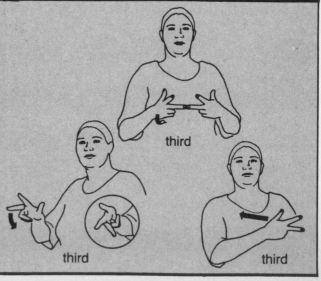

third

third

third

Numbers

ZERO
Curve all fingers, side by side, palm facing forward, to touch the bent thumb.

ONE
Point the index finger up, palm facing forward.

TWO
Point the separated index and middle fingers up, palm facing forward.

THREE
Point the separated index and middle fingers up, thumb extended, palm facing forward.

FOUR
Point the four separated fingers up, thumb across palm, palm facing forward.

FIVE
Point all four separated fingers up, thumb extended, palm facing forward.

SIX
Touch the thumb to the little finger, other fingers up and separated, palm facing forward.

SEVEN
Touch the thumb to the fourth finger, other fingers up and separated, palm facing forward.

EIGHT
Touch the thumb to the middle finger, other fingers up and separated, palm facing forward.

NINE
Touch the thumb to the index finger, other fingers up and separated, palm facing forward.

repeat movement

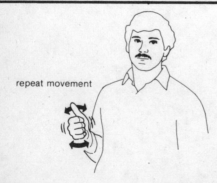

TEN
Shake the "a" hand, thumb extended up, palm left, back and forth from the wrist.

repeat movement

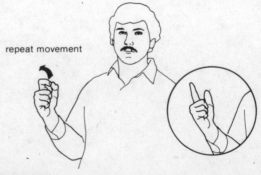

ELEVEN
Flick the index finger, twice, off the thumb, palm facing body, ending with the index finger pointing up.

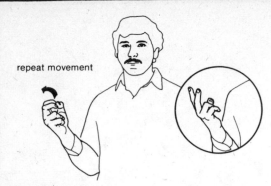

TWELVE
Flick both the index and middle fingers off the thumb, twice, palm facing body, ending with both fingers up and separated.

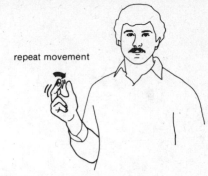

THIRTEEN
With the palm facing the body, thumb, middle, and index fingers extended upward, bend the index and middle fingers toward the body in and out repeatedly.

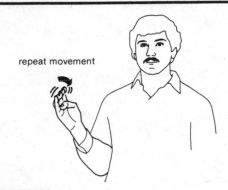

FOURTEEN
With all four fingers together, palm facing body and thumb across palm, bend the fingers toward the body in and out repeatedly.

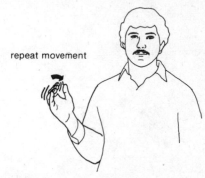

FIFTEEN
With all four fingers together, palm facing body and thumb extended, bend the fingers toward the body in and out repeatedly.

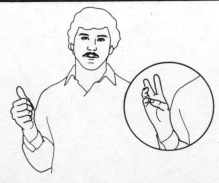

SIXTEEN
Start with the "a" hand, thumb extended, palm left, and knuckles forward. Then twist the wrist quickly to touch the thumb to the little finger, other fingers up and separated, palm forward.

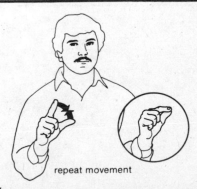

TWENTY
With the index finger and thumb extended forward and separated, bring the thumb and index finger together with a quick double motion.

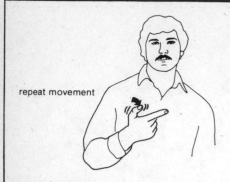

TWENTY-ONE

Extend the thumb and index finger toward the left, palm toward body. Repeatedly bend the thumb at knuckle.

TWENTY-TWO

With palm down, index and middle fingers extended, angled upward and away from the body, move the hand downward in a small arc to the right by bending down at the wrist.

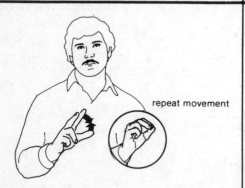

THIRTY

Bring the extended index and middle fingers, palm forward, down to touch the thumb.

ONE HUNDRED

Point the index finger up, palm facing forward. Curve the thumb and all four fingers forming a large semi-circle.

ONE THOUSAND

Point the right index finger up, palm left. Hit the fingertips of the bent right hand, palm left, against the open left hand, palm right.

ONE MILLION

Point the right index finger up, palm left. Hit the fingertips of the bent right hand, palm left, first to the left open palm and then to the left fingers.

COUNT
Move the right "9" fingertips from the heel of the left upturned palm toward the fingertips.
Hint: Moving across a column of numbers.

FIRST
Touch the extended right index finger, pointing left, palm toward body, to the extended thumb of the left "a" hand, palm facing right.
Hint: Pointing to the first finger.

SECOND
Touch the middle finger of the right "2" hand, palm toward body, to the index finger of the left "I" hand, palm facing right.
Hint: Pointing to the second finger.

THIRD
Touch the middle finger of the right "3" hand, palm toward body, to the middle finger of the left "3" hand, palm facing right.
Hint: Pointing to the third finger.

ONCE
Strike the right index finger, pointing left, against the left upturned palm with an upward motion.

TWICE, DOUBLE
With the right index and middle fingers extended and apart, strike the middle finger against the left upturned palm with an upward motion.

Quantity

ALL, WHOLE
With the open right hand, palm facing out, near the left shoulder, make a large loop to the right ending, palm up, in the upturned left palm.
Hint: The right hand seems to encompass everything as it moves.

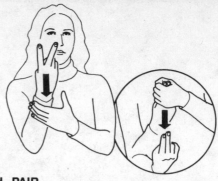

BOTH, PAIR
Bring the "v" right hand, palm toward body, downward through the left curved hand, palm toward body. As the right hand pulls downward, the left fingers squeeze the extended right fingers together into a "u" shape.
Hint: Two things join together to become one.

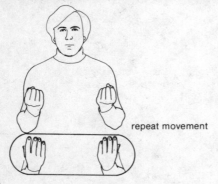

repeat movement

MANY, LOTS
Flick the fingers of both "s" hands upward into "5" hands several times, palms toward chest.
Hint: The flicking of the fingers indicates an indeterminable number.

MUCH, A LOT
Move both "claw" hands from touching each other outward in an arc, palms facing each other, in a deliberate movement.
Hint: Hands demonstrate a large amount of something.

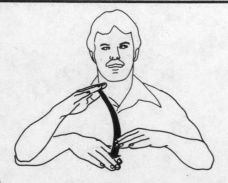

THAN
Bend down the fingers of the left open hand, palm down, with the fingertips of the right hand as it passes from above the left hand downward, palm down.

AND
Bring the "c" hand, palm left, from the left side of the chest across to the right, closing the fingertips to the thumb as it moves.
Hint: Similar in formation and concept to the sign for "add."

MORE
Tap the fingertips of both flattened "o" hands together several times, palms facing body.
Hint: Similar in formation and concept to the sign for "add."

MOST
Begin with the knuckles of both "a" hands touching each other, palms facing down. Bring the right hand upward in an arc ending with the thumb pointing upward and outward to the right.
Hint: The movement is used for "est" endings or "the greatest" when comparing things.

MEDIUM
Tap the little finger side of the right open hand, palm left, across the index finger side of the left "b" hand at right angles.
Hint: Indicating the middle of the finger or medium length.

ENOUGH, PLENTY, SUFFICIENT
Push the palm of the downturned right hand forward across the top of the left "s" hand, palm right.
Hint: Pushing away the excess of something that is already full.

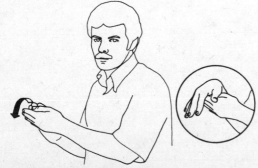

OVERFLOW, RUNNING OVER
Move the palm of the downturned right hand from down and behind the curved open left hand, palm toward body, smoothly up and over the index finger side of the left hand, spreading the right fingers apart as they move down the back of the left fingers.
Hint: Shows something overflowing.

FULL, FILL
Sweep the palm of the downturned right hand toward the left across the top of the left "s" hand, palm right.
Hint: Shows something full to the top.

SOME, PART, PORTION
Pull the little finger side of the open right hand, palm left, inward across the upturned open left palm.
Hint: Dividing something into parts.

VERY
Begin with the fingertips of both "v" hands touching, palms facing each other. Move fingers apart while holding the arms still.
Hint: Initialized sign formed similarly to "much."

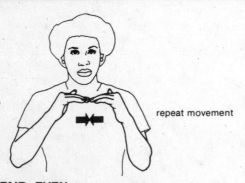

repeat movement

EQUAL, FAIR, EVEN
Tap the fingertips of the bent open hands, palms facing each other, together repeatedly.
Hint: Shows two things at an equal level with each other.

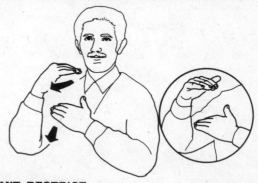

LIMIT, RESTRICT
With the right bent hand several inches above the left bent hand, both palms down, swing the fingertips of both hands outward a short distance.
Hint: The hands demonstrate the outside limits permitted.

INCREASE, GAIN WEIGHT
Bring the right "h" fingers, palm facing up, over and down across the left "h" fingers, palm down.
Hint: Formed similarly to "weight"; shows adding pounds on.

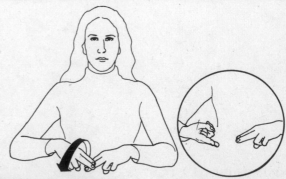

DECREASE, REDUCE
Move the right "h" fingers from crossed over left "h" fingers, both palms down, up and over ending with right palm up.
Hint: Formed similarly to "weight"; shows taking some pounds off.

WEIGH, WEIGHT
Rock the right "h" fingers, palm left, across the left "h" finger, palm right, by raising and lowering the right wrist.
Hint: Balancing things on a scale.

FULL, FED UP
Bring the back of the downturned open hand upward to under the chin.
Hint: Shows that you are full to the chin.

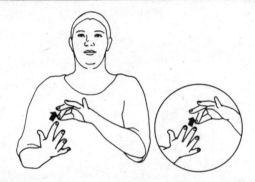

EITHER
Move the extended right index finger back and forth from first touching the thumb and then the index finger of the left "l" hand, palm right.
Hint: Trying to decide between one or the other.

ONLY
Beginning with the palm of the right "one" hand facing out, twist the wrist ending with the palm facing the body.
Hint: Shows only one thing.

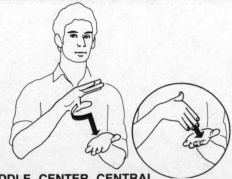

MIDDLE, CENTER, CENTRAL
Beginning with both open hands several inches apart, palms facing each other. Move the right hand forward in a circular motion suddenly dropping the fingers and bringing them sharply downward into the left palm.
Hint: Indicates the center of the palm.

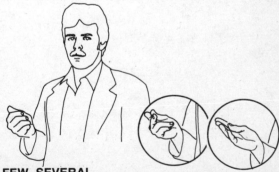

FEW, SEVERAL
Starting with an "a" hand, palm up, smoothly and quickly uncurl each finger, starting with the index finger, moving the thumb in toward the palm.
Hint: The fingers count out a few things.

A TINY BIT, BIT
Rub the thumb on the little fingertip of the right hand, palm facing up.
Hint: Feeling a tiny amount of something.

EMPTY, BARE, NAKED, BALD
Brush the bent middle fingertip of the right "5" hand, palm down, forward across the back of the left "s" hand, palm down, with a flick of the wrist.
Hint: The finger feels a bare spot on the back of the hand.

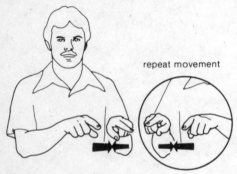

repeat movement

TOO, ALSO
Tap the extended index fingers, pointing forward and palms down, together first in front of chest and then again several inches to the right.
Hint: "Same" signed twice, showing something the same as something else.

LESS, DECREASE
Beginning with the right curved open hand several inches above the left open hand, palms facing each other, bring the right hand downward a short distance.
Hint: Demonstrates a decrease in distance.

ALMOST, NEARLY
Brush the fingers of the right bent open hand, palm up, upward from under the left upturned curved hand.

repeat movement

MEASURE, SIZE
Tap the thumbs of both "y" hands, palms down, together several times.
Hint: The little fingers indicate a unit of measure.

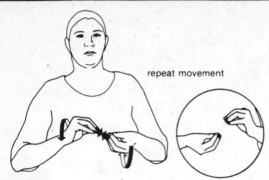

repeat movement

NUMBER
Starting with the fingertips of both flat "o" hands touching, left palm up and right palm down, twist wrists touching fingertips again, left palm down and right palm up.
Hint: Similar to sign for "add."

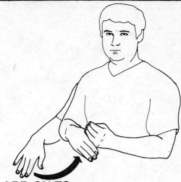

ADD, ADD ON TO
Starting with the right "5" hand several inches below and to the right of the left flattened "o" hand, bring the right hand up in an arc closing the fingertips to the thumb as it moves, ending with palms facing body.
Hint: Bringing a quantity to add on to an existing quantity.

PERCENT
Dip the "o" hand out to the right and then downward, palm left.
Hint: Trace the shape of a percentage sign in the air.

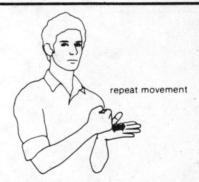

repeat movement

CREDIT CARD
Move the little finger side of the right "s" hand, palm facing in, back and forth across the palm of the up-turned left open hand.
Hint: Shows the action of a credit card machine taking an impression.

EXCEED, OVER, MORE THAN
Move the right bent hand from resting on the back of the fingers of the left bent hand, both palms down and fingers pointing in opposite directions toward each other, upward several inches above the left.
Hint: The right hand moves above a limit set by the left hand.

LESS THAN, BELOW
Move the right bent hand from under the fingers of the bent left hand, both palms down and fingers pointing in opposite directions toward each other, straight down several inches.
Hint: The right hand moves to a position less than the limit set by the left hand.

Money and Math

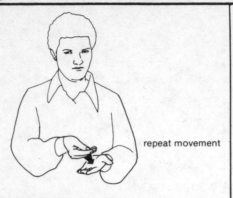

MONEY
Tap the back of the fingers of the right hand, fingertips touching the thumb and palm facing up, in the palm of the upturned left hand several times.
Hint: Holding money and laying it in the other hand.

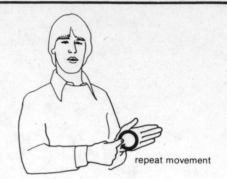

COINS
With the right extended index finger draw a small circle in the upturned left palm.
Hint: Shows the shape of a coin held in the hand.

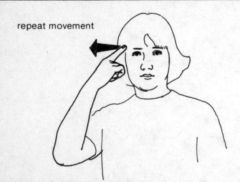

PENNY, ONE CENT, CENTS
Draw the extended index fingertip, palm toward face, from the right temple outward a few inches.
Hint: "Cents" plus "one."

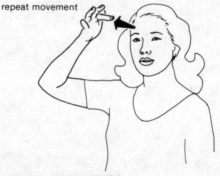

NICKEL, FIVE CENTS
Draw the index finger of the "5" hand, palm toward face, from the right temple outward a few inches.
Hint: "Cents" plus "five."

QUARTER, TWENTY-FIVE CENTS
Touch the extended index finger to the right temple, palm facing forward. Draw out, ending with the thumb, index finger, and little fingers extended, palm forward. Wiggle the down-pointing middle and fourth fingers.
Hint: "Cents" plus "twenty-five."

DIME, TEN CENTS
Touch the extended index finger to the right temple, palm facing shoulder. Pull away; change into an "a" handshape and wiggle it, palm facing back.
Hint: "Cents" plus "ten."

DOLLAR
With the right hand firmly holding the index finger side of the open left hand, palm toward body, drag the right hand along the top of the left hand from near the thumb outward off the fingertips.
Hint: Feeling the shape of a dollar bill.

ONE DOLLAR
With the hand in front of the right shoulder, twist the wrist of the "1" hand, palm left, ending with the palm toward body.
Hint: "One" plus a twist that means "dollar" for numbers under eleven.

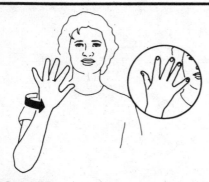

FIVE DOLLARS
Beginning with the "5" hand in front of the right shoulder, palm facing forward, turn it completely around with a twist of the wrist, ending with the palm facing body.
Hint: "Five" plus a twist that means "dollar" for numbers under eleven.

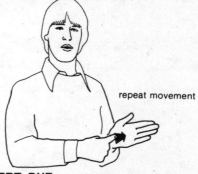

repeat movement

OWE, DEBT, DUE
Tap the palm of the open left hand, fingers forward and palm right, with the right bent extended index fingertip, palm left.
Hint: Similar action as the sign "against."

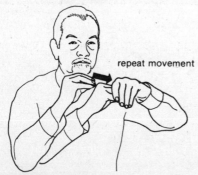

repeat movement

SAVE, SAVINGS, BANK
Shove the right thumb and fingers touching each other, pointing forward and to the left, into the left "c" hand, palm down, with a double motion.
Hint: Putting money away to save it.

DEPOSIT
With the thumbtip of the right "a" hand on the thumbnail of the left "a" hand, palms facing body, move the hands downward and apart by twisting the wrists.

BUY
Touch the back of the fingers of the right hand, fingertips touching the thumb and palm facing up, in the palm of the upturned left hand and then forward in a small arc.
Hint: "Money" plus "spend."

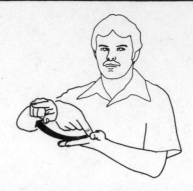

PAY
Sweep the right extended index finger, palm down, across the upturned left palm from the heel off the fingertips with a flick of the wrist.
Hint: Directing to pay off what is owed.

CHARGE, COST, FINE, TAX
Bring the back of the right "x" finger, palm toward body, down across the left palm, fingers forward and palm right, with a repeated motion.

repeat movement

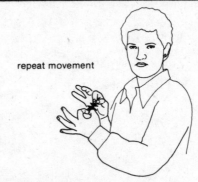

PRICE, COST
Touch the fingertips of both "9" hands to each other, palms facing, with a double motion.

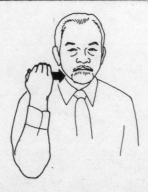

BROKE
Hit the little finger side of the "b" hand, palm facing down above the right shoulder and fingers pointing backward, against the neck.
Hint: Initialized sign; breaking the neck.

BEG
Hold the wrist of the right "claw" hand in the left hand, both palms up. Flex the right fingers in and out repeatedly.
Hint: Mime a beggar's motion.

EARN, SALARY, INCOME
Sweep the little finger side of the loose "5" hand from the fingers to the heel across the upturned left hand, ending with an "s" handshape.
Hint: Gathering money together.

SPEND
Starting with both "s" hands, palms up, in front of waist several inches apart. Move the hands upward and outward spreading the fingers into "5" hands.
Hint: Taking money in the hands and spreading it around.

BORROW
Beginning with both "k" hands, right on top of left in front of body, twist wrists to bring fingers up toward body, ending with fingers pointing up. Note: This means both "I borrow from you" and "You lend to me."
Hint: Bringing something borrowed to the body.

LEND
Place both "k" hands in front of body, right on top of left angled upward. Twist wrists to bring hands forward in an arc, ending with fingers pointing forward. Note: This means both "I lend to you" and "You borrow from me."
Hint: Giving something lent to the other person.

DIVIDE
With the right "b" hand on top of the left "b" hand, both palms facing each other and fingers pointing forward and angled inward, move the hands downward and apart.
Hint: Moving things apart from each other.

MULTIPLY, FIGURE, WORSE, ARITHMETIC
With the palms of both "k" hands toward body, right hand slightly higher than left, move hands past each other in opposite directions, touching the bottom of the right hand on top of the left as they pass.

ADD UP, SUM, TOTAL
Starting with the right "5" hand several inches above the left "5" hand, palms facing each other, gather the fingers to the thumbs of each hand bringing the hands toward each other until the fingertips touch.
Hint: Bringing two quantities together to add up.

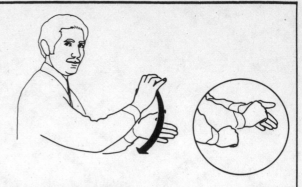

SUBTRACT, DISCOUNT
Sweep the right "claw" hand down, palm out, down across the left palm, fingers forward and palm right, changing into an "s" hand as it passes the left palm.
Hint: Taking something away.

ONE HALF
Bring the "1" hand from shoulder level downward, changing into a "2" handshape, palm toward body and fingers pointing up.
Hint: "One" plus "two" signed above each other similar to the written form.

ONE THIRD
Bring the "1" hand from shoulder level downward changing into a "3" handshape, palm toward body and fingers pointing up.
Hint: "One" plus "three" signed above each other similar to the written form.

ONE FOURTH
Bring the "1" hand from the shoulder level downward changing into a "4" handshape, palm toward body and fingers pointing up.
Hint: "One" plus "four" signed above each other similar to the written form.

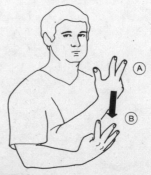

THREE FOURTHS
Bring the "3" hand from the shoulder level downward changing into a "4" handshape, palm toward body and fingers pointing up.
Hint: "Three" plus "four" signed above each other similar to the written form.

seven

TIME, DAYS, AND SEASONS

Time
Days and Holidays
Seasons and Weather

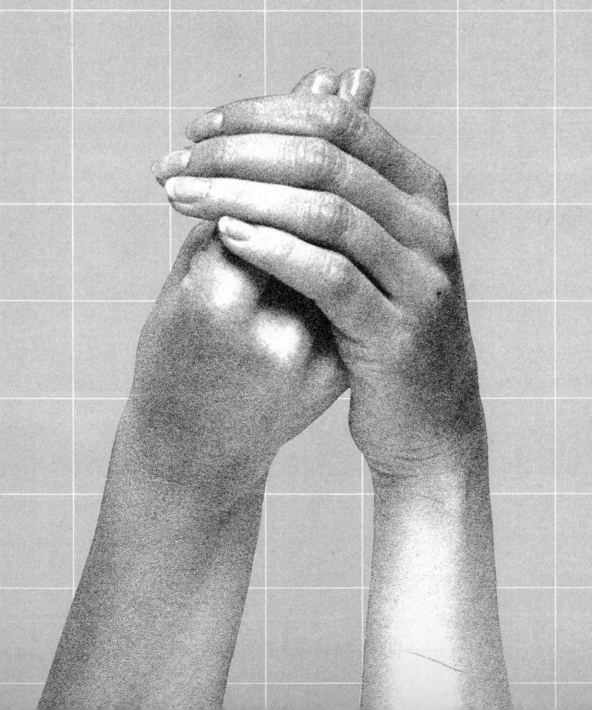

PAST, PRESENT, AND FUTURE TIME

Using the body as a present time referent, many of the time expressions fit logically into a pattern. Expressions which have a future connotation, such as "tomorrow," "later," and "still," have a forward movement from the body. Expressions indicating the past, such as "yesterday," "recently," and "previous," have a backward movement. Present time expressions, such as "today," "now," and "always," are formed directly in front of the body.

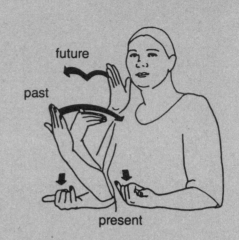

TIME OF DAY

With the left arm as an imaginary horizon, it is easy to visualize the sign which indicates the time of day. The right hand becomes the position of the sun over the horizon. Thus, "morning" brings the sun up over the horizon toward the body, and "afternoon" takes the sun down over the horizon away from the body. At "noon" the sun, hence the right hand, is up overhead, and at "midnight," it is directly below the horizon on the other side of the earth.

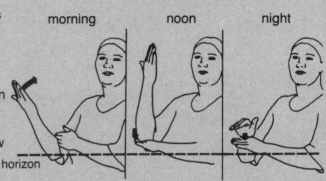

ADDING NUMBERS TO TIME

The numerals one through nine can be incorporated into the time signs "minute," "hour," "day," "week," and "month," forming signs like "six months" or "five days." In the same way, "next week," "last week," "last year," and "next year" can incorporate numbers to form concepts like "four years from now" and "three weeks ago."

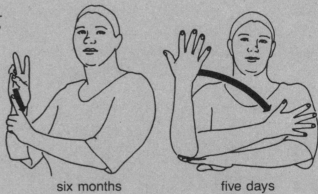

Time

TIME

Tap the curved extended index finger to the back of the left wrist.
Hint: Pointing to the location of a watch.

CLOCK

Tap the right index finger on the back of the left wrist; then place both wide "c" hands at the sides of the face.
Hint: "Time" plus an indication of a large clock face.

WATCH

Place the right "9" hand, palm down, on the back of the left wrist, encircling the location of a wristwatch.
Hint: Fingers encircle an imaginary wristwatch.

HOUR

Move the extended right index finger in a circular motion out, down, and around, ending at the starting position, palm facing open left palm and index finger pointing upward as it moves.
Hint: Indicates the minute hand making a complete hour movement around the clock.

MINUTE

Move the extended right index finger a small distance forward pivoting the closed fingers of the right hand on the palm of the left hand.
Hint: Indicates the movement of the minute hand on a clock.

SECOND (time)

Move the extended right index finger a tiny distance forward pivoting the closed fingers of the right hand on the palm of the left hand.
Hint: Indicates the movement of the second hand on a clock.

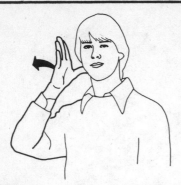

WILL, SHALL
Bring the open hand, palm left and fingers up, forward from the side of the face in one large arc, ending with the fingers pointing forward.
Hint: Indicates something in the future.

FUTURE
Bring the open hand, palm left and fingers up, forward from the side of the face in two arcs.
Hint: Indicates something in the future.

LATER, AFTER A WHILE
With the thumb of the "I" hand near lower cheek, twist wrist forward pointing the index finger of the "I" hand outward.
Hint: Initialized sign in a future movement.

FOREVER
Move the extended index finger, palm facing body, in a small circle toward right shoulder, moving smoothly into "y" hand arcing away from body, palm down.
Hint: "Always" plus "still."

repeat movement

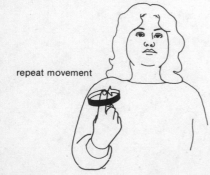

ALWAYS
Move the extended right index finger, palm facing body, in a small circle toward right shoulder.
Hint: The circular motion shows something never ending.

LAST, FINAL, FINALLY
Bring the right extended little finger down, striking the left extended little finger, both palms facing body.
Hint: Shows the last finger of the hand.

MONTH
Bring the right extended index finger, pointing left, palm facing the body, down the left extended index finger, pointing up, palm right.
Hint: With the left representing the weeks of a month, the right hand shows the passage of time over them all.

WEEK
With the right index finger extended, move the bent right fingers across the upturned left palm from the heel to the fingertips.
Hint: With the left hand representing a calendar, the right hand shows one row of dates.

NEXT WEEK, ONE WEEK FROM NOW
With the right, extended index finger pointing forward, palm down, move the bent right knuckles across the upturned left palm off the fingertips forward in an arc.
Hint: "Week" plus a future motion.

LAST WEEK, ONE WEEK AGO
With the right index finger extended, move the back of the right hand, palm up, across the upturned left palm off the fingertips back over the right shoulder.
Hint: "Week" plus a past motion.

repeat movement

WEEKLY
With the index finger extended, move the right hand across the left open hand, palms facing each other, from the heel to the fingertips several times, moving both hands slightly to the right each time.
Hint: The right finger traces several weeks across the calendar.

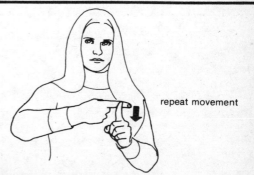

repeat movement

MONTHLY
Bring the right extended index finger, pointing left, palm facing body, down the left extended index finger, pointing up, palm right, several times, moving slightly to the right each time.
Hint: Shows several months passing.

PAST, AGO, LONG TIME AGO
Move the open hand from the side of the face, palm back, back over the right shoulder.
Hint: Past movement.

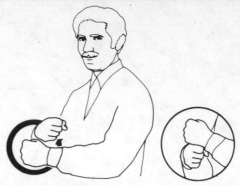

YEAR
With both "s" hands in front of body, palms facing body, right over left, move right hand forward and around left hand, landing on top of left hand.
Hint: The earth's movement around the sun.

LAST YEAR
Starting with right "s" hand on left "s" hand, palms out, move right hand back over right shoulder while extending index finger.
Hint: "Year" plus "one" in the past position.

NEXT YEAR
Starting with right "s" hand on left "s" hand, palms out, move right hand forward in an arc, extending index finger.
Hint: "Year" plus "one" in the future position.

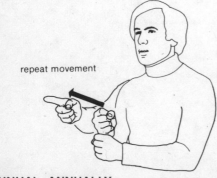

repeat movement

ANNUAL, ANNUALLY
Starting with the right "s" hand on the left "s" hand, palms out, move the right hand forward several times, flicking the index finger forward each time.
Hint: Sign "next year" several times quickly.

repeat movement

PREVIOUS, USED TO
Tap the bent open fingertips, palm facing back, on the right shoulder several times.
Hint: Past movement.

repeat movement

REGULARLY, REGULAR
With both extended index fingers pointing outward from body, strike the bottom of the right closed fingers to the top of the left hand repeatedly as the hand moves forward from body.
Hint: Indicates repeated action.

repeat movement

SOMETIMES, OCCASIONALLY
Sweep the extended right index finger pointing left, from the fingers to the heel of the upturned left palm, in a circular repeated motion. Note: "Occasionally" is signed more slowly than "sometimes."
Hint: Indicates a periodic repetition.

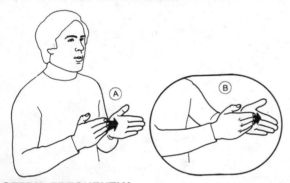

OFTEN, FREQUENTLY
Move the fingertips of the bent open right hand, palm left, against the open left palm. Move left hand forward and repeat.
Hint: "Again" repeated to show continued repetition.

AGAIN, REPEAT
Flip the upturned bent right hand over ending with the right fingertips on the upturned left palm, fingers pointing forward.
Hint: Right hand indicates a repetition.

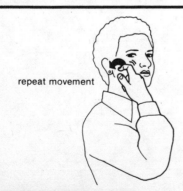

repeat movement

RECENTLY, LATELY, JUST
With palm facing back, rub the inside of the "x" index finger up and down on right cheek.
Hint: A brief past time.

repeat movement

DAILY, EVERYDAY, EVERY DAY
Rotate the side of the "a" hand, palm in, forward several times on side of chin with a twisting motion.
Hint: "Tomorrow" repeated several times.

NOW
Bring down both bent open hands in front of body, palms and fingers facing up.
Hint: In "present" position.

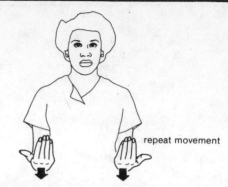

repeat movement

TODAY, NOW
Bring down both "y" hands in front of body, palms facing up.
Hint: In "present" position.

THEN, OR
Touch the extended right index finger first to the thumb and then to the index finger of the "l" left hand, palm right.
Hint: First one and then the other.

EARLY
Drag the bent middle finger of the "5" right hand, palm down, outward across the back of the down-turned left hand, fingers right.
Hint: The sun going over the horizon.

DURING, WHILE
With both index fingers extended pointing forward, palms down, move them out in a downward parallel arc.
Hint: Shows future movement of time.

STILL, YET
Starting with both "y" hands, palms facing chest, move down and outward in an arc.
Hint: Shows continuous future action.

UNTIL
Move the right extended index finger, palm left, in an arc to the left extended index fingertip, palm right.
Hint: Shows movement of time.

BE, AM, IS, ARE, WAS, WERE
Move the extended index finger, palm left and finger pointing upward, forward from the lips in a short straight movement.
Hint: Similar to the sign for "true" used to indicate a state of being.

BEFORE (time)
Starting with the back of the right curved open hand in the palm of the left curved open hand, both palms toward body, bring the right hand toward the chest.
Hint: Something happened prior to another thing. Past movement.

AFTER (time)
Starting with the palm of the right curved open hand against the back of the left curved open hand, both palms toward body, move the right hand outward from the left hand.
Hint: Something happened after another thing. Future movement.

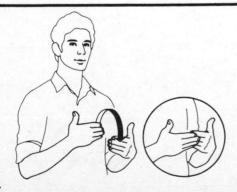

NEXT
Start with both open hands, palms facing body, left fingers pointing right and right fingers pointing left, right hand nearer body. Move the right hand in an arc over the left, ending directly behind it.
Hint: Shows something nearby.

repeat movement

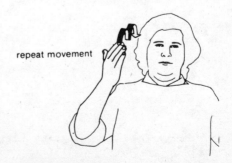

LONG TIME AGO
With the palm of the open hand facing left and fingers pointing up, move the hand backwards from in front of the right shoulder in two small arcs.
Hint: Past movement showing a long time in the past.

Days and Holidays

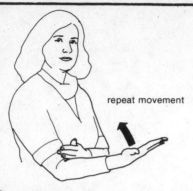

MORNING
With the fingers of the open left hand in the crook of the extended right arm, bring the right palm upward toward face.
Hint: Shows the movement of the sun coming up over the horizon in the morning.

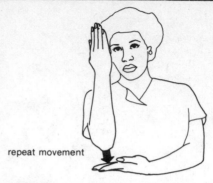

NOON
Place the elbow of the right arm, hand extended straight up, on the palm of the left hand, arm extended right in front of body.
Hint: Shows the sun straight up above the horizon.

AFTERNOON
With the fingers of the open downturned left hand under the elbow of the extended downturned right arm, lower the right palm slightly with a double motion.
Hint: Shows the movement of the sun going down toward the horizon in the afternoon.

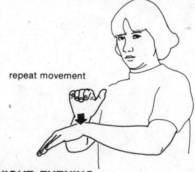

NIGHT, EVENING
Tap the wrist of the bent open right hand, palm down, on the top of the wrist of the downturned left arm, extended right.
Hint: Shows the sun setting below the horizon.

MIDNIGHT
Place the fingertips of the left hand in the crook of the right bent arm, extended downward, palm toward body.
Hint: Shows the sun halfway through its nighttime cycle.

BIRTHDAY
Move the right open hand, palm on chest, outward landing palm up on upturned left palm.
Hint: "Happy" plus "born."

DAY, ALL DAY
Place the elbow of the bent right arm, hand held straight up, palm left, on the downturned left hand. Move the extended right index finger downward toward the left elbow keeping the right elbow in place.
Hint: The sun moving across the horizon.

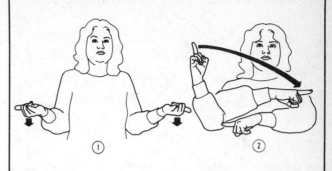

TODAY
Bring down both "y" hands in front of body, palms facing up. Place the elbow of the bent right arm, held straight up, palm left, on the back of the downturned left hand. Move the extended right index finger downward toward the left elbow.
Hint: "Now" plus "day."

TOMORROW
Move the thumbtip of the "a" hand forward in an arc from the right side of the chin.
Hint: Future motion.

YESTERDAY
Move the thumbtip of the "a" hand back from the right side of the chin to the center of the cheek.
Hint: Past motion.

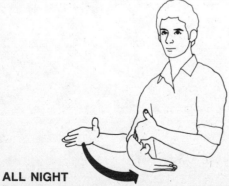

ALL NIGHT
Place the fingertips of the left hand in the crook of the right bent arm. Bring the right arm, palm down, in an arc from in front of body toward the body under the left arm.
Hint: Shows the movement of the sun through the entire nighttime cycle.

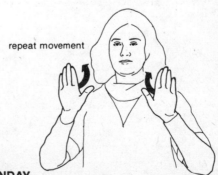

repeat movement

SUNDAY
Move both open hands, palms away from body, in circular motions upward and outward from each other.

MONDAY
Move the upturned "m," palm facing body, in a small circle.
Hint: Initialized sign.

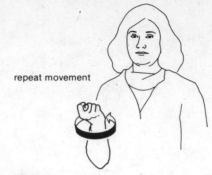

TUESDAY
Move the "t" hand, palm facing up, in a small circle.
Hint: Initialized sign.

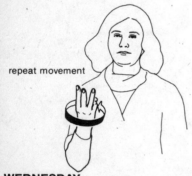

WEDNESDAY
Move the "w" hand, palm facing body, in a small circle.
Hint: Initialized sign.

THURSDAY
Flick the fingers quickly from a "t" to an "h" with a double motion.
Hint: Initialized sign.

FRIDAY
Move the "f" hand, palm facing body, in a small circle.
Hint: Initialized sign.

SATURDAY
Move the "s" hand, palm facing body, in a small circle.
Hint: Initialized sign.

HOLIDAY, VACATION, IDLE
Tap the thumbs of the "5" hands, palms facing, to the armpits with a double motion.
Hint: Sitting back with your thumbs under your suspenders with nothing to do.

VALENTINE'S DAY
Use both "v" hands, palms toward body, to trace the outline of a heart on the chest.
Hint: Initialized sign indicating the location of the heart.

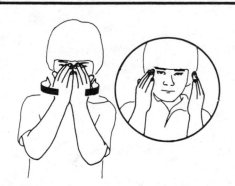

HALLOWEEN
Move open hands from together, palms toward face, outward to side of face.
Hint: Removing a mask.

THANKSGIVING
Starting with the open right hand, palm facing mouth, and the open left hand slightly forward, palm facing face, move both hands outward and upward drawing up and extending fingers as they move.
Hint: "Thank you" and "give" directed toward God.

CHRISTMAS
Flip the "c" hand, palm down and knuckles forward, to the right, ending with palm up. Note: Can be done with two hands.
Hint: Opening a present.

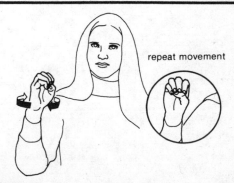

EASTER
Twist the "e" hand back and forth.
Hint: Initialized sign.

Seasons and Weather

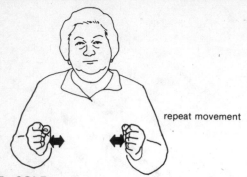

WINTER, COLD
Shake both "s" hands, palms facing, back and forth toward each other.
Hint: Shivering in winter.

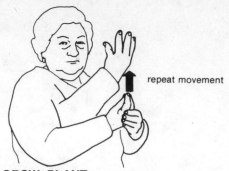

SPRING, GROW, PLANT
Smoothly bring the right hand, palm up with the fingertips touching the thumb, up through the left "c" hand, palm facing right, changing the right hand into a "5" handshape as it moves up. Repeat.
Hint: Mime a plant growing from a seed through the earth to a seedling.

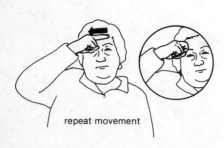

SUMMER
Drag the side of the index finger, pointing left, across the forehead changing it into an "x" hand ending at the right side of the forehead.
Hint: Wiping sweat off the brow.

FALL, AUTUMN
Brush the index finger of the right "b" hand down off the elbow of the raised left arm.
Hint: Leaves falling from a tree.

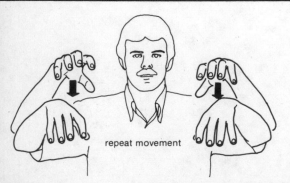

RAIN
Bring both loose "claw" hands, palms down, starting at shoulder level, down twice with a deliberate movement.
Hint: Raindrops falling.

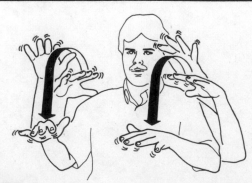

SNOW
Bring both loose "claw" hands, palms down, starting at shoulder level, down, gently wiggling each finger as the hands move.
Hint: Snowflakes falling.

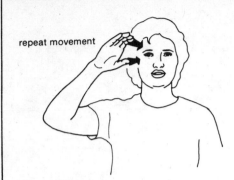

SUN
Bring the index finger side of the "c" hand to the right temple twice.
Hint: Shading the eyes from the sun.

MOON
Place the side of the curved index finger and thumb at the right temple encircling the right eye.
Hint: Fingers represent the crescent shape of the moon.

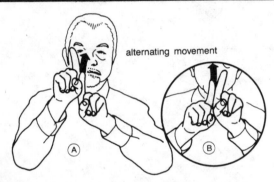

STARS
Brush the sides of both extended index fingers together, palms away from body, with an alternating motion as the hands move upward.
Hint: Fingers indicate the twinkling rays from the stars.

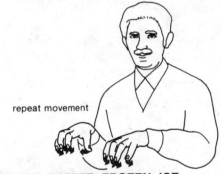

FROST, FREEZE, FROZEN, ICE
Keeping both "claw" hands, palms down, in front of body, draw fingers and thumbs inward toward palms.
Hint: A stiffening frozen position.

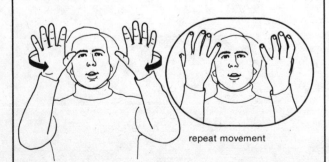

CLOUD
With loose "claw" hands, palms forward above shoulder level, move hands in outward arcs ending with palms facing body.
Hint: Follows the shape of fluffy, billowy clouds.

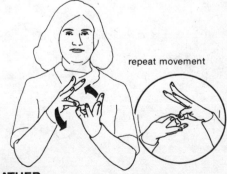

WEATHER
With the thumbs of both "w" hands touching, twist hands in opposite directions several times pivoting on the thumbs.
Hint: Initialized sign formed like "change," since weather changes so often.

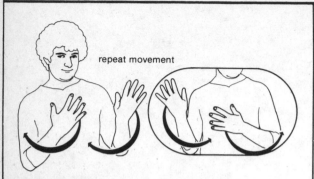

WIND, BREEZE
Starting with both "5" hands, fingers pointing right, right palm toward chest and left palm forward, bring hands across in front of body repeatedly, reversing hand positions on opposite side of body.
Hint: Shows the movement of the air.

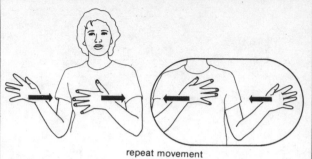

STORM
Starting with both "5" hands, fingers pointing right, right palm toward chest and left palm forward, swoop hands back and forth in front of body, reversing hand positions on opposite sides of the body.
Hint: Wind whipping the air around.

TORNADO
Starting with the right index finger near and pointing down to the left index finger, pointing up, spiral the right fingertip away in an upward motion.
Hint: Follows the shape of a tornado funnel.

HURRICANE
Starting with the "claw" hands, palms facing each other, right above left, spiral the right hand away in an upward motion.
Hint: Shows the whipping winds of a hurricane.

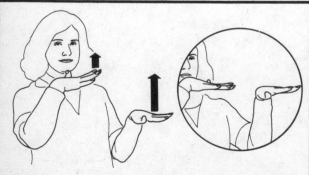

FLOOD
Begin with the thumb of the right "5" hand, palm down, fingers forward, on the chin and the left "5" hand parallel with the right hand, but somewhat lower. Raise both hands simultaneously to about mouth level.
Hint: Indicates water rising.

RAINBOW
Beginning with the right "4" hand near the left shoulder, fingers pointing outward, bring the hand upward in an arc, keeping the palm toward body and ending near right shoulder.
Hint: The fingers follow the colors and shape of a rainbow.

eight
PLACES

Cities and States
Countries
Location and Direction
Buildings

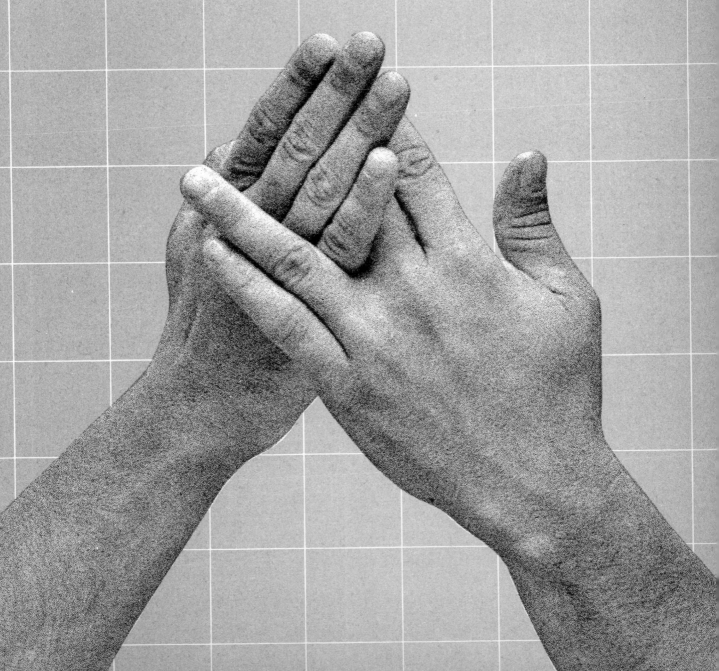

HERE, THERE

Pointing is used to indicate the adverbs "here" and "there." "Here" is signed by pointing down to the ground in front of the signer. "There" is signed by pointing in the direction of the object or person.

there

here

DIRECTION WITH "LOOK"

Using the extended index and middle fingers of either one or both hands to represent the eyes, point them in the direction of the object you are referring to. The hands should be held in front of the face at about nose level, and your eyes should peer down the fingers in the direction they are pointing. In this way you can form "look at," "look around," "look down," "look back," and so forth.

look at (the bat)

MAKING TWO SIGNS AT THE SAME TIME

It is possible in sign language to represent an object on each hand at the same time. For example, by using the index and middle fingers pointing downward on each hand to represent the legs of a person or animal, you can show how two people approached each other, or that a person stood behind another person. Both "3" hands with the thumbs pointing up can be used to represent vehicles; then you can demonstrate how their movement or location is related. There are other ways of representing people or objects such as using the extended index fingers. All of these representations are called "classifers."

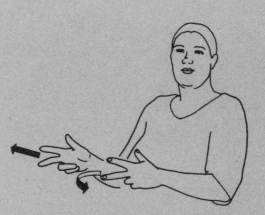

The car behind me turned left.

Cities and States

CHICAGO
Bring the "c" hand, palm facing left, first to the right
and then straight down.
Hint: Initialized sign.

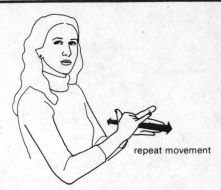

repeat movement

NEW YORK
Slide the palm side of the right "y" hand back and
forth on the palm of the upturned left hand.
Hint: Initialized sign.

ATLANTA
Touch the back of the thumb of the "a" hand, palm
left, first below the right shoulder and then below the
left shoulder.
Hint: Initialized sign.

BALTIMORE
Bounce the "b" hand, palm left and fingers pointing
forward, downward in front of the body and then
slightly to the right.
Hint: Initialized sign.

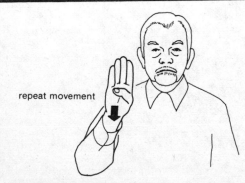

repeat movement

BOSTON
Bring the "b" hand, palm facing out, downward with a
double motion near the right shoulder.
Hint: Initialized sign.

DETROIT
Bring the "d" hand, palm facing left, first to the right
and then straight down in front of body.
Hint: Initialized sign.

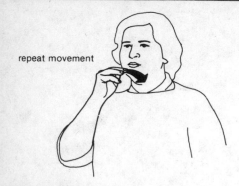

MILWAUKEE

Move the "m" hand, palm down, across the chin from right to left with a double movement.

Hint: Initialized sign. Wiping the famous Milwaukee beer from the chin.

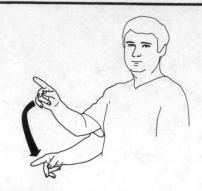

PHILADELPHIA

Bring the "p" hand, palm facing left, first to the right and then straight down in front of the chest.

Hint: Initialized sign.

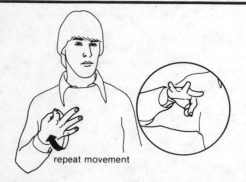

PITTSBURGH

Touch the index fingertip and thumb of the "9" hand on the upper right chest. Flip the hand down and out, ending with the palm down.

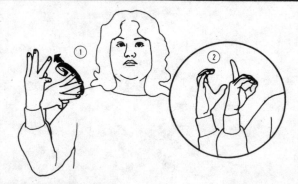

WASHINGTON, D.C.

Move the "w" hand upward in a circular movement from the right shoulder, palm facing back. Fingerspell "d" and "c" to designate "Washington, D.C."

Hint: Initialized sign formed in the position used for "boss" or "captain" to indicate the capital city.

NEW ORLEANS

Slide the thumb side of the flat "o" right hand, palm facing down, across the left open hand, palm facing right and fingers pointing forward.

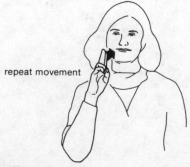

HOUSTON

Tap the index finger side of the "h" hand, palm facing left and fingers pointing up, at the right side of the chin with a double motion.

Hint: Initialized sign.

ARIZONA
Push the thumbnail of the "a" hand, palm left, from the right side of the chin to the left.
Hint: Initialized sigh formed like "dry" symbolizing the weather in Arizona.

TEXAS
Bring the "x" hand, palm facing out, to the right in front of the body, and then straight down.

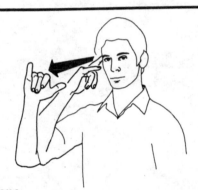

CALIFORNIA
With the thumb, index, and little fingers extended, touch the earlobe with the index finger. Then flick the wrist forward changing in a "y" hand, palm facing forward.
Hint: Similar to the sign for "gold"; California is known for the gold rush.

HAWAII, HAWAIIAN
With the fingers of the "h" hand, palm toward face, draw a counterclockwise circle in front of the face.
Hint: Initialized sign.

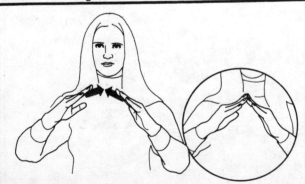

CITY, TOWN
Repeatedly bring the fingertips of both open hands together, palms angled facing each other, moving the hands to the right each time.
Hint: The hands represent the roofs of many buildings.

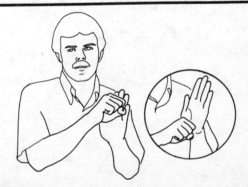

STATE
Bring the thumb side of the right "s" hand, palm facing out, down the open left hand, palm facing right and fingers pointing up, with a double motion.
Hint: Initialized sign.

Countries

COUNTRY, FOREIGN COUNTRY
Rub the knuckles of the right "y" hand in a circular movement near the bent left elbow, palm facing in.

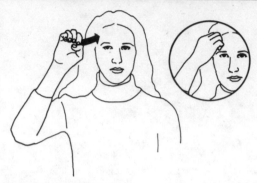

EUROPE, EUROPEAN
Starting with the "e" hand near the forehead, palm facing outward, twist the wrist bringing the knuckles of the hand to the forehead.
Hint: Initialized sign.

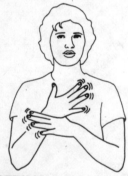

GERMANY, GERMAN
With the wrist of the right "5" hand between the thumb and index finger of the left "5" hand, palms toward chest, wiggle all the fingers.
Hint: Shows the double eagle symbol often used for Germany.

FRANCE, FRENCH
Starting with the palm of the "f" hand facing the right shoulder, flick the wrist forward, ending with the palm facing out. Note: Can be signed in reverse.
Hint: Initialized sign; flicking of a Frenchman's handkerchief out of his cuff.

AMERICA, AMERICAN
Loosely mesh the fingers of both "5" hands to each other, fingers pointing forward and palms angled toward each other. Move the hands in a horizontal, clockwise circle a couple of times.
Hint: The split-rail fences of early America.

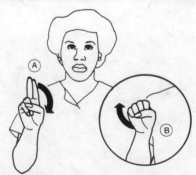

UNITED STATES
Bring the "u" hand slightly downward in an arc. Then bring the "s" hand slightly upward in an arc.
Hint: Initialized sign, "U.S."

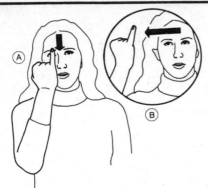

ITALY, ITALIAN
Using the extended right little finger, palm toward face, draw an small cross on the forehead.
Hint: Initialized sign; demonstrates the religious nature of many Catholics in Italy.

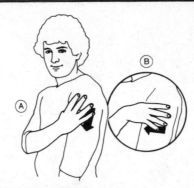

SCOTLAND, SCOTTISH
Bring the fingertips of the right "4" hand, fingers pointing up and palm in, down the left upper arm. Then bring the right "4" fingers, pointing back, forward across the side of the upper arm.
Hint: Fingers for the plaid of Scotch fabric.

SPAIN, SPANISH
With the extended curved index fingers pointing inward at either shoulder, bring them toward each other, hooking them together in front of the chest.
Hint: Fingers follow the shape of the Spanish mantilla.

IRELAND, IRISH
Bring the fingertips of the right crooked "v" hand, palm down, in a circular movement down to touch the back of the downturned left hand.
Hint: Similar to the sign for "potatoes," symbolizing the Irish potato.

HOLLAND, DUTCH, NETHERLANDS
Start with the thumb of the "y" hand at the forehead, palm left. Move the hand down and forward in an arc.
Hint: Hand follows the shape of the traditional Dutch hat.

repeat movement

ENGLAND, ENGLISH
Curl the fingers of the downturned right hand over the back of the left "s" hand, palm down. Use the right hand to pull the left hand toward the chest with a double movement.
Hint: Mime an Englishman's posture holding his hands over the head of his cane.

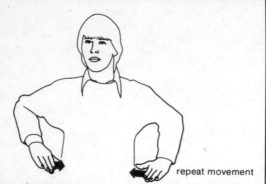

repeat movement

RUSSIA, RUSSIAN
Tap the index finger side of both downturned open hands below the waist on either side of the body.
Hint: Hand position for a familiar Russian dance.

repeat movement

SWEDEN, SWEDISH
Starting with the spread fingertips and thumb of the right downturned hand on the back of the open left downturned hand, draw the right hand upward bringing the fingertips and thumb together. Repeat.

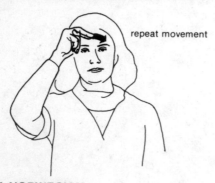

repeat movement

NORWAY, NORWEGIAN
Tap the "n" fingers, palm left, downward across the forehead a couple of times.
Hint: Initialized sign.

repeat movement

DENMARK, DANE, DANISH
Bring the "d" hand, palm left, downward across the forehead with a double motion.
Hint: Initialized sign.

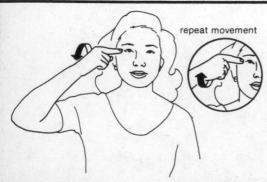

repeat movement

CHINA, CHINESE
Twist the extended index finger back and forth at the corner of the right eye, palm down.
Hint: Points to distinguishable eye shape of a Chinese person.

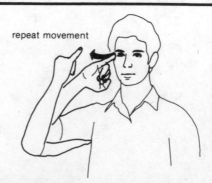

repeat movement

JAPAN, JAPANESE
With the extended little finger at the corner of the right eye, palm facing outward, twist the wrist down, forming a tight "j," ending with the palm facing back.
Hint: Initialized sign pointing to the distinguishable eye shape of a Japanese person.

repeat movement

repeat movement

CANADA, CANADIAN
Beat the palm side of the "a" hand on the right side of the chest a couple of times. Note: Fingers may grasp the clothing and pull it in and out with the "a" hand.
Hint: Shows that the Canadian Mounted Police reportedly "always get their man."

GREECE, GREEK
Bring the "g" hand, fingers pointing up and palm toward face, down the bridge of the nose.
Hint: Initialized sign following the shape of a Greek nose.

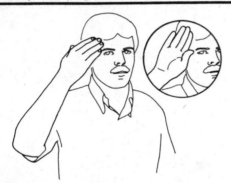

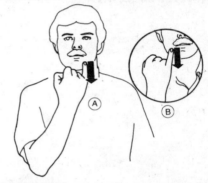

AUSTRALIA, AUSTRALIAN
Start with the fingertips of the open hand touching the forehead, palm facing in. Then flip the wrist and touch the back of the open hand against the forehead, palm facing out.
Hint: Represents a traditional Australian hat.

ISRAEL, ISRAELI
Bring the extended little finger downward, first on the left side of the chin and then the right side.
Hint: Initialized sign following the shape of a traditional Jewish beard.

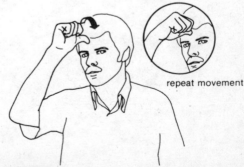

repeat movement

AFRICA, AFRICAN
Bring the thumb of the "a" hand, palm facing left, in a large circle in front of the face.
Hint: Initialized sign.

INDIA, INDIAN
With the thumb of the "a" hand in the center of the forehead, twist the knuckles downward toward the left. Note: This sign is not used for the American Indian.
Hint: Shows the dot worn on the forehead of many Indian women.

Location and Direction

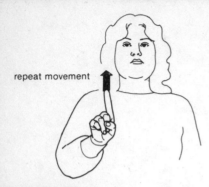

UP, UPSTAIRS
Move the extended index finger pointing up, palm facing out, upward.
Hint: Natural gesture.

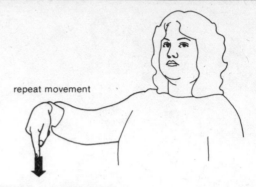

DOWN, DOWNSTAIRS
Move the extended index finger pointing down, palm facing in, downward.
Hint: Natural gesture.

NEAR, CLOSE TO, APPROACH
Bring the back of the right open hand, palm toward body and fingers pointing left, out near to the palm of the left open hand, palm facing body and fingers pointing right.
Hint: Something comes near another thing.

FAR
With both "a" hands touching in front of body, palm toward each other, bring the right hand forward.
Hint: Something is a distance away from another thing.

ABOVE, OVER
Starting with the downturned right open hand laying on the back of the downturned left open hand, elbows out, bring the right hand upward first toward the body and then arc outward.
Hint: Something is above another thing.

BELOW, BENEATH
Starting with the downturned right open hand under the palm of the downturned left open hand, bring the right hand in an arc toward the body and downward.
Hint: Something is below another thing.

TOGETHER
With the "a" hands together, palms facing each other, make a horizontal clockwise circle.
Hint: Two things moving together.

SEPARATE, APART
Start with the knuckles of both bent hands together, palms toward body. Then pull them apart.
Hint: Two things moving apart.

AHEAD, BEFORE
With the "a" hands together, palms facing each other and thumbs extended, arc the right hand forward a short distance.
Hint: Something moves ahead of another thing.

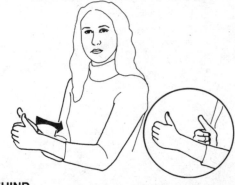

BEHIND
With the "a" hands together, palms facing each other and thumbs extended, move the right hand backward toward the lower chest.
Hint: Something moves behind another thing.

OUT
With the fingers pointing down, draw the right open hand up and out of the left "c" hand, palm right. Draw the right fingertips and thumb together as the hand moves.
Hint: Taking something out of another thing.

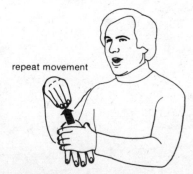

repeat movement

OUTSIDE
With the fingers pointing down, draw the right open hand up and out of the left "c" hand, palm right. Draw the right fingertips and thumb together as the hand moves. Repeat.
Hint: Taking something out of another thing.

AROUND, SURROUND
Move the extended right index finger, palm and finger pointing down, around the left index finger pointing up, palm toward body.
Hint: Something moving around another thing.

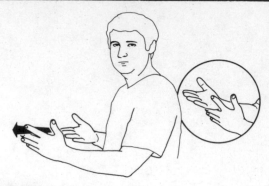

THROUGH
Bring the open right hand, palm angled up, between the index and middle fingers of the left open hand, palm angled in and right.
Hint: Something goes through another thing.

LEFT
Move the "l" hand, palm facing out, to the left with a deliberate motion. Note: May be done with the left hand instead.
Hint: Initialized sign pointing left.

RIGHT
Move the "r" hand, palm facing out, to the right with a deliberate motion.
Hint: Initialized sign pointing right.

IN
With the right fingertips touching the thumb, palm toward body and fingers pointing down, insert them down into the left "c" fingers, palm right.
Hint: Put something inside another thing.

repeat movement

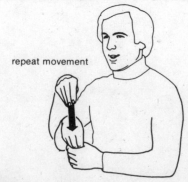

INSIDE
With the right fingertips touching the thumb, palm toward body and fingers pointing down, insert them down into the left "c" fingers, palm right, with a double movement.
Hint: Put something inside another thing.

AWAY
Extend the right arm with the bent open hand held at shoulder level, palm and fingers down. Flick the wrist up, ending with the open palm facing out.
Hint: Brushing something away.

GONE, LEFT
Bring the "c" hand, palm and fingers toward right cheek, outward to the side of the body, drawing the fingertips and thumb together.
Hint: Something disappearing into the distance.

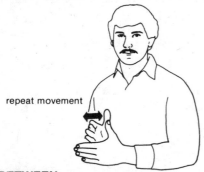

repeat movement

BETWEEN
Move the little finger side of the right open hand, palm left and fingers pointing forward, back and forth on the index finger of the left open hand, palm right and fingers pointing forward at cross angles.
Hint: Indicating a location between the finger and the thumb.

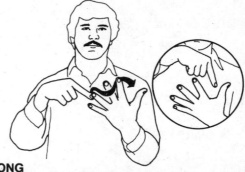

AMONG
Hold the left "5" hand in front of the chest, palm facing the body. Starting at the fourth finger, move the right extended index finger in and out between the left fingers, ending between the index finger and thumb.
Hint: Something moving among other things.

AFTER, ACROSS, OVER
Move the right "b" hand, palm left and fingers pointing forward, in an tight arc over the left "b" hand, palm toward body and fingers pointing right.
Hint: Something moves over another thing.

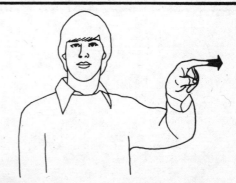

THERE
Point the extended index finger at a specific location.
Hint: Something in a location away from you.

NORTH
Move the "n" hand, palm facing out, upward.
Hint: Initialized sign moving north on a map.

EAST
Move the "e" hand, palm facing out, to the right from the shoulder.
Hint: Initialized sign moving east on a map.

SOUTH
Move the "s" hand, palm facing out, downward.
Hint: Initialized sign moving south on a map.

WEST
Move the "w" hand, palm facing out, to the left in front of the chest.
Hint: Initialized sign moving west on a map.

DIRECTION
Move both "d" hands, palms facing each other and index fingers pointing forward, back and forth in front of the body in alternating movements.
Hint: Initialized sign indicating movement in a non-specific direction.

PLACE
With the middle fingers of both "p" hands touching, palms facing up, bring the hands outward in a circle toward the body, ending by touching the middle fingers again close to the lower chest.
Hint: Initialized sign outlining an area.

AGAINST, SUE
Bring the fingertips of the bent right hand, palm toward body, firmly against the left palm, facing right.
Hint: Something coming up against another thing.

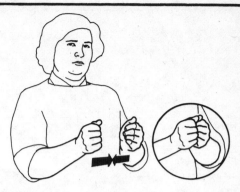

WITH
Bring both "a" hands together, palms facing each other.
Hint: Something moves with another thing.

TO
Bring the extended right index finger, palm down and finger pointing left, a short distance to the extended left index finger, palm right and finger pointing up.
Hint: Bringing something to another thing.

TOWARD
Bring the extended right index finger, palm left and finger pointing up, in an arc from near the right shoulder to the extended left index finger, palm right and finger pointing up.
Hint: Bringing something toward another thing.

UNDER
Bring the right "a" hand, palm facing left, from the chest down in an arc under the downturned left hand held at shoulder level.
Hint: Something moves under another thing.

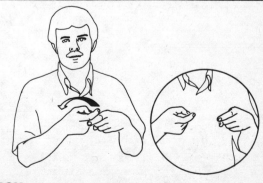

FROM
Bring the right "x" index finger, palm facing body, toward the body from the left extended index finger, palm facing right and finger pointing up.
Hint: Taking something from another thing.

FOLLOW
With the left "a" hand in front of the right "a" hand, palms facing toward each other, move both hands forward simultaneously.
Hint: The right hand is following the left hand.

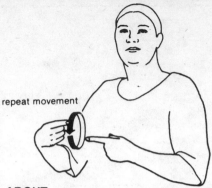

repeat movement

ABOUT
Move the extended right index finger, palm toward body and finger pointing left, around the fingertips of the left thumb and fingers held together and pointing right, palm toward body.
Hint: Something moving about another thing.

ON
Lay the palm of the downturned right hand across the back of the downturned left hand.
Hint: Something is on another thing.

OFF
Bring the downturned right hand from off the back of the downturned left hand, upward a few inches.
Hint: Something moves off another thing.

APPEAR, SHOW UP
Bring the right extended index finger, palm facing out, upward between the index and middle fingers of the downturned open left hand.
Hint: Pop up out of nowhere.

DISAPPEAR, DROP OUT
Pull the extended right index finger, pointing up and palm out, down between the index finger and middle finger of the downturned left open hand.
Hint: Something drops out of sight.

Buildings

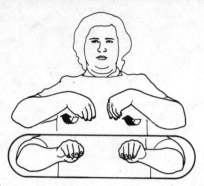

STORE
Starting with both flat "o" hands pointing downward and inward toward the lower chest, palms toward body, move the wrists upward flipping the fingertips out.
Hint: Similar to "sell" only with a single movement.

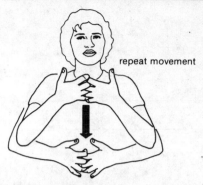

repeat movement

FACTORY, MACHINE
Loosely mesh the fingers of both curved "5" hands, thumbs extended up and palms toward body. Bend the wrists up and down, keeping the fingers loosely meshed with each other.
Hint: Shows the moving of the gears in machinery.

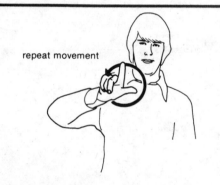

repeat movement

LIBRARY
Move the "l" hand, palm facing out, in a large circle in front of the shoulder.
Hint: Initialized sign.

RESTAURANT
Touch the fingertips of the "r" hand at the right side of the chin and then at the left, palm facing in.
Hint: Initialized sign formed near where you eat.

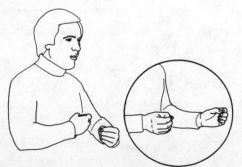

OFFICE
Place both "o" hands in front of body, the left hand farther out than the right, both palms facing in. Move the hands to the side, palms facing each other.
Hint: Initialized sign formed like "room" and "box."

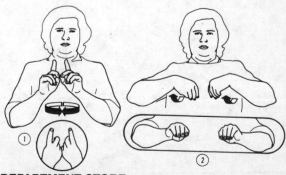

DEPARTMENT STORE
With the fingertips of both "d" hands touching each other, palms facing, move the hands around in a small circle, coming together with the little fingers touching and the palms toward the body.
Hint: "Department" is an initialized sign. "Store" is like "sell," only with one movement.

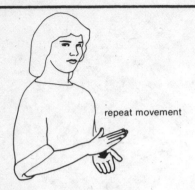

SCHOOL
Clap the palm of the downturned right hand, fingers forward, crosswise across the upturned palm of the left hand, with a double motion.
Hint: Clapping your hands to get the students' attention.

COLLEGE
Bring the downturned right hand, fingers forward, from laying across the upturned left palm up and out in a circular motion.
Hint: "School" plus showing that it is higher.

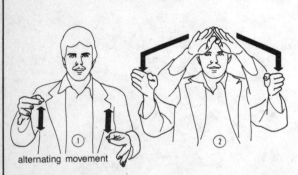

COURTHOUSE
Alternately raise and lower both "f" hands, palms facing each other and fingers forward. Follow by bringing both open hands down at shoulder width, palms facing each other and fingers pointing out.
Hint: "Judge" plus "house."

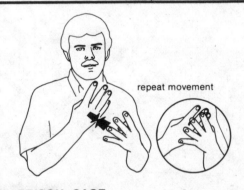

JAIL, PRISON, CAGE
Bring the back of the right "4" hand, palm facing body, and the palm of the left "4" hand crosswise against each other.
Hint: Fingers represent the cell bars.

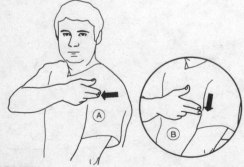

HOSPITAL
With the fingertips of the "h" hand, draw a small cross on the upper left arm.
Hint: Initialized sign tracing the symbolic cross of some medical personnel's uniforms.

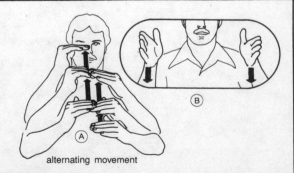

BUILDING
With the fingertips of both bent open hands overlapping slightly, alternatingly move the hands over each other. Follow by bringing both open hands down. at shoulder width, palms facing each other
Hint: "Build" plus the hands follow the outer walls of a building.

nine

HEALTH AND SURVIVAL

Health and Medical
Parts of the Body
Survival

SIGNS THAT EXPRESS DIFFICULTY

Many signs that express difficulty are formed with a bent "v" handshape. Some examples are "hard," "strict," "difficult," and "problem."

hard

SIGN PLACEMENT

Some verbs can carry additional information by their placement on the body. For example, "hurt," "sore," "cut," and "operation" will be understood more easily if you sign them near the location on the body where the pain or surgery has occurred.

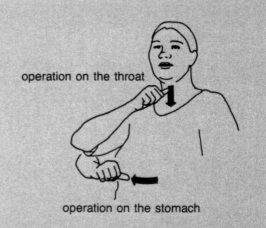

operation on the throat

operation on the stomach

COMPOUNDS

Compounds are formed in spoken language by joining two words together to form a new word with a different meaning from that of either contributing word. For example, "notebook" has a completely different meaning than either "note" or "book." Similarly, in sign language, two signs may be combined to form a new sign with a different meaning. An example of a sign compound is "pale," which is made up of the two signs "white" plus "face." Often, knowing the two signs that make up a compound helps you remember it.

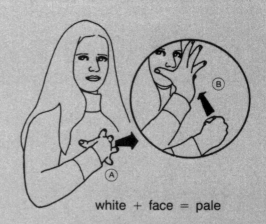

white + face = pale

Health and Medical

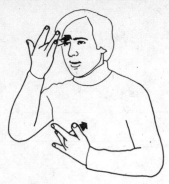

SICK, ILL, DISEASE
Touch the right bent middle finger of the "5" hand to the forehead simultaneously while touching the left bent middle finger of the "5" hand to the stomach, both palms facing in.
Hint: Indicates a bad feeling in the head and body.

HURT, PAIN, ACHE, SORE
Jab the extended index fingertips toward each other in front of body several times without making contact with each other, palms facing chest. Note: Can be signed near the point of pain.
Hint: Shows the piercing pains.

OPERATION, SURGERY
Drag the thumbtip of the right "a" hand, palm down, on the upturned left palm, fingers pointing forward, from the fingertips to the heel toward the body. Note: Can be signed near the place surgery occurred.
Hint: Shows where the incision occurred.

INJECTION, SHOT
Point the index finger of the right "I" hand to the upper left bent arm. Push the index fingertip into the forearm while lowering the thumb.
Hint: Mime giving yourself an injection.

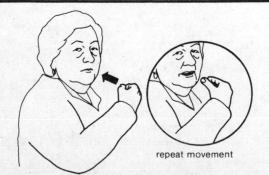

repeat movement

PILLS, TAKE A PILL
With the fingertips of the extended thumb and index finger together, palm toward body, move the hand toward the mouth, spreading the fingertips apart as they approach the mouth.
Hint: Dispensing a pill into the mouth.

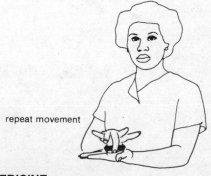

repeat movement

MEDICINE
Rub the tip of the bent middle finger of the right "5" hand, palm down, back and forth on the upturned left palm.
Hint: Miming the old way of grinding medicine with a pestle and mortar.

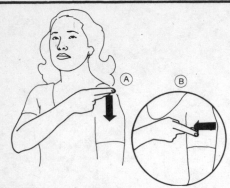

PATIENT
With the middle fingertip of the "p" hand, palm toward body, draw a small cross on the side of the upper left arm.
Hint: Initialized sign formed like "hospital."

SKELETON, POISON
With the arms crossed on the chest at the wrists, tap the opposite shoulders with the crooked "v" fingertips, palms toward body.
Hint: Forms the crossbones from the skull and crossbones symbol on poison.

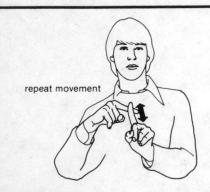

repeat movement

TEMPERATURE
Move the right extended index finger, palm down, up and down on the back of the left extended index finger, pointing up and palm facing out.
Hint: Shows the mercury moving up and down in a thermometer.

THERMOMETER
Insert the extended index finger, palm down, between the lips.
Hint: Mime taking a person's temperature.

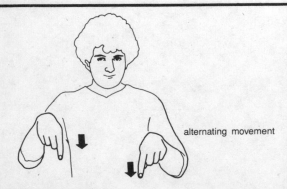

alternating movement

CRIPPLED, LAME
With both extended index fingers pointing down, palms toward the lower chest, move them up and down with alternating movements.
Hint: The fingers represent two legs limping.

repeat movement

WHEELCHAIR
With both extended index fingers pointing in at either side of the waist, palms facing up, make large circles simultaneously.
Hint: The fingers follow the motion of a wheelchair's wheels.

BLIND
Bring the crooked "v" fingers, palm toward face, close to the eyes on either side of the nose.
Hint: The eyes are put out.

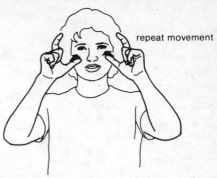

repeat movement

GLASSES
With both extended index fingers and thumbs curved on either side of the face, palms facing each other, tap the thumbs on the cheeks with a double movement.
Hint: The fingers encircle the shape of the glasses frames and lenses.

DEAF
Bring the right extended index finger from touching the ear, palm left, down, changing into a "b" hand to meet the left "b" hand in front of the chest, both palms down.
Hint: Shows that the ears are closed.

DEAF
Touch first the mouth and then the ear with the extended index finger, palm left.
Hint: The mouth and ear are closed.

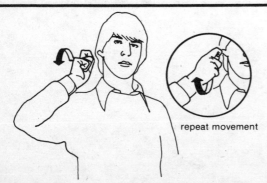

repeat movement

HEARING AID
Twist the "x" finger touching the thumb, palm left, back and forth in front of the ear.
Hint: Screwing the hearing aid mold firmly in the ear canal.

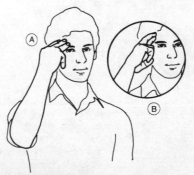

MENTALLY RETARDED
With the palm toward the face, fingerspell "m" and "r" against the right side of the forehead.
Hint: Initials for "mentally retarded."

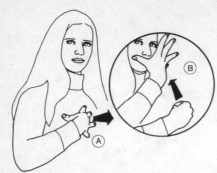

PALE

Draw the fingertips of the loose "5" hand from touching the chest, palm facing in, outward while drawing the thumb and fingertips together. Raise the hand, opening back into a "5" hand in front of the face.
Hint: "White" plus "face."

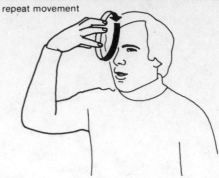

DIZZY

Move the "claw" hand, palm toward face, in a counterclockwise circle in front of the forehead.
Hint: The head is spinning.

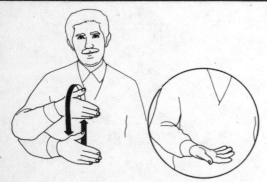

UPSET

Bring the palm of the open hand upward on the stomach, turning the wrist up and outward. Lower the hand with the palm facing up.
Hint: Shows a stomach turning over.

FAINT

Bring the extended right index finger from touching the right temple, palm left, downward, changing into a loose "5" hand at waist level by the left loose "5" hand.
Hint: The head falls forward loosely.

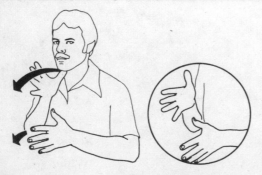

VOMIT

With the right "5" hand under the chin, palm left, and the left "5" hand held lower, palm right, move both hands forward in an arc simultaneously.
Hint: Shows the path vomit comes from the stomach and mouth.

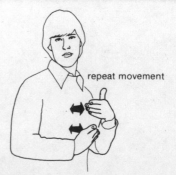

BREATH, BREATHE

With the left open hand above the right open hand, both palms toward the chest, simultaneously move both hands slowly back and forth repeatedly.
Hint: The hands follow the sinking and rising of the chest during breathing.

repeat movement

COLD, HANDKERCHIEF, TISSUE
Bring the thumb and index fingertips of the "g" hand, palm toward face and fingers pointing up, downward with a double motion, closing the thumb and index fingertips together.
Hint: Mime wiping the nose with a handkerchief.

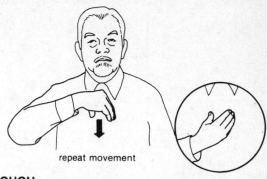

repeat movement

COUGH
Roll the fingertips of the "c" hand, palm toward body, downward on the chest, keeping the fingers in place.
Hint: Shows the action of a cough deep in the chest.

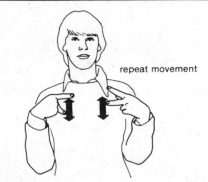

repeat movement

PNEUMONIA
Rock the middle fingertips of both "p" hands up and down on the chest, palms toward body.
Hint: Initialized sign showing difficulty breathing from pneumonia.

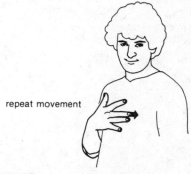

repeat movement

HEART
Touch the center of the chest with the bent middle finger of the "5" hand, palm toward body.
Hint: Shows location of the heart.

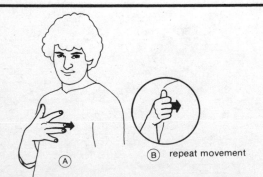

Ⓐ   Ⓑ repeat movement

HEARTBEAT
Touch the center of the chest with the bent middle finger of the "5" hand, palm toward body. Change into an "a" hand and tap the chest twice.
Hint: "Heart" plus the pounding of the heart.

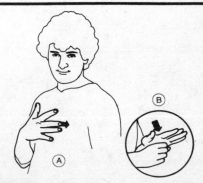

Ⓑ

Ⓐ

HEART ATTACK
Touch the center of the chest with the bent middle finger of the "5" hand, palm toward body. Slam the downturned right palm on the top of the left "s" hand, palm right.
Hint: "Heart" plus having an attack.

MUMPS
Form both "claw" hands, palms facing each other, at the sides of the neck below the jaws.
Hint: Shows the shape and location of mumps.

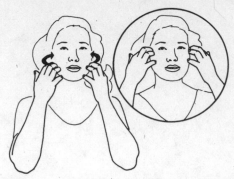

MEASLES
Lightly tap the fingertips of both loose "claw" hands to the lower cheeks and then to the upper cheeks, palms toward face.
Hint: Shows the spots on the face from measles.

BLOOD, BLEED
With the left "5" hand in front of the chest, palm toward body and fingers pointing right, bring the right "5" hand, palm toward body and fingers pointing left, from touching the lips down past the left hand, wiggling the fingers as the hand moves.
Hint: Blood streaming down.

PREGNANT
Bring the fingertips of the curved "5" hand upward and outward from the lower belly, palm toward body.
Hint: Shows the size and shape of a pregnant woman's belly.

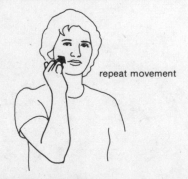

repeat movement

MENSTRUATION, PERIOD
Tap the cheek with the knuckles of the "a" hand, palm toward face.

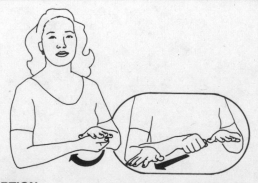

ABORTION
Bring the upturned right "a" hand from under the downturned left "5" hand, twisting the wrist and ending with a downturned right "5" hand to the right side of the body.
Hint: Taking out the fetus and throwing it away.

Parts of the Body

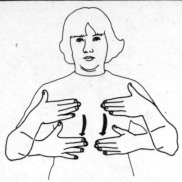

BODY, HEALTH
Touch the upper chest and then the lower chest with the palms of both open hands.
Hint: Shows the location of the body.

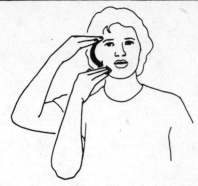

HEAD
Touch the temple and then the cheek with the fingertips of the bent open hand, fingers and palm facing left.
Hint: Shows the location of the head.

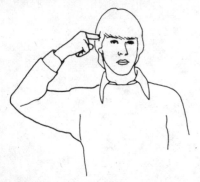

BRAIN, MIND
Touch the index fingertip to the right temple with the elbow out and the palm toward the face.
Hint: Shows the location of the brain.

FACE, LOOKS, APPEARANCE
Make a counterclockwise circle around the face with the extended index finger, palm toward face.
Hint: The hand outlines the shape of the face.

HAIR
Hold a bit of hair between the index finger and thumb of the "9" hand.
Hint: Shows the location of the hair.

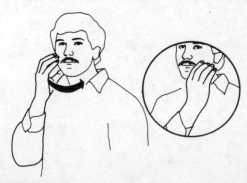

BEARD
Move the thumb and fingertips of the "c" hand, palm toward face, from the right cheek along the jawline, ending with the index finger side of the "c" hand against the left cheek.
Hint: Shows the location and shape of a beard.

MOUTH
Circle the mouth with the extended index finger, palm toward face.
Hint: Shows the location and shape of the mouth.

LIPS
Trace over the lips with the extended index finger in a counterclockwise oval.
Hint: Shows the location and shape of the lips.

TONGUE
Touch the extended tongue with the extended index fingertips, palm toward face.
Hint: Shows the location of the tongue.

TEETH
Tap the fingernail of the extended crooked index finger against the front teeth, palm toward face.
Hint: Shows the location of the teeth.

NOSE
Touch the extended index fingertip to the tip of the nose, palm toward face.
Hint: Shows the location of the nose.

EYES
Use the extended index finger to point upward to each eye, palm toward face.
Hint: Shows the location of the eyes.

EAR
Grab the right earlobe between the thumb and index finger of the "a" hand.
Hint: Shows the location of the ear.

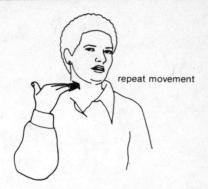

repeat movement

NECK
Bring the fingertips of the bent open hand, palm and fingers back, against the neck.
Hint: Shows the location of the neck.

repeat movement

BACK
Tap the back of the right shoulder with the fingertips of the downturned hand.
Hint: Shows the location of the back.

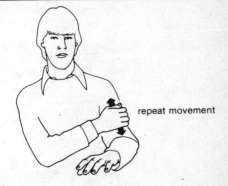

repeat movement

ARM
Drag the palm of the curved right hand up and down on the bent left arm from the armpit to the elbow.
Hint: Shows the location and shape of the arm.

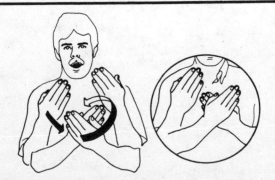

HANDS
Wipe the right palm on the back of the left open hand, both palms facing the neck; repeat the action with the left palm on the back of the right hand.
Hint: Displays the location of the hands.

FEET
Point downward toward each foot with the hand above waist level, palm facing body.
Hint: Points out the location of the feet.

Survival

SURVIVE
Bring both "a" hands with thumbs extended upward, palms toward the body, upward from the waist to the chest.
Hint: Formed similar to the sign for "live."

LIVE, LIFE
With the index fingers of both "l" hands pointing toward each other, palms toward the waist, move the hands upward toward the chest.
Hint: Initialized sign showing life moving through the body.

HELP, AID, ASSIST
Raise the left "a" hand, palm toward body, upward with the upturned right palm.
Hint: The right hand is giving assistance to the left hand.

repeat movement

DEFEND, PROTECT, GUARD
With both "s" hands crossed at wrists in front of upper chest, right palm facing left and left palm facing right, move both hands forward with a double motion.
Hint: The hands are held up to protect the body.

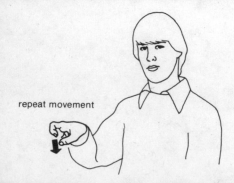

repeat movement

NEED, NECESSARY, OUGHT TO, SHOULD
Tap the "x" index finger up and down in a double motion.

MUST, HAVE TO
Bring the "x" index finger downward once.

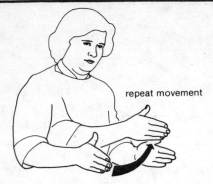

SPANK
Swing the open right hand, palm facing left, across and upward against the open left palm, facing right and fingers pointing forward. Repeat.
Hint: Mime spanking the hand across someone's bottom.

PUNISH, PENALTY
Strike the extended right index finger, pointing left, downward on the elbow of the raised bent left arm.

HIT, STRIKE, PUNCH
Strike the left extended index finger, pointing up and palm out, with the knuckles of the right "s" hand, palm toward body.
Hint: Striking something.

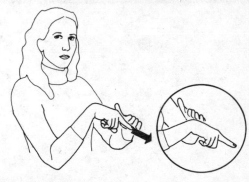

KILL, MURDER
Push the extended right index finger, palm down, forward and down under the left downturned open palm.
Hint: Stabbing into someone.

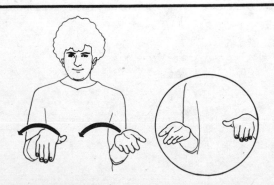

DIE, DEATH, DEAD
With the upturned right hand beside the downturned left hand, fingers pointing forward, side by side, flip the hands to the left so that the right palm faces down and the left palm faces up.
Hint: Mime a bug turning over to die.

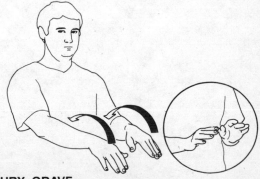

BURY, GRAVE
Move both downturned open hands, fingers pointing forward, back toward the body in an arc.
Hint: Hands follow the mound of dirt on a grave.

MATCH
Bring the knuckle of the extended crooked index finger in an arc upward off the left open palm facing right.
Hint: Mime striking a match.

alternating movement

SMOKE
With the right curved "5" fingertips pointing down at the upturned left curved "5" fingertips, palms facing each other, move them in alternating circles.
Hint: Smoke billowing up from a fire.

FLAME
Wiggle the fingers of the right "5" hand upward, palm toward chest, while holding the left "s" hand, palm down, against the back of the right wrist.
Hint: Shows the flames billowing.

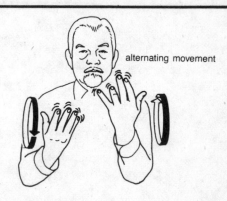

alternating movement

FIRE
While wiggling the fingers of both "5" hands, move them in alternating circles upward, palms toward chest.
Hint: Shows the flames rising.

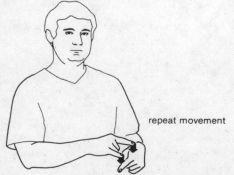

repeat movement

CIGARETTE
Tap the right extended index and little fingers, palm down, on the top of the left extended index finger, palm right.
Hint: Tapping the tobacco down in a cigarette.

repeat movement

SMOKING
Move the extended "u" fingertips from the lips, palm toward face, outward twisting the wrist, ending with the palm facing out.
Hint: Mime holding and smoking a cigarette.

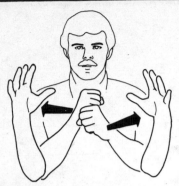

BOMB, EXPLODE
Bring both "s" hands, right hand over left, apart in a sudden movement, opening into "5" hands, palms facing each other at shoulder width.
Hint: A bomb exploding outward.

HURRY
Move both "h" hands, palms facing each other and fingers pointing forward, in a bouncing movement up and down while moving forward.
Hint: Initialized sign moving forward quickly.

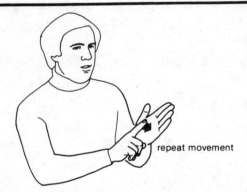

repeat movement

ALARM
Quickly tap the side of the right extended index finger, palm down, against the open left hand, palm right.
Hint: The striking of the bell on an alarm.

WARNING, SIGNAL
Strike the back of the downturned left "s" hand with the fingers of the right open hand, palm down.
Hint: Slapping someone to warn them.

repeat movement

DANGEROUS, DANGER
Brush the back of the right "a" thumb, palm left, upward on the back of the left "s" hand, palm toward lower chest, several times.

DAMAGE, DESTROY
Move the right downturned "claw" hand over the upturned left "claw" hand toward the chest, changing the right hand into an "a" handshape while the hand moves. Bring the right "a" hand back out across the left hand which has changed into an "a" handshape.
Hint: Taking something and tearing it into shreds.

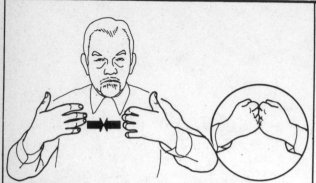

ACCIDENT

Move both curved "5" hands, palms toward body, from in front of the shoulders toward each other, closing into "s" hands and making contact in front of the chest.
Hint: Two objects running into each other.

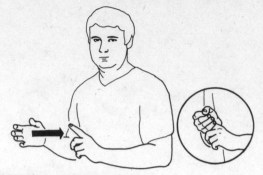

CAPTURE, ARREST, CATCH

Grab the extended left index finger, pointing up, with the loose open right hand, palm left.
Hint: Surrounding and capturing someone.

STEAL

Bring the right "v" hand, fingers pointing left and palm down, from the bent left elbow toward the wrist, pulling up the fingers into a "claw" right hand.
Hint: Stealthily taking something.

GUN

Move the "l" hand, index finger pointing forward and palm left, forward in a small arc from the waist.
Hint: Mime holding a play gun.

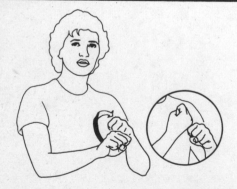

LOCK

With the right "s" knuckles on the back of the left "s" hand, both palms down, twist the right hand over, hitting the back of the left hand with the back of the right hand, palm facing up.
Hint: Turning the lock for protection.

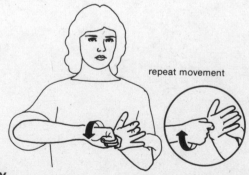

repeat movement

KEY

Twist the knuckle of the right "x" hand into the open left palm, facing right.
Hint: Turning the key in a lock.

ten

RECREATION

Sports
Leisure and Hobbies
Travel and Transportation
Geography

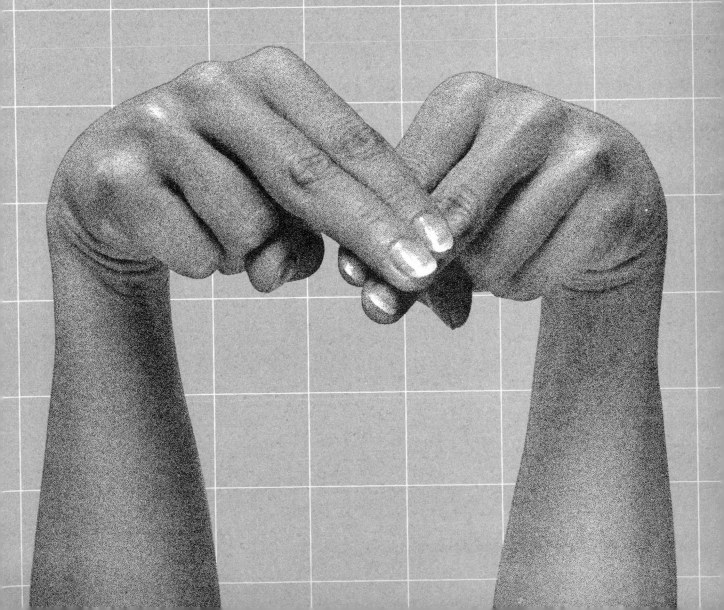

INITIALIZED SIGNS

The sign for "class" is formed with both "c" hands, palms facing each other, moving out and around until the little fingers touch and the palm is facing the body. The sign for "group" is formed in exactly the same way, except that the hands have a "g" shape. "Family" is formed the same with an "f" shape, "association" with an "a" shape, "society" with an "s" shape, and so forth. These signs are formed with the fingerspelled handshape of the first letter of the English gloss. The initialized formation helps distinguish the literal meaning of many signs.

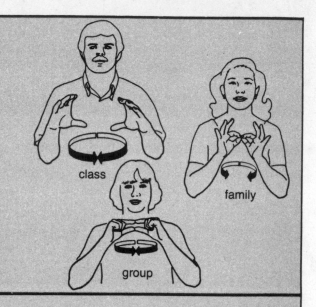

class

family

group

REPEATING SIGNS

Many signs, when they are repeated three or more times, indicate that the action or feeling lasted a long time, or that it happens habitually. A verb sign executed with a repeated slow circular orbit toward the body means "a continuous action." A verb sign quickly repeated means "a repeated action." For example, "wait, wait, wait," signed with a slow circular motion toward the body means "I waited for a long time." If you sign "worry, worry, worry" quickly, it means "I keep worrying."

alternating movement

worry—worry—worry = I keep worrying.

THE "ICONICITY" OF SIGNS

Many signs resemble some aspect of the objects they represent. These signs are said to be "iconic" or "transparent." Often people unfamiliar with sign language will recognize and guess the meaning of these signs. Most signs for sports are very iconic. For example, "baseball" looks like you are ready to swing your bat, and for "basketball," your hands seem to encircle and throw an imaginary basketball. Many other signs are less iconic, but once the relationship between the sign and its meaning is explained, they are easier to remember than those signs which seem to be more arbitrarily formed.

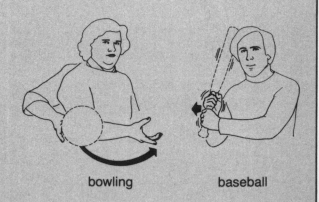

bowling   baseball

Sports

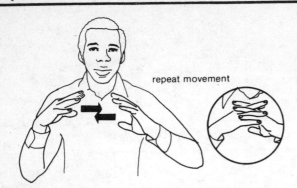

FOOTBALL
Bring both "5" hands, palms facing each other, forward toward each other meshing the fingers together repeatedly.
Hint: The fingers represent the two lines of scrimmage.

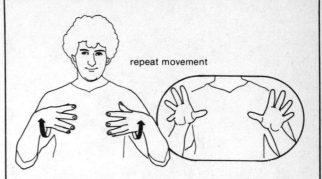

BASKETBALL
Bring both "5" hands, palms facing body and fingers pointing toward each other, upward by flicking the wrists outward in a double motion.
Hint: Mime throwing a basketball.

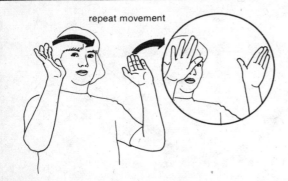

VOLLEYBALL
Flick both open hands, palms facing upward and fingers pointing back, forward from the wrist in a double movement.
Hint: Mime hitting a volleyball.

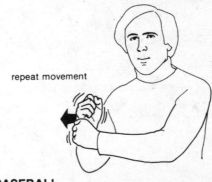

BASEBALL
Hold the right "s" hand, palm facing left, on top of the left "s" hand, palm facing right, shaking them forward and back slightly at the right shoulder.
Hint: Mime holding a baseball bat.

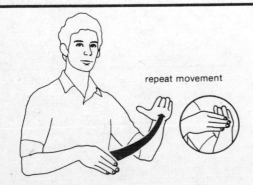

SOCCER
Bring the right "b" hand, palm facing down, upward in an arc striking the index finger against the left downturned palm twice.
Hint: Kicking a soccer ball.

HOCKEY
Bring the knuckle of the right "x" hand, palm toward body, in an arc upward across the upturned left palm.
Hint: The hockey stick striking a puck.

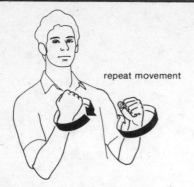

BOXING
Make circles in opposite directions with both "s" hands in front of chest, palms facing body.
Hint: Mime defending yourself during boxing.

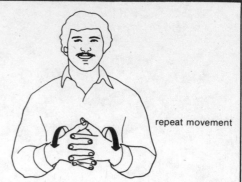

WRESTLING
With the fingers of both "5" hands meshed together, palms toward body, twist the wrists outward with a double motion.
Hint: Shows the limbs of two people intertwined and struggling.

FIGHTING, FIGHT
Bring both "s" hands, palms facing each other, from near the shoulders toward each other in a double motion, brushing the right little finger across the left index finger as they pass, ending with the wrists crossed in front of chest.
Hint: Mime fighting.

GOLF
Bring both "a" hands, right over left and palm facing each other, down from above the right shoulder in a large arc to the left.
Hint: Mime swinging a golf club.

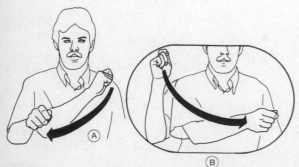

TENNIS
Bring the "a" hand, palm left, from the left shoulder down in an arc to the right. Then bring the "a" hand from the right shoulder down in an arc to the left.
Hint: Mime swinging a tennis racquet.

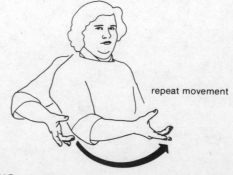

BOWLING
With the middle and fourth fingers together of the curved "5" hand, palm facing out, move hand in an arc from behind the right side of the body forward.
Hint: Mime throwing a bowling ball.

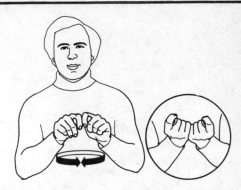

GAME, CHALLENGE
Bring both "a" hands, palms facing body and thumbs extended, in an arc upward in a double motion touching each other in front of the chest.
Hint: Shows two people meeting each other in challenge.

TEAM
Starting with the index fingers of both "t" hands, palms facing out, touching in front of body, bring the hands outward in a circle ending with the little fingers touching, palms facing in.
Hint: Initialized sign formed like "group" and "class."

OLYMPICS
Repeatedly interlock the thumbs and index fingers of both "f" hands, turning the wrists back and forth and moving the hands toward the left each time.
Hint: The five Olympic rings.

SWIMMING
Move both downturned open hands from together in front of the waist outward in arcs with a double motion to either side of the body.
Hint: Mime swimming.

repeat movement

alternating movement

SKIING
Bring both "x" hands, palms facing up and fingers pointing forward, smoothly forward in an arc.
Hint: Pushing yourself forward with ski poles.

RACE, COMPETE
With an alternating movement, move both "a" hands, palms facing each other and thumb pointing up, quickly back and forth past each other by twisting the wrists.
Hint: Two people passing each other while racing.

Leisure and Hobbies

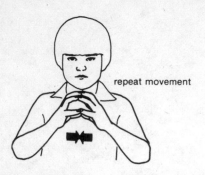

BALL
Tap the fingertips of both "claw" hands together in front of chest a couple of times.
Hint: Fingers form the shape of a ball.

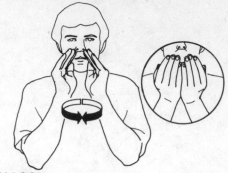

BALLOON
Move both curved hands, palms facing each other, from in front of the chest, out and around in a circle, ending with the little fingers touching, palms facing body.
Hint: Hands encircle the shape of a balloon.

DOLL
Stroke the side of the "x" index finger, palm facing left, up and down on the tip of the nose with a double motion.

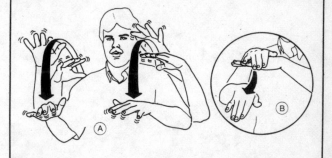

SLED
Bring both "5" hands, palms down, from above either shoulder down and forward in an arc, wiggling the fingers as the hands move. Then bring the down-turned right hand from resting across the back of the downturned left hand forward in a swoop.
Hint: "Snow" plus showing the movement of a sled.

FUN
Bring the right "n" fingers, palm facing left, sideways right from the nose and then downward, tapping the fingertips of the left "n" fingers, pointing right, as they pass.

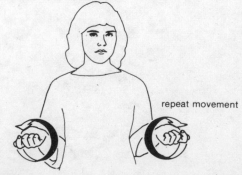

JUMPROPE
Move both "a" hands, with the index finger knuckles slightly extended and palms facing up, in circles moving outward in opposite directions at the sides of the body.
Hint: Mime turning the rope for jumping.

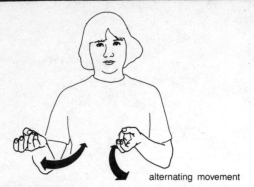

ROLLER SKATING
With an alternating movement, swing the both up-turned crooked "v" hands forward and back in front of the waist.
Hint: Shows the action of the legs while skating.

alternating movement

ICE SKATING
With an alternating movement, swing both upturned "x" hands back and forth in front of the waist.
Hint: Shows the action of the legs on ice skates.

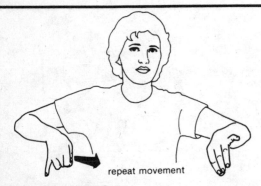

repeat movement

POOL, BILLIARDS
Holding the right "9" hand near the right side of the body, palm facing in, elbow out, and little finger extended, and the left "9" hand forward of the left side of the body, palm down, elbow out, and little finger extended, move the right hand toward the left.
Hint: Mime holding the cue stick.

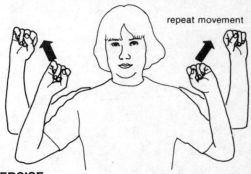

repeat movement

EXERCISE
Start with loose "s" hands, palms forward, above shoulders with the elbows sticking out. Move the hands upward and outward a few times.
Hint: Mime doing exercises.

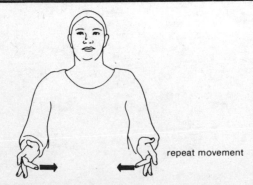

repeat movement

PINBALL
Jab the bent middle fingers of both "5" hands toward each other with a double motion.
Hint: The action for playing a pinball machine.

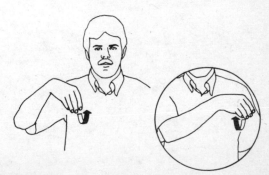

PING PONG
With the fingers of the flat "o" hand pointing downward, palm toward body, flip the fingers outward first in front of the right shoulder and then the left shoulder.
Hint: Mime the action for playing ping pong.

TENT
Bring both extended index and little fingers from touching in front of the face, palms facing each other, downward and apart.
Hint: Fingers follow the shape of a tent.

CAMPING
Bring both extended index and little fingers from touching in front of the face, palms facing each other, downward and apart with a double motion.
Hint: Fingers follow the shape of a tent.

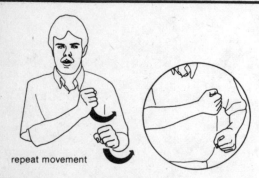

repeat movement

CANOEING
With the right "s" hand, palm left, near the left shoulder and the left "s" hand, palm right, by the left side, move both hands backward and upward in small arcs a few times.
Hint: Mime rowing a canoe.

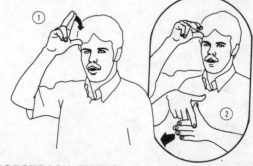

HORSEBACK RIDING
With the fingers of the "3" hand pointing downward, palm toward body, place the index and middle fingers on either side of the open left hand, palm facing right and fingers pointing forward. Move hands forward in small arcs.
Hint: The fingers are legs straddling the horse.

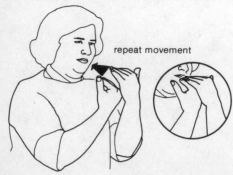

repeat movement

PICNIC
With the left bent hand over the back of the right bent hand, both palms facing down and fingers pointing toward mouth, move the hands toward the mouth with a double motion.
Hint: Shoving a lot of food in your mouth at a picnic.

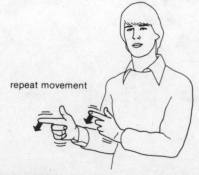

repeat movement

HUNTING
Point the index fingers of both "I" hands, palms facing each other and right hand slightly in front of the left. Move the hands downward twice with short deliberate motions.
Hint: Mime shooting at something.

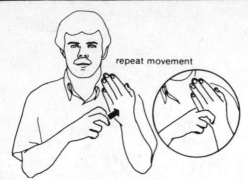

TICKET
Move the fingers of the right crooked "v" hand, palm facing down and fingers pointing left, in and out on either side of the little finger side of the open left hand, palm toward body and fingers pointing up.
Hint: Punching a used ticket.

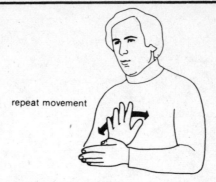

MOVIE, FILM, SHOW
With the heel of the right "5" hand, palm facing forward and fingers pointing up, on the heel of the heel of the left open hand, palm toward body and fingers pointing right, twist the right hand back and forth from the wrist.
Hint: The flickering of the pictures on the screen.

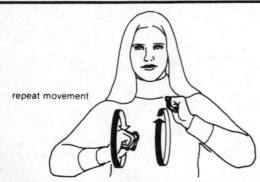

THEATER, DRAMA, PLAY, ACT
Move the thumbtips of both "a" hands, palms facing each other, in alternating circles toward the chest.

STAGE
Move the right "s" hand, palm facing out, from the wrist to the hand of the left arm extended right, palm facing in. Repeat.
Hint: Initialized sign following the shape of a stage floor.

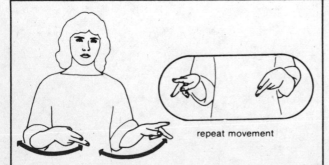

PARTY
Swing both "p" hands, palms facing each other, from side to side in front of the body a few times.
Hint: Initialized sign.

ART, ILLUSTRATE, DRAW
Bring the extended right little finger, palm toward body, downward in a wiggling movement on the palm of the left hand, facing right.
Hint: Drawing a line on paper.

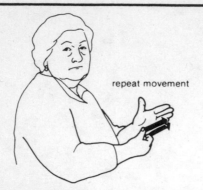

MAGAZINE, BROCHURE
Move the extended right index finger and thumb, palm toward body, along either side of the open left hand, palm right, from heel to fingers with a double movement.
Hint: Fingers follow the spine of a magazine.

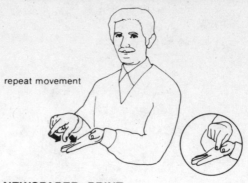

NEWSPAPER, PRINT
Bring the right "g" fingers across the upturned left palm, closing the finger to the thumb as the hand moves from the left fingers to the heel.
Hint: Placing hot type into place for printing newspapers.

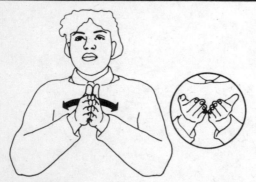

BOOK, NOTEBOOK
Starting with both palms touching in front of chest, fingers pointing forward, move the hands apart at the top, keeping the little fingers together.
Hint: Mime opening a book.

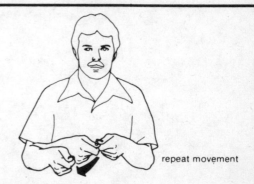

PLAY CARDS
With the bent index finger of both "a" hands slightly extended and touching each other, move them away to the right and back repeatedly, moving both hands slightly to the right each time.
Hint: Dealing cards.

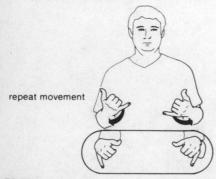

PLAY
Twist both "y" hands, palms toward body, up and down a couple of times.

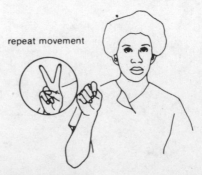

TV, TELEVISION
Fingerspell "t" and "v" with a rapid repeated movement which will appear almost like a flicking downward of the middle finger.
Hint: Fingerspelled sign which has become a formal sign.

MUSIC, SONG, SING
Swing the right open hand, palm toward body, back and forth on the extended left arm, fingers forward and palm right.
Hint: Directing music.

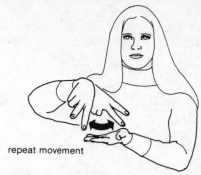

DANCE
Swing the downturned "v" hand, palm toward body, back and forth above the upturned left palm.
Hint: The two fingers represent legs dancing on the dance floor.

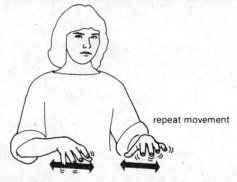

PIANO, PLAY PIANO
Move the downturned "5" hands to the right and then to the left while wiggling the fingers.
Hint: Mime playing the piano.

GUITAR
Move the loosely curved right hand, palm facing body, up and down on the chest while holding the left "a" hand, palm facing back, somewhat out from the left shoulder.
Hint: Mime strumming a guitar.

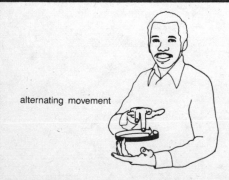

RECORD
Move both bent middle fingers of "5" hands, palms facing each other, in alternate circles around each other.
Hint: Shows the needle moving around a record.

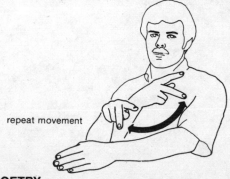

POETRY
Swing the right "p" hand, palm toward body, back and forth on the extended left arm, fingers forward and palm right.
Hint: Initialized sign formed like "music."

Travel and Transportation

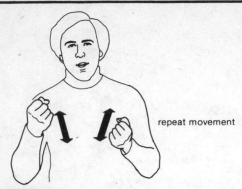

CAR, AUTOMOBILE
Move both "s" hands, palms toward body, up and down at an angle repeated with an alternating movement.
Hint: Mime driving a car.

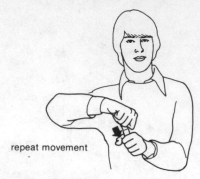

GASOLINE, FILL UP
Dip the extended thumb of the right "a" hand, palm right, downward into the top of the left loose "s" hand, palm facing right, a couple of times.
Hint: Pouring gas into the gas tank.

STREET, HIGHWAY, ROAD
With both open hands a few inches apart in front of the waist, palms facing each other and fingers angled forward and down, move the hands straight forward and slightly upward.
Hint: The hands follow the outline of a straight highway.

ROAD, PATH
With both open hands a few inches apart in front of the waist, palms facing each other and fingers angled forward and down, move the hands forward and slightly up with a zigzag movement.
Hint: The hands follow the outline of a winding road.

TRAFFIC
Move the right and left "5" hands, palms facing each other and fingers pointing up, forward and back repeatedly with an alternating movement, brushing the palms against each other as they pass.
Hint: Shows cars whizzing past each other in both directions.

PARK
Tap the little finger side of the right "3" hand, palm left and fingers pointing forward, on the upturned left palm.
Hint: The right hand represents a vehicle parking on the left hand.

BOAT
With the little finger side of both cupped hands together, palms up and fingers pointing forward, move the hands forward in front of the waist in small arcs.
Hint: The hands form the hull of a boat moving forward.

SHIP
With the little finger side of the right "3" hand, palm left and fingers pointed forward, on the upturned left palm, move both hands forward in small arcs.
Hint: The right hand represents a ship moving forward on the waves.

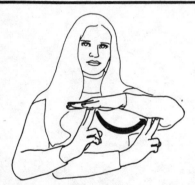

BRIDGE
With the left downturned hand extended in front of the chest, touch the fingertips of the right "v" hand, palm left and fingers pointing up, first to the left palm and then near the left elbow.
Hint: Shows the span of a suspension bridge.

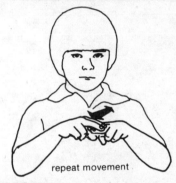

repeat movement

TRAIN, RAILROAD
Move the right "h" fingers, palm facing down, back and forth repeatedly on the back of the fingers of the downturned left "h" hand.
Hint: Shows the cross ties on a railroad.

repeat movement

HELICOPTER
With the palm of the downturned right "5" hand on the thumbtip of the left "3" hand, palm right and fingers pointing forward, move both hands forward as the right hand wiggles.
Hint: The right hand represents the propeller turning on a helicopter.

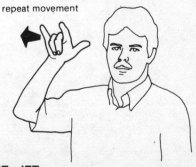

repeat movement

AIRPLANE, JET
With the right extended thumb, index finger, and little finger, palm down, above the right shoulder, move the hand a short distance forward with a double motion.
Hint: The hand represents an airplane moving.

TRAVEL, TRIP
Sweep the crooked "v" hand, palm down, from in front of the chest up to the right and out to shoulder level.
Hint: The fingers represent legs going somewhere.

TRAVEL AROUND, RUN AROUND, TRAVEL
With the right extended index finger pointing down at the left extended index finger which is pointing up, move both fingers in small counterclockwise circles while moving the hands forward.
Hint: Shows a person moving around within a specific area.

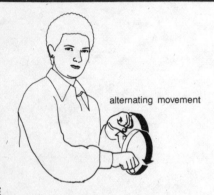

alternating movement

BICYCLE
Move both "s" hands side by side in front of waist, palms facing down, in alternating circles outward.
Hint: Mime the movement of the feet on bicycle pedals.

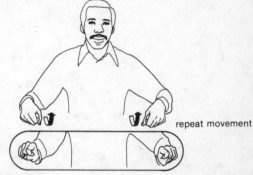

repeat movement

MOTORCYCLE
With both "s" hands at either side of the waist, palms facing the body, move them upward a few times from the wrist.
Hint: The motion of hands on a motorcycle's handlebars.

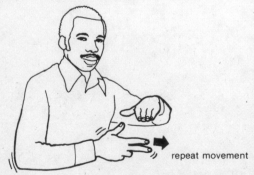

repeat movement

GARAGE
Move the right "3" hand, palm facing left and fingers pointing forward, out from the waist under the down-turned left palm held at chest level.
Hint: The right hand represents the vehicle moving into the garage.

RIDE
Hook the curved fingers of the right "h" hand, palm facing down, on the thumb of the left "c" hand, palm right. Move both hands forward.
Hint: The curved fingers represent legs sitting while the vehicle moves forward.

GO
With both extended index fingers pointing up in front of waist, palms facing out and left hand closer to the body than the right, flick the wrists to point both fingers forward.
Hint: Something going away from the body.

COME
With both extended index fingers pointing forward, palm facing up, at waist level, bring the index fingers up toward the body in a large arc.
Hint: Something coming toward the body.

ARRIVE
Bring the right open hand, palm left and finger pointing up, from in front of the right shoulder forward, landing the back of the right hand in the palm of the left hand, both palms toward chest.
Hint: The right hand represents something coming and arriving in the left hand.

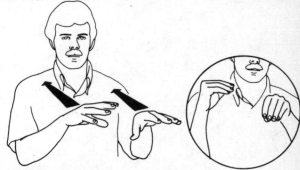

LEAVE, DEPART
Draw both loose downturned "5" hands back toward the right shoulder drawing the thumbs and fingertips together as the hands move.
Hint: Something moving off into the distance.

FLY
With the right extended thumb, index finger, and little finger, palm down, above the right shoulder, move the hand forward.
Hint: Shows an airplane flying.

VISIT
Bring the middle finger of the right "v" hand, palm toward face, from the corner of the right eye down, moving it in alternating circles with the left "v" hand in front of the chest.
Hint: Initialized sign showing people going around seeing each other.

Geography

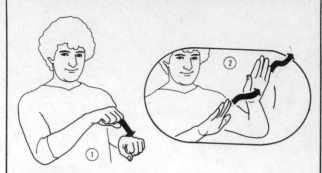

HILL
Move both open hands, angled forward, upward to the left with a wavy movement, left hand higher than the right.
Hint: Hands follow the shape of a hill.

MOUNTAIN
Tap the knuckles of the right "s" hand on the back of the downturned left "s" hand. Move both open hands, angled forward, upward to the left with a wavy movement, left hand higher than the right.
Hint: "Rock" plus the shape of a rocky mountainside.

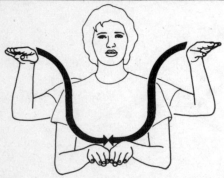

VALLEY
Beginning with both downturned "b" hands above either shoulder, fingers pointing out, bring the hands down in an arc meeting at the waist.
Hint: The hands outline the shape of a valley.

ISLAND
Draw a circle with the right extended little finger, palm toward body, on the back of the downturned left hand.
Hint: Initialized sign showing a small area surrounded by water.

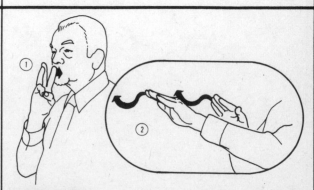

RIVER
Tap the index finger side of the right "w" hand, palm left, to the chin. Bring both downturned open hands, left hand closer to body than right, forward while wiggling the fingers.
Hint: "Water" plus the action of a rolling river.

OCEAN, SEA
Tap the index finger side of the right "w" hand, palm left, to the chin. Move both downturned open hands, right hand closer to body than left, forward with an up and down wavy motion.
Hint: "Water" plus the action of the ocean waves.

FARM, COUNTRY
Rub the fingers of the right open hand on the elbow of the left arm raised across the chest.

FARM
Drag the thumbtip of the "5" hand, palm left and fingers forward, across the chin from left to right.

repeat movement

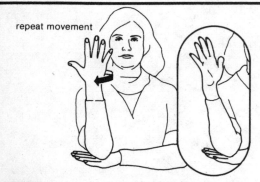

TREE
Place the elbow of the right raised arm, palm toward the right shoulder, on the back of the downturned left hand. Twist the right palm in and out a number of times.
Hint: The arm represents the tree trunk and the hand its branches.

repeat movement

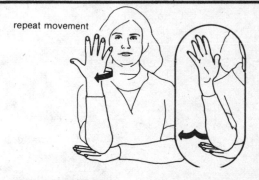

FOREST, WOODS
Place the elbow of the right raised arm, palm toward the right shoulder, on the back of the downturned left hand. Twist the right palm in and out a number of times. Repeat while moving arms toward the right.
Hint: The sign repeats "tree" many times making a forest.

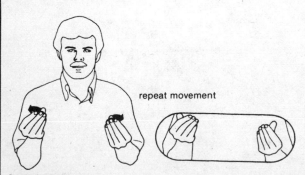

repeat movement

DIRT, SOIL
Rub the thumbs of both hands across the fingertips from the little finger to the index finger.
Hint: Feeling soil between the fingers.

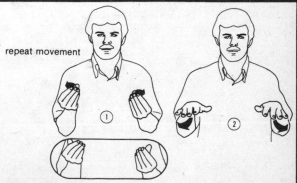

repeat movement

LAND, FIELD
Rub the thumbs of both hands across the fingertips from the little finger to the index finger. Push both downturned "5" hands forward and outward, fingers pointing forward.
Hint: "Dirt" plus the flat land before you.

repeat movement

EARTH

While holding the back of the downturned left hand, fingers right, with the thumb and middle finger of the downturned right hand, rock the right hand from side to side with a double movement.
Hint: The earth moving around on its axis.

WORLD

Bring the right "w" hand, palm left and fingers forward, in a circle over and around the left "w" hand, palm right and fingers forward.
Hint: Initialized sign following the shape of the globe.

repeat movement

ROCK, STONE

Tap the knuckles of the right "s" hand on the back of the downturned left "s" hand.
Hint: Knocking on a rock to show its hardness.

NATURE, NATURALLY

Move the right "n" hand, palm down, in a circle over and down on the back of the downturned left open hand.
Hint: Initialized sign.

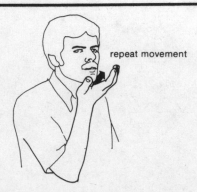

repeat movement

GRASS, HAY

Move the heel of the curved upturned hand upward under the chin with a double movement.

FLOWER

With the thumb and fingertips together, touch first the right side of the nose and then the left.
Hint: Smelling a flower.

eleven

ACTIONS

Actions of the Body
Actions at School and Work
Other Actions

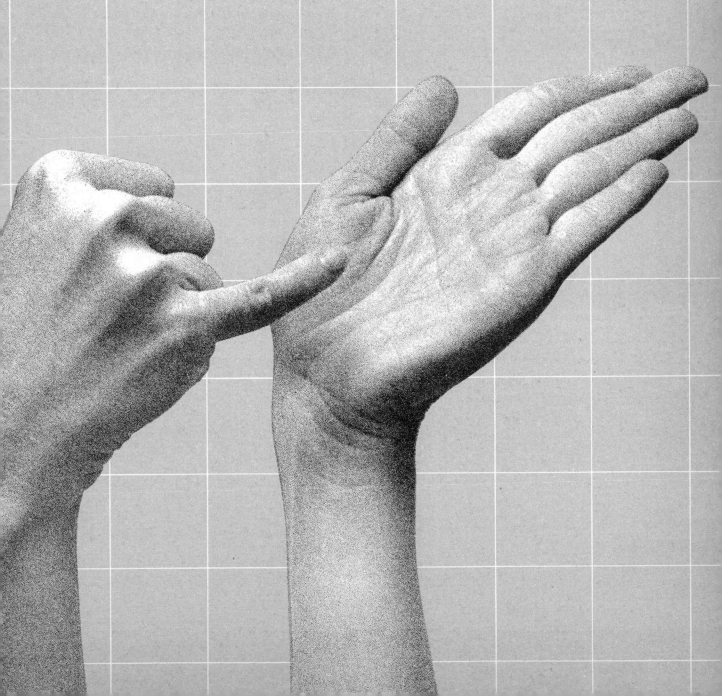

THE DIRECTION OF THE SIGN

Some verbs can carry information about the subject and object of the sentence by the direction in which the sign moves. For example, if the sign "show" is pulled back toward the body, it means that "you showed something to me." If "show" moves from the body outward, it means that "I showed something to you." Other verbs in this category are "inform," "ask," "help," "tell," "give," "send," and "look at."

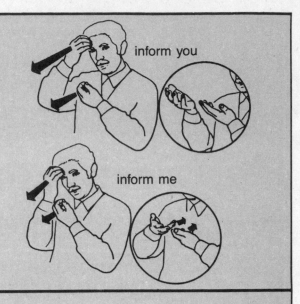

inform you

inform me

PAST, PRESENT, AND FUTURE VERBS

In English, verb tense is expressed by changing the verb form to indicate past, present, or future. In sign language, verb tense is indicated by establishing a time reference. All discussion remains in the established time frame until a new one is introduced. The time reference may be set by signing "past," "now," "future," or any other indication of time, such as "two weeks ago."

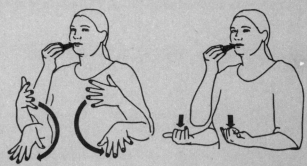

eat + finished = ate   eat + now = is eating

THE "TO BE" VERB

Native sign language users do not always sign the verb "to be" because verb tenses are designated by establishing a time frame. However, many signers prefer using "am," "is," "are," "was," or "were," especially, when they are signing in an English word order. The same sign is used in sign language for all tenses of "to be." That sign is similar to the sign for "true" and adds emphasis to the sentence.

am; be; is; are; was; were

Actions of the Body

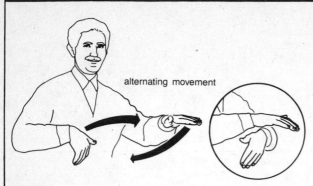

WALK

Alternately swing both open hands back and forth from in front of the body, palms facing down, back to the sides, palms facing back.

Hint: The arms represent the movements of the legs while walking.

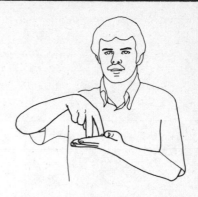

STAND

Place the fingertips of the right "v" hand, palm toward body, down into the upturned left open palm.

Hint: The fingers represent the legs standing up.

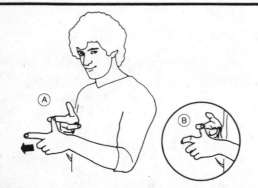

RUN

With the thumb of the right "l" hand in front of and touching the index finger of the left "l" hand, palms facing each other and index fingers pointing forward, repeatedly crook both index fingers and the right thumb while moving the hands forward.

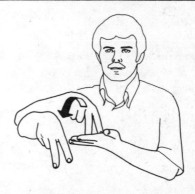

JUMP

With the fingertips of the right "v" hand pointing down into the upturned left open palm, move the right fingers forward off the palm in an arc.

Hint: The fingers represent legs jumping off something.

THROW, THROW AWAY

Hold the curled index and middle fingers under the thumb, palm toward body. Thrust the hand down and forward, flicking the two fingers forward.

Hint: Mime discarding something.

CATCH

Hold the loose curved "5" hand, palm down at shoulder level. Bring the hand downward, closing into an "s" hand on the back of the left downturned "s" hand.

Hint: Mime catching something.

SMILE
Point the extended index fingers to the corners of the mouth while smiling.
Hint: Pointing to the expanse of a smile.

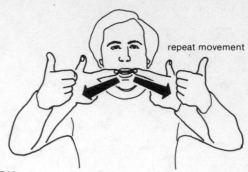

repeat movement

LAUGH
Bring the index fingers of both "I" hands, palms toward face, from pointing at the corners of the smiling mouth outward, changing into "a" hands with extended thumbs pointing up.
Hint: Initialized sign showing a smile broadening into a laugh.

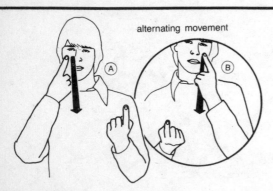

alternating movement

CRY, TEARS
Alternately stroke downward on the cheeks with the fingertips of both extended index fingers, palms toward face.
Hint: Tears streaming down the face.

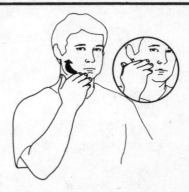

KISS
Touch the fingertips of the bent hand, palm facing down, first to the lips and then to the cheek.
Hint: Planting a kiss on the cheek.

REST, RETIRE
Lay the palms of both open hands near the opposite shoulder, crossing the arms on the chest at the wrists.
Hint: Laying back to rest.

SLEEP, NAP
Bring the loose "5" hand, palm in front of face and fingers pointing upward, downward, bringing the thumb and fingertips together.
Hint: Drawing the eyes closed for sleep.

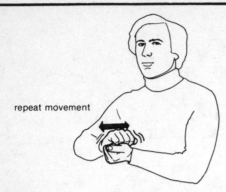

WASH
Rub the knuckles of the right "a" hand, palm facing down, back and forth repeatedly across the upturned knuckles of the left "a" hand.
Hint: Rubbing something to wash it.

DUST
Move the "a" hand, palm facing down, from left to right in a wavy movement in front of chest.
Hint: Mime cleaning with a dust rag.

MOP
With the right "a" hand, palm toward body, closer to the body than the left "a" hand, palm facing up, push both hands forward a short distance with a double movement.
Hint: Mime pushing a mop.

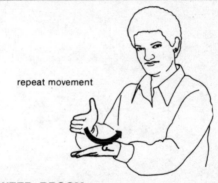

SWEEP, BROOM
Brush the little finger side of the right open hand, palm facing left, across the upturned left palm, from the fingers toward the heel.
Hint: The right hand is sweeping away dirt.

BAKE, OVEN
Move the upturned "b" hand forward and upward slightly.
Hint: Putting something in the oven.

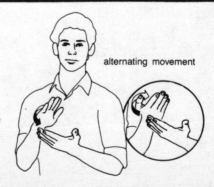

COOK
Starting with the downturned palm of the right hand laying across the upturned left palm, flip the right hand over and back again repeatedly.
Hint: Flipping food over to cook both sides.

PUT, MOVE
With the thumbs and fingertips of both hands together, hands side by side in front of body, palms facing down, move the hands in an arc forward and to the left.
Hint: Mime moving something from one place to another.

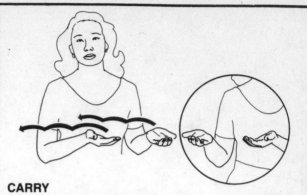

CARRY
Bring the upturned open hands from left to right in small arcs.
Hint: Mime carrying something.

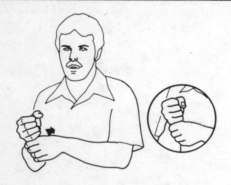

HOLD
Bring both "s" hands, right over left and palms toward body, in toward the chest a short distance.
Hint: Mime holding on to something.

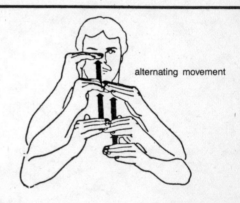

alternating movement

BUILD
With the fingertips of both bent open hands overlapping slightly, alternatingly move the right and left hands over each other, moving the hands upward each time.
Hint: Move hands as if constructing something.

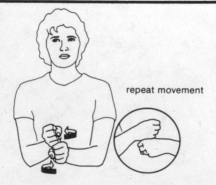

repeat movement

MAKE
With the right "s" hand on top of the left "s" hand, palms facing toward each other, twist the wrists in opposite directions repeatedly, touching the hands together each time.
Hint: Constructing something.

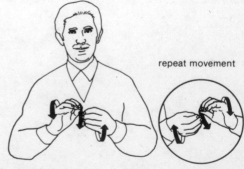

repeat movement

FIX
Repeatedly touch the fingertips of both "o" hands as the wrists are twisted in opposite directions.
Hint: Putting the parts of something together.

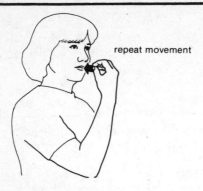

EAT, FOOD
With the thumb and fingertips together, palm facing down, repeatedly move the fingertips toward the lips with short movements.
Hint: Putting food in the mouth.

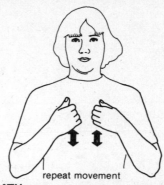

BATHE, BATH
Rub the knuckles of both "a" hands, palms facing in and knuckles pointing toward each other, up and down on the chest with a double movement.
Hint: Mime washing the chest during a bath.

CUT
With the right "3" hand, fingers pointing forward and palm left, move the index and middle fingers together repeatedly across the fingertips of the downturned left open hand.
Hint: Mime cutting with some scissors.

SIT
Lay the fingers of the right "h" hand across the fingers of the left "h" hand, both palms facing down.
Hint: The right fingers represent legs which are put down to sit on something.

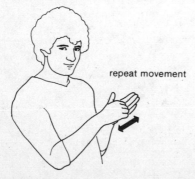

RUB
Rub the knuckles of the right "a" hand on the left open hand, palms facing each other.
Hint: Mime rubbing something.

PUSH
Move both open hands, palms facing forward, away from the body with a short deliberate motion.
Hint: Mime pushing something.

Actions at School and Work

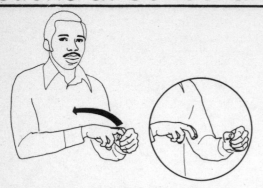

RESIGN, GET OUT
Bring the bent right "h" fingers, palm down, out of the left "o" hand, palm facing right, back toward the body.
Hint: The fingers represent legs which you are withdrawing from a situation.

QUIT
Bring the right "h" fingers, palm left, up from inside the left "o," palm facing right, in an arc toward chest.
Hint: The fingers represent legs which pull away from a situation.

STOP
Bring the little finger side of the right open hand, palm facing left, down into the upturned left palm.
Hint: A natural gesture for stopping something.

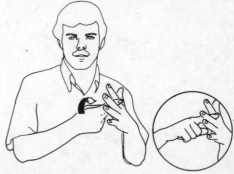

START, BEGIN, INITIATE
Twist the right extended index finger, palm facing body, between the index and middle fingers of the left "5" hand, palm facing right.
Hint: Turning a key in the ignition.

PARTICIPATE, JOIN
Bring the right "h" fingers, palm left and fingers pointing up, down from in front of chest into the left "c" hand, palm facing right.
Hint: The fingers represent legs which you are moving toward a situation.

COMPLETE, END, FINISH, DONE
Starting with the little finger side of the right "b" hand, palm left, crossed on top of the index finger side of the left "b" hand, palm right, slide the right hand down the left index finger and off the end of the left fingertips.
Hint: Showing the end of something.

WORK, EMPLOYMENT
Tap the heel of the right "s" hand, palm facing down, on the back of the downturned left "s" hand with a double movement.

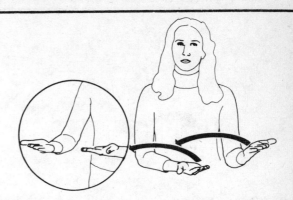

BRING
Bring both upturned hands from right to left in a long arc in front of the waist.
Hint: Mime bringing something in your arms.

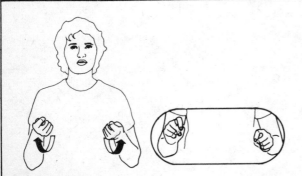

TRY, ATTEMPT
Starting with both "t" hands, palms facing up, in front of the waist, move the hands forward in an arc, turning the wrists over while moving, ending with the palms facing down.
Hint: Initialized sign showing effort.

ALLOW, LET, PERMIT
Move both open hands, palms facing each other and fingers forward, outward and upward in an arc in front of the waist.
Hint: Providing an open path to permit someone to do something.

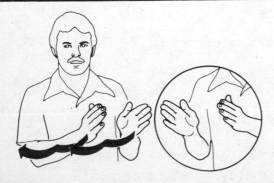

PREPARE
Move both open hands, palms facing each other and fingers forward, to the right side in several small arcs.
Hint: Making plans by preparing parts of the job at a time.

PLAN, SCHEDULE, ARRANGE
Move both open hands, palms facing each other and fingers forward, to the right side in a smooth movement.
Hint: Showing an orderly flow of events.

KEEP
Tap the little finger side of the right "k" hand, palm left, and the index finger side of the left "k" hand, palm right, to each other.
Hint: Initialized sign. The fingers represent the eyes looking in all directions to keep something safe.

HIRE, WELCOME, INVITE
Swing the upturned curved right hand from in front of body inward toward the waist in an arc.
Hint: Bringing something in close to you.

ACCEPT, RECEIVE
Bring both bent "5" hands from in front of the chest, palms facing down, inward, bringing the thumbs and fingertips together against the chest.
Hint: Taking something and bringing it to oneself in acceptance.

RECEIVE, GET
With the right "5" hand, palm facing left, on top of the left "5" hand, palm facing right and all fingers pointing forward, bring the hands toward the chest, closing the fingers into "s" handshapes.
Hint: Taking something for yourself.

REJECT
Touch the fingertips of the bent right hand, palm down and knuckles forward, on the heel of the upturned left hand. Flick the fingers away, ending with the right downturned palm above the left palm.
Hint: Pushing away something that you reject.

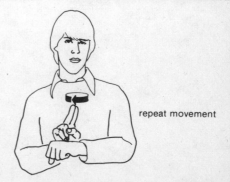

USE
Move the right "u" hand, palm facing out and fingers pointing up, with a circular motion across the back of the downturned left "s" hand.
Hint: Initialized sign.

INVESTIGATE, INSPECT, EXAMINE, CHECK
Touch the extended right index finger from under the right eye down to the palm of the upturned left hand, forward off the left fingertips.
Hint: Moving the vision from the eye down to examine something.

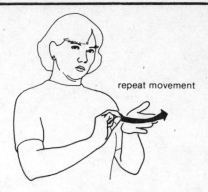

WRITE
Move the extended right thumb and index finger together, across the palm of the left open hand, palms facing each other.
Hint: Mime holding a pencil and writing on paper.

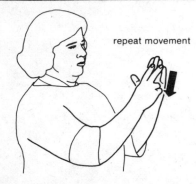

READ
Bring the fingertips of the right "v" hand down the palm of the left open hand, palms facing each other.
Hint: The fingers represent the eyes moving across a page.

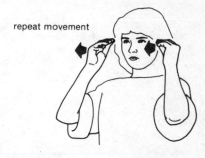

TEACH
With the thumbs touching the fingertips of both hands, palms facing down, move the hands forward from near the temples in a short deliberate double motion.
Hint: Taking information from your head and giving it to another.

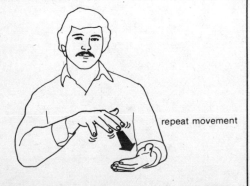

STUDY
Wiggle the fingers of the downturned right "5" hand as the fingertips move down toward the upturned left palm with a double motion.
Hint: Reading and rereading a book.

LEARN
Bring the downturned "5" right hand, palm facing down, from the upturned left palm upward toward the head, closing the thumb to the fingertips as the hand moves.
Hint: Taking information from the page and putting it in the head.

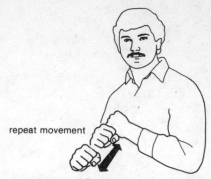

SUCCEED, FINALLY, AT LAST
Starting with both index fingers pointing toward each other from in front of either shoulder, both palms facing in, twist the wrist outward, ending with the index fingers pointing upward, palms forward.
Hint: A natural sign for success.

repeat movement

ADVERTISE, PUBLICIZE, COMMERCIAL
Move the right "s" hand up and down with a double motion on the little finger side of the left "s" hand held against the lower chest.
Hint: Stretching the truth.

CHOOSE, PICK, SELECT
Bring the bent thumb and index finger of the right "5" hand from the fingers of the left "5" hand, palms facing each other, back toward the right shoulder, closing the thumb to the index fingertip together.
Hint: Making a selection of the fingers on the left hand.

FIND, DISCOVER
Starting with the loose downturned "5" hand in front of the right shoulder, draw the hand upward from the wrist, closing the thumb and index fingertip together.
Hint: Picking up something you found.

PROVE
Bring the open right hand, palm facing back and fingers pointing up, from the right cheek forward and down, landing on the upturned left palm.
Hint: Taking something and laying it out for examination.

DEMONSTRATE, SHOW, EXAMPLE
Touch the extended right index finger into the open left hand, palms facing each other. Move both hands forward and down in a short arc.
Hint: Pointing out something as an example.

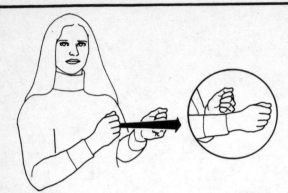

PASS, BY
Move the right "a" hand forward past the left "a" hand, palms facing each other and knuckles pointing out.
Hint: Something passing another thing.

FAIL
Move the back of the upturned right "k" hand forward from the heel of the upturned left palm toward the fingertips.

CANCEL, CORRECT, CRITICIZE
Using the extended right index finger, draw a large X across the upturned left palm.
Hint: Cross out something that is incorrect.

ESTABLISH, APPOINT, APPOINTMENT
Starting with the right "a" hand, palm facing out, above the left downturned hand, twist the right wrist forward, landing the little finger side of the right "a" hand on the back of the left hand.
Hint: Take something and firmly establish it.

REQUIRE, DEMAND
Strike the fingertips of the right "x" hand, palm left, against the open left palm, facing right. Bring both hands toward the chest.
Hint: Demanding that something be placed in your palm as required.

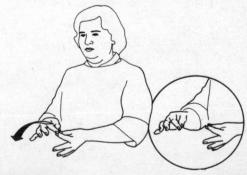

POSTPONE
Starting with the fingertips of both "9" hands touching in front of the waist, palms facing each other, move the right hand forward a short distance in an arc.
Hint: Put something off from the present into the future.

DEVELOP
Move the index finger side of the right "d" hand, palm facing out and index finger pointing up, from the heel of the open left palm upward toward the fingertips.
Hint: Initialized sign showing an idea growing upward.

repeat movement

SUPERVISE
With the right "k" hand, palm left, crossed on top of the left "k" hand, palm right, move the hands together in a horizontal circle.
Hint: The fingers represent eyes looking in every direction to supervise.

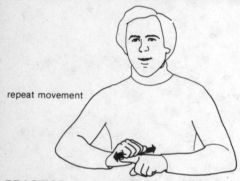

repeat movement

PRACTICE
Rub the knuckles of the downturned right "a" hand on the extended index finger of the downturned left hand in a double movement.
Hint: Repetitive action.

MANAGE, DIRECT, CONTROL
Move both "x" hands, palms facing each other and fingers pointing forward, in alternating movements in and out in front of chest.
Hint: Holding the reins to control a horse.

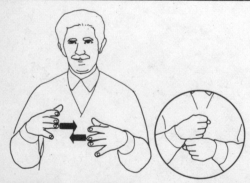

SUMMARIZE, CONDENSE
With both loose "5" hands apart, palms facing each other and fingers forward, bring the hands together closing into "s" handshapes and ending with the right hand on top of the left.
Hint: Bringing information together in a summary.

LINE UP
Hold the right "4" hand in front of the chest, palm facing left. Place the left "4" hand in line near the right little finger, palm facing right. Move the hands apart, right toward chest and left outward.
Hint: People standing in a line.

CHALLENGE, DARE

Bring the extended thumbs of both "a" hands, palms facing out, from near the shoulders in an arc inward and upward toward the center of the chest.
Hint: Two things coming together in order to compete.

IMPROVE

Move the little finger side of the right open hand, palm left, across the index finger side of the left "b" hand at right angles, and then to the forearm.
Hint: Moving up on the chart.

LOSE, LOST

With the knuckles of both "c" hands touching, palms toward the chest and the knuckles pointing toward each other, bring the hands downward and apart, dropping the fingertips down.
Hint: Dropping or losing what you have.

WIN

Swoop the right "5" hand from right side of body, palm facing left, down in an arc across the top of the left "s" hand, palm right, changing the right hand in an "s" as it moves.
Hint: Grabbing to take the trophy.

SUPPORT

Push the knuckles of the right "s" hand, palm toward body, at an angle upward under the little finger side of the left "s" hand, palm facing back, forcing it to move in the same direction.
Hint: The right hand is giving support to the left hand.

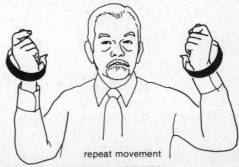

repeat movement

CELEBRATE, VICTORY, FESTIVAL

Make small circles above either shoulder with both "a" hands, palms facing back and index finger knuckles extended.
Hint: Waving a flag to celebrate.

Other Actions

SEE
Move the "v" hand, palm toward face and fingers pointing up, from in front of the eyes outward in an arc.
Hint: The fingers represent the eyes looking at something.

LOOK
Swing the "v" hand, palm down and fingers pointing forward, outward from the face in an arc.
Hint: The extended fingers represent the eyes looking around.

NOTICE, OBSERVE
Move the extended right index finger from under the right eye downward to point at the upturned left open palm.
Hint: Direct your eye to carefully inspect something in your hand.

WATCH
Rest the heel of the right "v" hand, palm and fingers forward, on the back of the downturned left "s" hand.
Hint: The extended fingers represent the eyes watching something.

PREDICT
Move the right "v" hand, palm toward face and fingers pointing up, from in front of the eyes downward under the downturned left palm, coming out on the other side.
Hint: Looking into the future.

repeat movement

SEARCH, EXAMINE, LOOK FOR
Make a circle with the "c" hand, palm facing left, in a counterclockwise double movement in front of the face.
Hint: Moving things aside to search everywhere.

OPEN
Bring the downturned "b" hands from side by side in front of the chest upward and outward, ending with the palms facing each other.
Hint: Pulling the lid back on either side of a container.

CLOSE
Bring both "b" hands, palms apart and facing each other, toward each other, ending with palms down.
Hint: Closing the lid on a container.

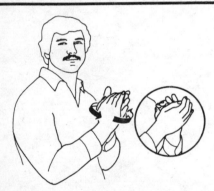

BECOME
With the right open palm against the left open palm, twist the wrists to put the hands in reverse positions.
Hint: Change one thing into something else.

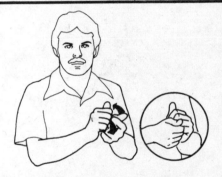

CHANGE, ADAPT, ALTER
With the knuckles of the right "a" hand on the knuckles of the left "a" hand, twist the wrists in opposite directions putting the hands in reverse positions.
Hint: Turn something into something else.

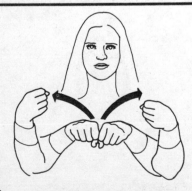

BREAK
With both "s" hands side by side in front of chest, jerk the hands up and apart by twisting the wrists outward.
Hint: Taking something in your hands and breaking it in half.

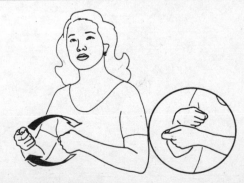

EXCHANGE, TRADE
With both "a" hands, palms facing each other and index finger knuckles extended, move the hands in a circle around each other, exchanging places.
Hint: Taking one thing and exchanging its location for another's.

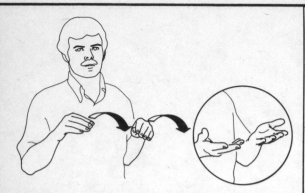

GIVE
Move both downturned hands with the thumbs touching the fingertips forward, flipping the hands over and opening into "5" hands, palms facing up.
Hint: Taking something and presenting it to another person.

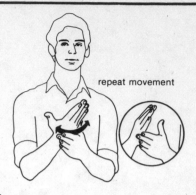

repeat movement

SHARE
Brush the little finger side of the right open hand, palm left, back and forth between the thumb and index finger of the left open hand, palm right.
Hint: Dividing something to give out shares.

HAVE, POSSESS
Bring the fingertips of both bent hands against the chest, palms facing in opposite directions away from each other.
Hint: Bringing something you own in toward yourself.

OFFER
Bring both upturned open hands, fingers angled up and forward, in an upward arc in front of chest.
Hint: Taking something and presenting it to another person.

WAIT
Wiggle the fingers of the loose upturned "5" hands, with the left hand more forward than the right.
Hint: Drumming the fingers in boredom while waiting.

SAVE, SAVIOR, SAFE, SALVATION
Bring both "s" hands, wrists crossed in front of chest and palms facing in, outward by twisting the wrists away from each other ending with palms forward at sides of body.
Hint: Unloosing the chains binding the wrists together.

HIDE

With the back of the "a" thumb touching the lips, palm left, move the hand down and forward, ending with it under the downturned left bent hand.

Hint: "Secret" plus hiding something out of sight.

AVOID

Move the right "a" hand, palm left, from the thumb side of the left "a" hand, palm right, back in a wavy motion to the right.

Hint: Moving away from something to avoid it.

FORCE, DEFEAT

Roll the right "c" hand, palm facing forward, across and down the other side of the downturned left hand, ending with the "c" palm facing down.

Hint: The right hand pushes against something and forces it down.

PREVENT

With both bent open hands at chest level, left hand just outside the right and both palms facing down, move the right hand forward to hit against the index finger side of the left hand.

Hint: Put up a barricade.

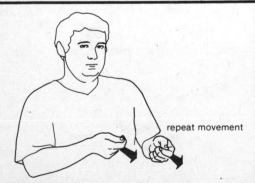

repeat movement

URGE, PERSUADE

With the left "a" hand forward of the right "a" hand, index knuckles extended forward and palms angled up, draw the hands forward and back a short distance with a double motion.

Hint: Using the reins to urge a horse forward.

MISS

Move the "c" hand, palm facing left, across in front of the face, changing into an "s" handshape as it moves.

Hint: Something gets away that you grab for.

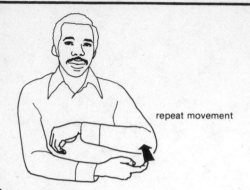

TEMPT
Tap the elbow of the bent left arm with the index fingertip of the right "x" hand.
Hint: Direct someone's attention away.

BLAME
Move the right "a" hand, palm left and thumb extended upward, in a downward arc across the back of the downturned left "s" hand.
Hint: Pushing the blame away from yourself to another.

TEND, INCLINED TOWARD
Touch the chest with the bent middle fingers of both "5" hands, palms facing body. Bring the hands forward in an arc.
Hint: Bring the heart outward toward something.

SEND, MAIL
Touch the fingertips of the right bent hand, palm and fingers down, to the back of the downturned left hand. Flick the right fingertips up and forward.
Hint: Brush something away to send it.

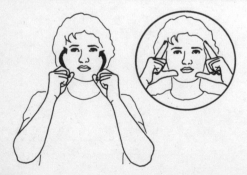

BLUSH
Starting with the thumbtips of both "a" hands near either side of the chin, raise the index fingers to the temples, palms facing in.
Hint: Fingers indicate a blush rising in the cheeks.

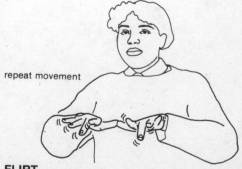

FLIRT
Wiggle the fingers of both downturned "5" hands, fingers pointing forward and thumbs touching.
Hint: Mime fluttering your eyelashes when flirting.

CONTINUE
With the right thumbtip on the left thumbnail, both palms facing down, move the hands forward in two small arcs.
Hint: Move the action into the future.

STAY
With the thumbs of both "y" hands touching, palms facing down, move the right hand forward and downward.
Hint: Moving something into a location to stay.

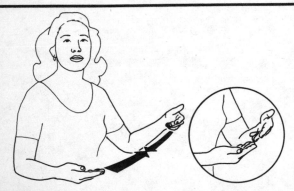

INTRODUCE
With both upturned open hands apart at either side of the body, swing the hands together to touch fingertips.
Hint: Bring two people together to meet each other.

MOVE ON, FORWARD, CONTINUE
With both open hands in front of body, palm facing in and fingers pointing toward each other, move the hands forward in a smooth motion.
Hint: Moving on with things; a natural motion.

ENTER, INTO
With the right fingertips touching the thumb, palm toward body and fingers pointing down, insert them down into the left "c" fingers, palm right, spreading the right fingers as they move through the left hand.
Hint: Something moving into another thing.

INCLUDE
Move the right downturned "5" hand to the left between the thumb and index finger of the left "c" hand, palm right, closing the right thumb to the fingertips as the hand moves.
Hint: Taking something and putting with others to include it.

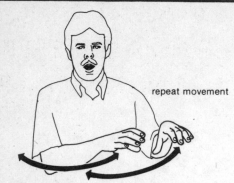

DO, ACT, ACTION
Swing both downturned "c" hands back and forth in a double motion in front of the waist.
Hint: Shows the hands actively doing something.

MEET
Bring both extended index fingers, pointing up and palms facing, toward each other until they meet in front of the chest.
Hint: Two people walking up to each other.

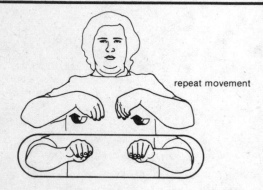

SELL
With the fingertips touching the thumbs of both hands, palms facing down, swing the fingertips up and down several times.
Hint: Taking something and holding it up for sale.

EXCUSE, FORGIVE, PARDON
Brush the fingertips of the right downturned hand across the fingertips of the left upturned hand with a repeated movement.
Hint: Brushing aside a mistake.

GUIDE, LEAD
Grab the fingertips of the left open hand, palm right, with the fingers of the right hand, palm toward body. Let the right hand pull the left hand forward.
Hint: The right hand is guiding the left hand.

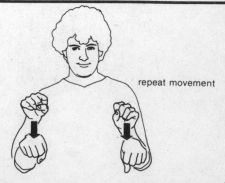

POSSIBLE
Move both "s" hands, palms facing out, downward twice with deliberate movements by bending the wrists.
Hint: The hands represent the head shaking up and down in affirmative.

twelve

BEING AND FEELING

Actions of the Mind
Feelings

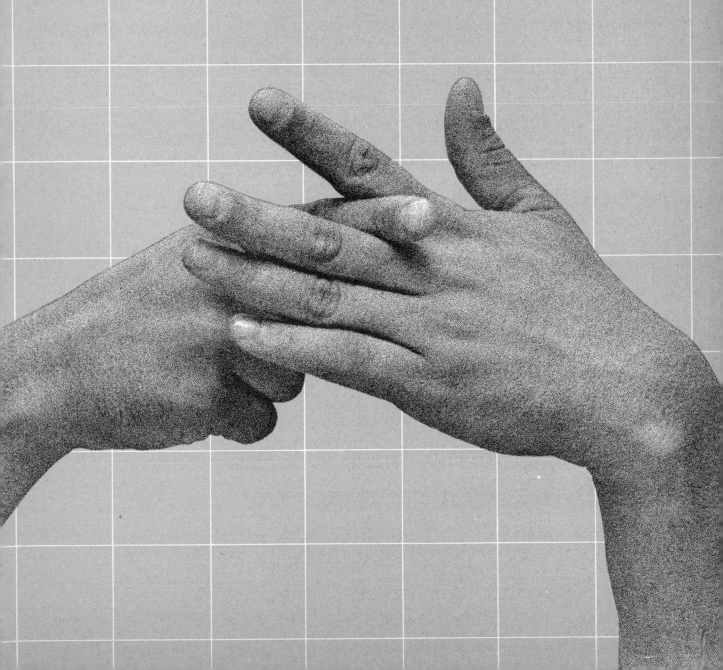

SIGNS FOR THINKING ACTIVITIES

The signs for many mental activities are formed against the forehead near the brain. Some examples of mental signs are "think," "remember," "stupid," "memory," "dream," and "forget."

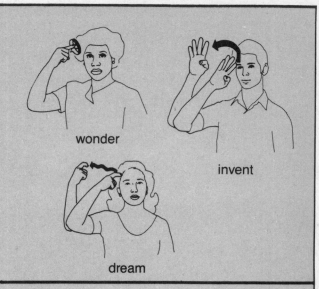

wonder

invent

dream

SIGNS FOR FEELING

A group of signs using a handshape with the middle finger of the "5" hand bent forward relate to feelings or sensitivity. Some signs in this group are "feel," "sick," "thrilled," "pity," and "depressed."

repeat movement

pity

SLANG AND SOCIALLY RESTRICTED SIGNS

A number of signs, usually formed near the nose, are considered socially restricted. Some of these signs are "don't care," "lousy," "bug," "urinate," and "boring." In a polite atmosphere, these signs would not be used. For example, the slang word for "boring" would be signed by twisting the extended index finger at the side of the nose; but in a polite conversation, the concept of "boring" would be expressed by the more delicate sign for "dry."

don't care

Actions of the Mind

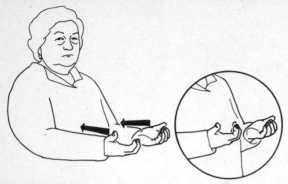

WANT, DESIRE
Draw both upturned "claw" hands toward the body at waist level.
Hint: Bringing something to yourself that you want.

WISH, DESIRE
Drag the tips of the thumb and fingers of the "c" hand down the center of chest, palm facing in.

LOVE, HUG
Cross the arms of both "a" hands at wrists, palms toward body, across the chest.
Hint: Holding something dear to oneself.

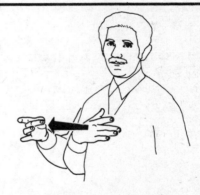

LIKE
Draw the thumb and middle finger of the open hand, palm facing body, forward from the chest, pulling the tips of the thumb and middle finger together as the hand moves.
Hint: Taking something from the heart.

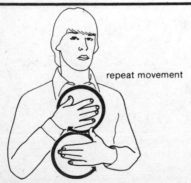

repeat movement

ENJOY, APPRECIATE
Move the palms of both open hands in a circular motion in opposite directions on the chest and stomach, right hand above left.
Hint: Rubbing the chest in pleasure.

PREFER, RATHER
Place the palm of the open hand on the chest. Draw the hand to the right and up, ending with an "a" handshape near the shoulder, palm toward body.

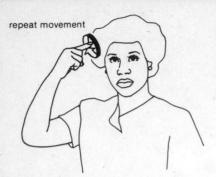

WONDER, CONSIDER
Move the extended index finger in a small circle pointing at the right temple.
Hint: Shows the brain pondering over something in a continuous action.

IMAGE, IMAGINATION
Bring the extended little finger from the right side of the forehead outward.
Hint: Taking a little thought from the head.

INVENT, CREATE
Bring the index finger of the "4" hand, palm left, upward on the forehead and then outward in an arc.

DREAM, DAYDREAM
Bring the extended index finger from the right temple outward with a wiggly motion, palm toward head.
Hint: Taking a little thought a way off.

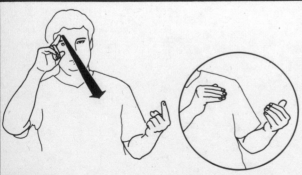

EXPECT
With the right extended index finger near the right side of the forehead and the left extended index finger forward of the left shoulder, palms facing each other, bring the right finger down toward the left, changing into bent hands facing each other near the left shoulder.

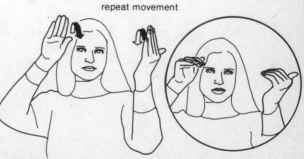

HOPE
With the right open hand near the right side of the forehead and the left open hand forward of the left side of the forehead, palms facing each other, bend the fingers down on both hands toward each other twice.
Hint: Taking a thought and looking for it in the future.

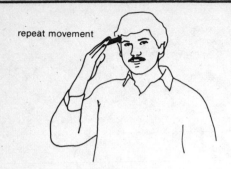

KNOW, KNOWLEDGE
Tap the fingertips of the bent hand to the temple, palm facing down.
Hint: Hand indicates that knowledge is in the brain.

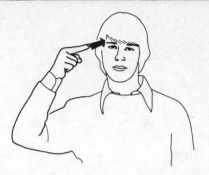

THINK, THOUGHTS
Bring the extended index finger to touch the right temple.
Hint: Pointing to where thinking takes place.

MEMORIZE, MEMORY
Touch the fingertips of the "c" hand to the forehead, palm toward face. Bring the hand forward closing the fingers into a "s" handshape.
Hint: Take information from the brain and hold on to it.

REMEMBER
Bring the thumb of the "a" right hand from the right side of the forehead down to touch the thumbnail of the left hand held at waist level, palms facing each other.
Hint: Taking something from the head and looking at it.

DECIDE, DECISION
Bring both "f" hands, palms facing each other and fingers extended forward, downward with short deliberate motions.
Hint: Take a thought from the head and set it down firmly.

BELIEVE, BELIEF
Move the extended right index finger smoothly down from the temple to clasp the left hand in front of the body.
Hint: Take a thought from the head and hold on to it.

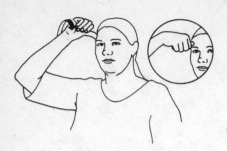

REMIND

Place the thumbtip of the "a" hand on the right side of the forehead, palm left. Twist the wrist downward, grinding the thumb into the forehead.
Hint: Embedding a thought in the mind.

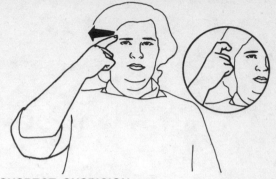

SUSPECT, SUSPICION

Move the extended index finger away from the temple, palm toward face, changing into an "x" handshape in a double movement.
Hint: Take something from the mind and question it.

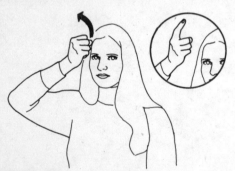

UNDERSTAND

Start with the "s" hand near the right side of the forehead, palm toward face. Flick the index finger up.
Hint: A light goes on in the head.

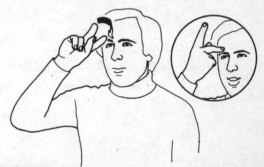

MISUNDERSTAND

Touch the index finger of the "k" hand to the center of the forehead, palm facing out. Turn the wrist and touch the middle finger to the forehead, palm facing in.
Hint: Taking something and turning it around in the head.

GUESS

Move the "c" hand from the right side of the face to the left in an arc, ending with an "s" handshape.
Hint: Grabbing at a thought.

FORGET

Bring the open hand, palm on forehead and fingers pointing left, across the forehead, closing into an "a" handshape.
Hint: Wiping a thought out of the mind.

HATE
Flick the middle finger of both open hands, palms facing each other, off the thumbs outward from the body.
Hint: Flick something away from the body.

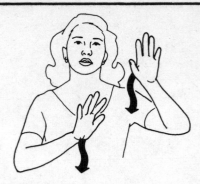

FEAR, DREAD
Start with both raised "5" hands held on left side of body, left held higher than right, palms facing outward. Move both hands downward simultaneously with wavy motions.
Hint: Hands are held up to protect body against the unknown fear.

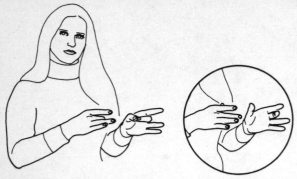

DENY
Bring the thumbs of both "a" hands from under the chin, palms facing each other, forward and outward to shoulder width with a deliberate movement.
Hint: This is "not" formed with both hands for emphasis.

IGNORE
Bring the "4" hand from the index finger touching the side of the nose, palm left, down and forward, ending with the fingers forward and the palm facing down.

AGREE
Move the thumb of the "g" right hand, palm down and index finger pointing forward, from the forehead down and forward to the left extended index finger pointing forward about chin level.

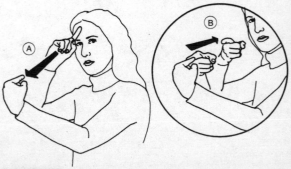

DISAGREE
With the right extended index finger near the right side of the forehead and the left extended index finger forward of the left shoulder, palms facing each other, bring the right finger down to meet the left finger, then pull the right finger back toward the right shoulder.

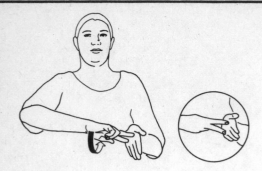

MEAN, INTEND
Point the index and middle fingers of the "p" right hand, palm the body, down into the upturned left palm. Twist the right wrist outward, touching the fingers down again, palm facing left.

SUFFER, BEAR
Twist the thumbnail of the "a" hand, palm left, on the lips, ending with the palm toward the neck.
Hint: Silently bearing a burden.

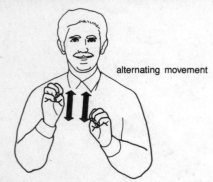

alternating movement

EVALUATE
Move both "e" hands up and down with an alternating movement in front of the chest, palms facing out.
Hint: Initialized sign showing indecision.

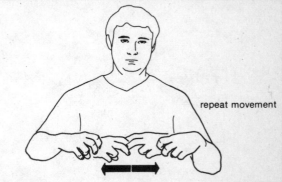

repeat movement

ANALYZE
Bring both crooked "v" hands from touching in front of the chest, palms facing down, outward toward the shoulders with a double motion.
Hint: Tearing something apart to inspect it carefully.

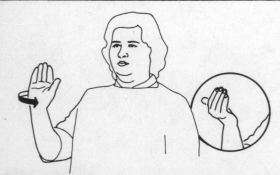

SEEM, APPEAR
Hold the cupped open hand near the right shoulder, palm facing out. Twist the hand, ending with the palm facing the shoulder.
Hint: Similar to "mirror."

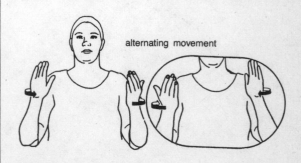

alternating movement

COMPARE
Hold both cupped open hands out from either side of the face, palms facing each other. Twist the hands forward and back with alternating movements, keeping the palms toward each other.
Hint: Taking two things and looking first at one and then the other.

DUMB
Tap the knuckles of the "a" hand against the forehead, palm toward face.
Hint: Showing a thick-headed, dumb person.

IGNORANT, STUPID
Tap the back of the "v" hand against the forehead, palm facing out.
Hint: Blocking the head from ideas.

CLEVER
Bring the bent middle finger of the "5" from the center of the forehead outward with a twist of the wrist, ending with the palm facing out.
Hint: Shows clever thoughts coming from the head.

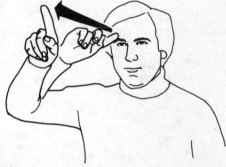

SMART
Bring the extended index finger, palm left, straight forward from the middle of the forehead.
Hint: Shows smart thoughts coming out of the brain.

repeat movement

WISE
Shake the "x" index finger, pointing downward and palm left, up and down in front of the forehead.
Hint: Shows very deep thinking.

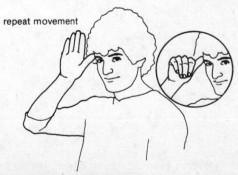

repeat movement

STUBBORN, OBSTINATE
With the thumb of the open hand held at the right temple, palm forward, bend the fingers forward and back twice.
Hint: The sign is made like "donkey," indicating "stubborn like a mule."

Feelings

DISCOURAGED, DISAPPOINTED
Touch the center of the chest with both bent middle fingers of the "5" hands, palms toward body and fingers pointing toward each other. Drag fingers down toward waist.
Hint: Feelings that are pulling the mood down.

DEPRESSED
Drag the thumbs of both "5" hands, palms toward body and fingers pointing down, from the upper chest down toward the waist.
Hint: Feelings that are suppressed and down.

SAD, SORROWFUL, SORROW
Bring both loose "5" hands downward from the sides of the face, palms facing the body.
Hint: Hands show the downturned expression.

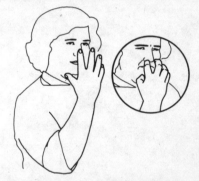

CROSS, GROUCHY, ANGRY, MAD
With the palm of the loose "5" hand in front of the face, bend the fingers down into a "claw" hand.
Hint: Shows bringing the facial features into an angry shape.

ANGER
Bring both "claw" hands, knuckles pointed toward each other and palm toward body, upward from near each other at the waist, out toward the shoulders.
Hint: Shows angry feelings rising up in the body.

repeat movement

BOILING MAD, BURNING MAD
Wiggle the right "5" fingers, pointing up, in a circular movement under the downturned left hand.
Hint: Deep penetrating feelings smoldering in the body.

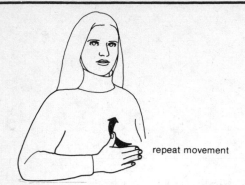

HAPPY, GLAD, JOY
Bring the flat palm, fingers pointing left, upward and outward on the chest.
Hint: The upward movement shows an "up" mood.

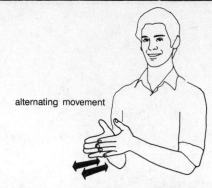

ENTHUSIASTIC, EAGER, ANXIOUS
Rub the open palms together with the fingers pointing forward.
Hint: A natural gesture of rubbing the hands together in enthusiasm.

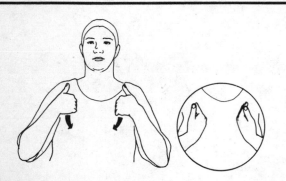

TIRED
With the fingertips of both bent hands on the chest, allow the hands to drop down and rest the little finger side of the hands against the chest.
Hint: The energy seems to drop.

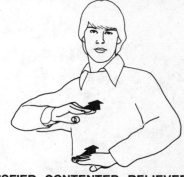

SATISFIED, CONTENTED, RELIEVED
Hold the right downturned "b" hand, fingers pointing left, above the left downturned "b" hand, fingers pointing right, a few inches in front of the chest with the elbows pointing out. Move both hands simultaneously against the chest.
Hint: Shows that you are full or satisfied after eating.

FINE
Bring the "5" hand, palm left, forward with a flick of the wrist from the middle of the chest.
Hint: Similar to "fancy," indicating the old-time fancy ruffles on a shirt.

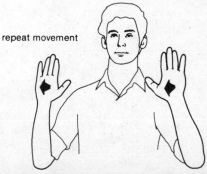

TERRIFIC, WONDERFUL, GREAT, FANTASTIC
Pat the air repeatedly with both "5" hands, palms forward near the shoulders.
Hint: A natural gesture for exclaiming delight.

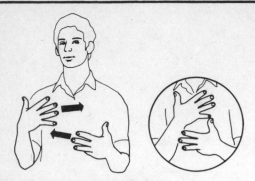

AFRAID, SCARED, FRIGHTENED
With the right "5" hand near the shoulder and the left "5" hand near the armpit, palms facing chest and fingers pointing toward each other, move both hands toward the center of the chest with a deliberate motion.
Hint: Protecting the body against the unknown.

COMFORTABLE, COMFORT, SOOTHE
Bring the palm of the downturned curved right hand down over the fingers of the downturned curved left hand. Repeat with the left over the right.
Hint: Stroking the hands in a smooth comforting manner.

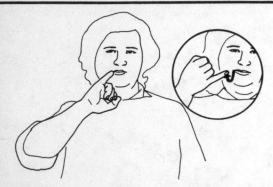

JEALOUS
Make a small "j" at the right corner of the mouth with the extended little finger, starting with the palm facing out and twisting the wrist to face the palm inward.
Hint: Initialized sign.

SELFISH
With the "3" hands apart in front of the waist, palms down, draw the hands toward the body, crooking the fingers and thumbs.
Hint: Keeping something for oneself.

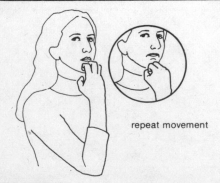

repeat movement

STINGY, MISERLY
Bring the fingers of the "claw" hand, palm toward body, downward from the chin changing into an "s" hand at the neck.

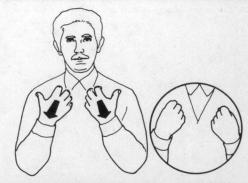

COURAGEOUS, BRAVE, WELL, HEALTHY
Bring the fingers of both loose "claw" hands from in front of the shoulders, palms toward body, outward, changing into "s" hands a few inches from the chest.
Hint: Taking strength from the body.

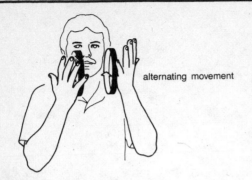

EMBARRASSED

Bring both "5" hands, palms toward face, in circular alternating movements upward in front of the face.
Hint: Shows the blush rising in the face.

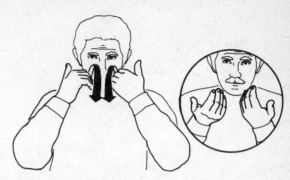

ASHAMED, SHAME

Place the back of the fingers of both curved hands on the cheeks, palms down and fingers pointing back. Twist the hands forward, ending with them cupped upward in front of the chin.
Hint: Shows the blush rising in the face.

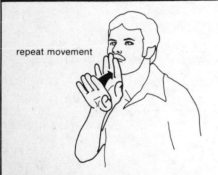

FRUSTRATED

Bring the back of the open hand, palm facing out, back to in front of the mouth.
Hint: Coming up to an obstacle.

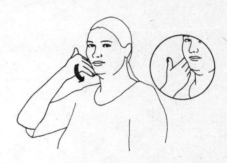

SHY

Place the back of the fingers of the curved hand on the cheek, palm down and fingers pointing back. Twist the hand forward, ending with it cupped upward in front of the chin.
Hint: A blush rising in the cheeks.

HUMBLE, MEEK

Move the extended index finger, palm left, down from the lips, changing into a "b" and moving under the downturned left hand in an arc.
Hint: Placing yourself beneath others.

FEEL, FEELING, SENSATION

Bring the bent middle finger of the "5" hand, palm toward body and fingers pointing left, upward in the center of the chest.
Hint: Bringing feelings out of the heart.

DISAPPOINTED, MISS
Touch the extended index finger to the chin, palm toward body.

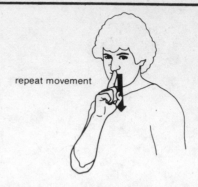

repeat movement

LONELY, LONESOME
Move the extended index finger, palm left, from in front of the lips downward in a slow, smooth motion.
Hint: A combination of the handshape for the sign "alone" signed like "patience."

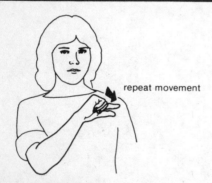

repeat movement

GUILT, GUILTY, CONSCIENCE
Tap the index finger side of the "g" hand on the upper left chest several times.
Hint: Initialized sign over the heart.

PATIENT, PATIENCE, ENDURE
Bring the thumbnail of the "a" hand, palm left, down from the lips to the chin.
Hint: Silently enduring a burden.

DOUBT, DISBELIEF
Move both "s" hands, palms down, in front of the chest in alternating up and down movements.
Hint: The alternating movement indicates indecision.

PROUD, PRIDE
Drag the thumbtip of the "a" hand up the center of the chest, thumb pointing down and palm facing out.
Hint: Feelings rising from within.

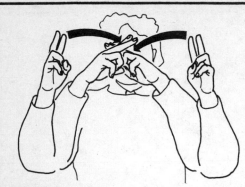

CARELESS
Wave both "v" hands, palms facing, from the sides of the head, about shoulder width, toward each other in front of the face in an arc a couple of times.
Hint: Hands are waved carelessly in front of the face.

LOUSY
Start with the thumb of the "3" hand on the nose, palm left. Throw the hand forward and down in an arc.

repeat movement

LAZY
Tap the palm side of the "l" hand, thumb pointing up, on the heart a couple of times.
Hint: Initialized sign.

repeat movement

SORRY, APOLOGIZE
Rub the "a" hand, palm facing in, over the heart in a circular motion repeatedly.
Hint: Beating the heart in sorrow.

SURPRISED, SURPRISE
Flick the index fingers of both "s" hands upward near the eyes on the sides of the face, palm facing each other.
Hint: The eyes opening wide in surprise.

SHOCKED, DUMBFOUNDED
Move the right extended finger from pointing at the right temple, palm forward, downward, ending with both curved hands moving a short distance downward in front of lower chest, palms down.
Hint: Taking a thought and dropping it in shock.

HUNGRY, STARVED

Bring the fingertips and thumb of the "c" hand, palm toward chest and knuckles pointing left, downward from near the throat to the chest.
Hint: Shows an empty passage to the stomach.

THIRSTY

Scratch the throat with the extended index fingertip, palm toward body.
Hint: Shows a dry throat.

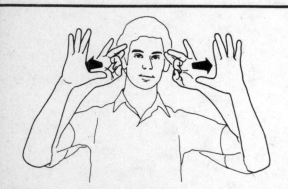

TERRIBLE, HORRIBLE, AWFUL

Flick the bent middle fingers of both "5" hands off the thumbs near either temple, palms forward.
Hint: Flicking something terrible away from the mind.

repeat movement

CRAZY

Draw a large circle in the air at the side of the head with the extended index finger, palm facing down.
Hint: Natural gesture for showing that someone's brains are all mixed up.

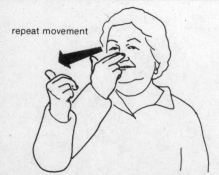

repeat movement

FUNNY

Bring the extended index and middle fingers, palm toward face, down the nose and outward, dropping the fingers toward palm as it moves. Repeat twice.
Hint: The nose twitches when something is funny.

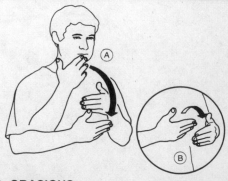

KIND, GRACIOUS

Move the right open hand from the lips, palm facing the body, down and outward over the left open hand, palm facing chest and the fingers of both hands pointing toward each other in opposite directions.
Hint: "Good" plus a modification of "comfortable."

thirteen

RELIGION AND COMMUNICATION

Religion
Abstract Concepts
Communication

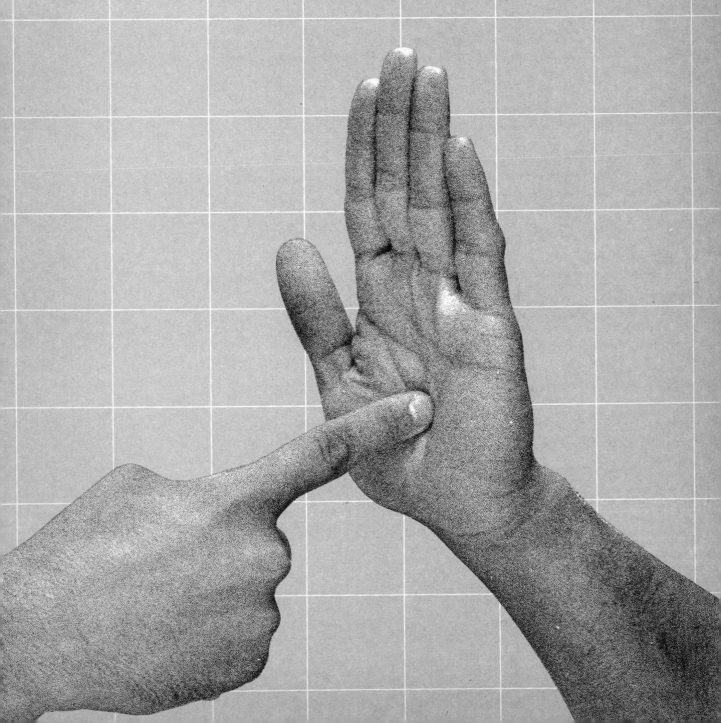

EMPHASIS

Emphasis can be added to any word in a signed sentence in one of four ways. One way is to add the sign for "true" or "really" before the sign. The sign which might best be translated as "whew" or "wow" can be added after the sign that is to be emphasized. A third way is to execute the sign itself in an emphatic way. Or, fourth, you can fingerspell the word to add emphasis.

heroic + whew = very heroic

SIGNS SHOWING JUDGMENT

A group of signs which are two-handed and use an alternating movement indicate indecisiveness. Some of the signs in this group are "maybe," "judge," "which," and "doubt."

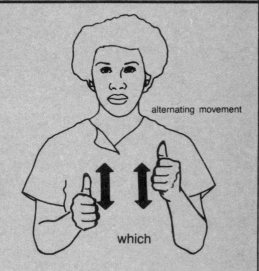

alternating movement

which

RELIGIOUS SIGNS

Many religious signs are governed by the specific beliefs of the religion they describe. In other words, the same English word may be signed in different ways depending on which religion is being discussed. A Protestant "Bible" is a compound of "Jesus" plus "book," whereas a Jewish "Bible" is signed as the compound "God" plus "book." The sign for "baptism" depends on whether the religion requires immersion or not.

God + book = Bible

Jesus + book = Bible

Religion

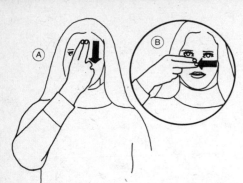

CATHOLIC
Draw the "u" hand downward from the forehead to in front of the nose, palm toward face and fingers pointing up. Then bring the "u" hand, fingers pointing left, from left to right in front of nose.
Hint: Crossing oneself.

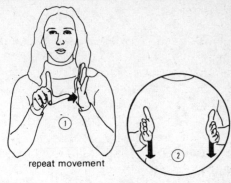

repeat movement

LUTHERAN
Tap the thumbtip of the right "l" hand, palm facing out, against the palm of the open left hand, palm facing right.
Hint: Initialized sign in the position for "Jesus."

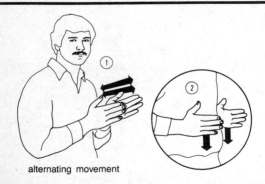

alternating movement

METHODIST
Rub the palms of both hands together with alternating back and forth movements, fingers pointing forward.
Hint: Shows the enthusiasm of the early Methodists.

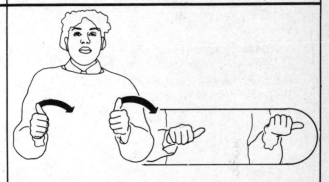

BAPTIST, BAPTIZE
Starting with both "a" hands, palms facing, several inches apart in front of chest, dip wrists to the right twice.
Hint: Dipping the head under water for baptism.

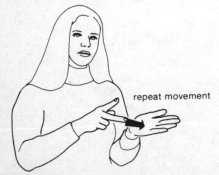

repeat movement

PRESBYTERIAN
Tap the middle finger of the right "p" hand into the center of the upturned left palm.
Hint: Initialized sign.

EPISCOPAL
With the extended right index finger, palm toward body, touch wrist and then the elbow of the bottom of the left arm extended across chest.
Hint: Follows the sleeve shape of the minister's robe.

RELIGION, RELIGIOUS
Touch the fingertips of the "r" hand to the right chest, palm facing body. Then move the "r" smoothly down and outward, ending with the palm facing left and the finger pointing outward.
Hint: Initialized sign taking religious feelings from the heart.

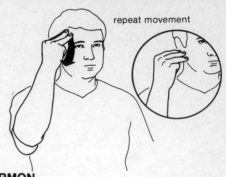

repeat movement

MORMON
Brush the fingertips of the "m" hand from right temple downward and slightly outward near the right cheek.
Hint: Initialized sign.

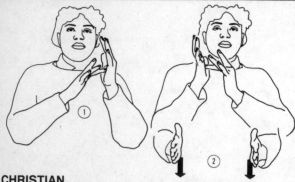

CHRISTIAN
Touch the bent middle finger of the right "5" hand into the center of the left palm, palms facing each other. Reverse the action using the left hand. Follow by moving both open hands with a parallel movement down the sides of the body, palms facing each other.
Hint: "Jesus" plus "person marker."

repeat movement

JEW, JEWISH
With the "5" hand, palm toward neck, draw the fingertips from chin downward, gathering the fingertips to the thumb as the hand moves. Repeat.
Hint: Hand follows the shape of the traditional Jewish beard.

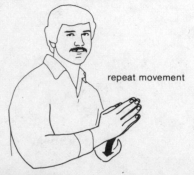

repeat movement

PRAY, PRAYER, AMEN
With both open hands, palms against each other and fingers angled up and forward, move hands inward and downward slightly.
Hint: Mime folding hands in prayer.

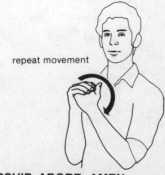

repeat movement

WORSHIP, ADORE, AMEN
Cup the fingers of the right hand over the left "a" hand, palms downward. Move hands upward in an arc toward the body.
Hint: Mime a worshipful pose.

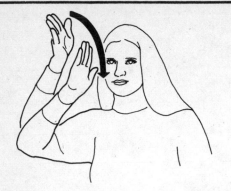

GOD
Move the open hand, palm left, from above the head downward in an arc toward the face.
Hint: The hand comes down from heaven.

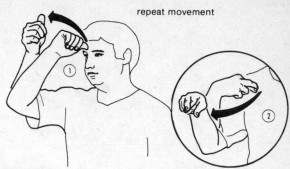

BUDDHA
Drag the thumbtip of the "a" hand, palm left, upward and outward off the center of the forehead. Then move the "r" fingertips from touching the right shoulder, palm facing down, outward in an arc, ending with the "r" fingers pointing outward.
Hint: "India" plus "religion."

CHRIST
Touch the index finger side of the "c" hand, palm left, first to the left shoulder and then to the right hip.
Hint: Initialized sign following the sash worn by royalty.

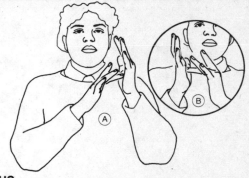

JESUS
Touch the bent middle finger of the right "5" hand into the center of the left palm, palms facing each other. Reverse the action by touching the bent middle finger of the left "5" hand into the right palm.
Hint: Fingers touch the location of the nail holes in Jesus' hands.

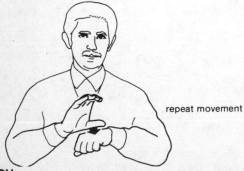

CHURCH
Tap the thumb side of the right "c" hand on the back of the left "s" hand, palm facing down.
Hint: Initialized sign indicating that the church is built on a rock.

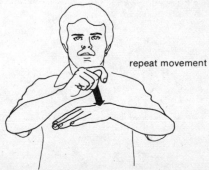

TEMPLE
Tap the heel of the right "t" hand, palm down, on the back of the left "s" hand, palm down.
Hint: Initialized sign formed like "church."

ANGEL
Touch the fingertips of both bent hands to the shoulders, palms facing down and elbows close at the sides. Turn the wrists outward and bend the hands up and down.
Hint: Represents the moving of angels' wings.

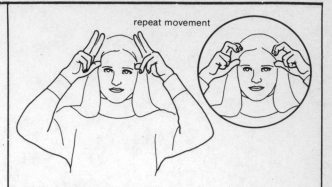

DEVIL, MISCHIEVOUS
With the thumbs of both "3" hands touching temples, palms facing each other, crook the extended index and middle fingers twice. Note: May be produced with one hand.
Hint: Fingers represent the devil's horns.

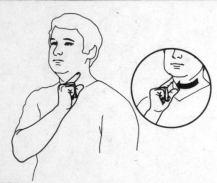

PRIEST
Drag the fingertips of the "g" hand from the left side of the neck, palm facing body, around the neck to the right.
Hint: Fingers follow the shape of a priest's collar.

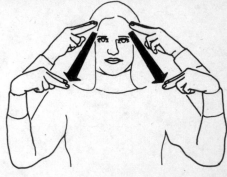

NUN
Move both "n" hands, palms facing each other, from touching the temples down to touching the shoulders.
Hint: Initialized sign following the outline of a nun's headwear.

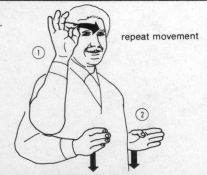

PREACHER, MINISTER, PASTOR
Move the "f" hand, palm forward, at the side of the face, forward with several small jerky motions. Follow with both open hands moving with a parallel movement down the sides of the body, palms facing each other.
Hint: "Preach" plus "person marker."

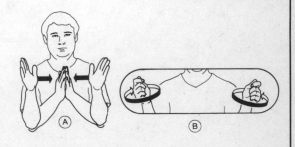

HALLELUJAH
Clap the palms of the open hands together in front of chest. Then make a small circle with both "a" hands near the shoulders, palms facing each other.
Hint: "Praise" plus "celebration."

COMMANDMENTS

Move the index finger side of the right "c" hand, palm facing outward, down across the left open palm, facing right with fingers pointing up, touching first the left fingertips and then the heel.
Hint: Initialized sign formed like "law."

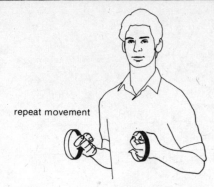

repeat movement

SIN, EVIL

With both "x" hands, palms facing each other, make simultaneous circles by moving the hands upward and outward.

HEAVEN

Starting with both open hands, palms up, on either side of the head, move them toward each other in a waving movement, ending with the arms crossed at the wrists in front of forehead.
Hint: Indicates the spaciousness of the sky.

HELL

Thrust the "h" hand, palm facing body, from the center of the chest downward and outward to the side of the waist.
Hint: Initialized sign.

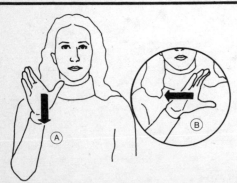

CROSS

Bring the "c" hand, palm forward and fingers toward the right, from chin level to upper chest. Then move the hand in front of chest from left to right, palm forward and fingers up.
Hint: Initialized sign following the shape of a cross.

SPIRIT, HOLY GHOST

Touch the thumbs and index fingers of both "f" hands to each other, right hand over left, palms facing. Draw hands apart.

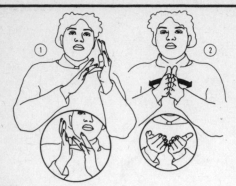

BIBLE
Touch the bent middle finger of the right "5" hand into the center of the left palm. Reverse the action using the left hand. Then with the palms of both hands together, fingers pointing forward, bring the palms apart, keeping the little fingers together.
Hint: "Jesus" plus "book."

HOLY
Move the right "h" hand, palm facing body, from over the heel of the upturned left hand forward, changing into an open hand as it brushes down over the left fingertips.
Hint: Initialized sign formed like "clean."

repeat movement

PREACH
Move the "f" hand, palm forward, at the side of the face forward with several small jerky motions.
Hint: Giving out of information.

BLESS, BLESSING
Place the thumbnails of both "a" hands from near the mouth, palms facing each other. Move hands forward and outward, opening into downturned "5" hands.
Hint: Taking a blessing from the mouth and speading it outward.

ALTAR
Bring both "a" hands from touching in front of chest, palms facing down, sideways to shoulder width and then straight downward.
Hint: Initialized sign formed like "table."

FAST
Move the fingertips of the "f" hand, palm toward face, from left to right across the lips.
Hint: Initialized sign pointing to the closed lips preventing eating.

Abstract Concepts

HABIT, CUSTOM
With the "a" right hand on the back of the "a" left hand, both palms facing down, move both hands downward.
Hint: The downward movement indicates a continued action.

INFLUENCE, COUNSEL, ADVISE
Move the right flattened "o" hand forward across the back of the left flat hand, fingers pointing right, spreading the fingers into a "5" hand, palm down, as the right hand moves forward.
Hint: The distribution of advice.

HONOR
Move the "h" hand, palm left and fingers pointing up, in a slight arc toward the forehead and down to the chest.
Hint: Initialized sign.

RESPECT
Move the "r" hand, palm left and fingers pointing up, in a slight arc toward the forehead and down to the chest.
Hint: Initialized sign.

repeat movement

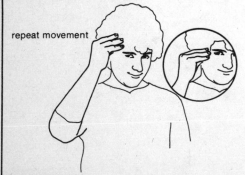

EXPERIENCE
Brush the fingertips of the "c" hand, palm facing right cheek, downward with a double motion from right temple to touching the thumb.
Hint: Feeling the greying at the temples from experience.

RESPONSIBILITY, BURDEN
With the fingertips of both bent hands on the right shoulder, palms down, roll hands forward slightly on fingertips.
Hint: Having a heavy burden on your shoulders.

GOAL, OBJECTIVE
Touch the extended right index finger to the right forehead, palm left, and then move it outward toward the extended left index finger held forward of the left forehead.
Hint: Directing your mind to a specific point or goal.

CONCEPT
Move the "c" hand from the right side of the forehead forward in two small arcs, palm left.
Hint: Initialized sign showing concepts coming out of the head.

IDEA
Move the "i" fingertip from the right side of forehead, palm toward face, upward and outward with a deliberate movement.
Hint: Initialized sign showing an idea coming out of the head.

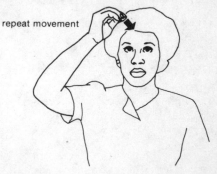

OPINION
Bounce the "o" hand up and down near the center of the forehead, palm left, by bending the wrist.
Hint: Initialized sign in the "thinking" position.

PHILOSOPHY
Bounce the "p" hand up and down near the center of the forehead, palm left, by bending the wrist.
Hint: Initialized sign in the "thinking" position.

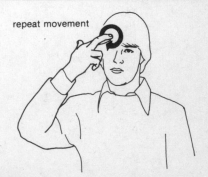

REASON
Move the "r" hand in a small circle at the right side of the forehead, palm toward the face.
Hint: Initialized sign in the "thinking" position.

TROUBLE, WORRY, CARE
With an alternating movement, bring both "b" hands, palms facing down, from the forehead level downward across the face several times.
Hint: Things are coming at you from all sides causing worry.

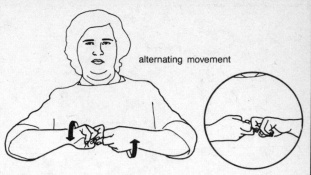

PROBLEM
Rub the knuckles of the curled index and middle fingers of both hands against each other, palms toward body, by twisting the wrists back and forth in opposite directions.
Hint: Handshape is typical of signs indicating "difficulty."

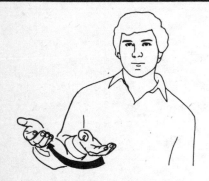

THING
Move the upturned curved hand in two arcs from the center lower chest outward to the right.

FAULT, BLAME
Thrust the right "a" hand, palm left and thumb extended up, down, striking the back of the downturned left "a" hand.
Hint: The thumb is directing the blame toward the other person.

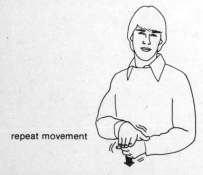

PRESSURE
With the palm of the open right hand, push downward on the top of the left "s" hand, palm right, with two deliberate movements.
Hint: Demonstrates putting pressure on someone.

LIE
Push the right extended index finger, palm facing down, across the chin from right to left.
Hint: Speaking out of the side of the mouth.

MERCY, PITY, SYMPATHY
With the bent middle finger of the right "5" hand, palm facing body, stroke upward on the middle of the chest. Then with both bent middle fingers of "5" hands, stroke outward with a double motion.
Hint: Using the "feeling" fingers, taking feeling from your own heart to another's.

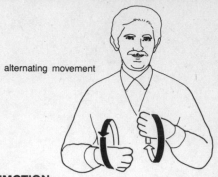

alternating movement

EMOTION
Move both "e" hands, palms facing body, in alternating circular motions upward on the chest.
Hint: Initialized sign showing feelings coming from the heart.

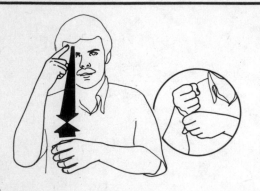

repeat movement

FAITH
Move the extended right index finger from the forehead smoothly down, changing into an "s" hand, meeting the left "s" hand in front of chest, both palms facing body.
Hint: Taking information from the brain plus "faith."

PEACE
Bring both open hands, palms facing angled outward, in a smooth movement from in front of the mouth downward and outward to about shoulder width at lower chest level.
Hint: Shows a quieting effect over everything.

TRUTH, HONESTY, HONEST
Move the right "h" hand, palm left and fingers pointing forward, across the upturned left palm, fingers pointing forward, from the heel outward toward the fingertips.
Hint: Initialized sign showing splitting the left palm in equal parts.

TRUST, CONFIDENCE
Hold the right "c" hand a few inches above the left "c" hand, palms facing each other, slightly away from the body. Bring the hands together and toward the body, changing them into "s" hands as they move.
Hint: Holding on to something with trust.

LAW
Move the right "l" hand across the left open palm, touching first at the fingers and then at the heel, palms facing each other.
Hint: Recording a law on the books.

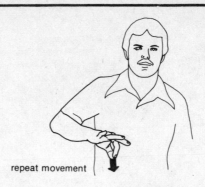

repeat movement

BENEFIT, PROFIT, ADVANTAGE
Bounce the fingertips of the "9" hand, palm facing down, at the right lower chest several times.
Hint: Putting money in an imaginary pocket.

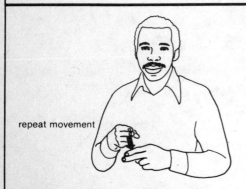

repeat movement

NAME, TITLE
Tap the right "h" fingers across the left "h" fingers, palms facing each other.

PROMISE, VOW
Bring the open right hand from the mouth, palm facing body, down to land palm down on top of the left "s" hand, palm right.
Hint: Bringing your words down to seal them in a contract.

ATTENTION, PAY ATTENTION, CONCENTRATE
Move both open hands from the sides of the face, palms facing outward, keeping the fingers pointing upward.
Hint: Wearing blinders to keep the eyes directed to the task at hand.

VANITY, VAIN
Move the fingers of both "v" hands, palms toward body, up and down above the shoulders simultaneously in a double movement.
Hint: Initialized sign indicating that everyone is looking at you.

Communication

SPEAK, TALK
Tap the index finger of the "4" hand at the mouth, palm facing left and the fingers pointing up, several times.
Hint: Shows a lot of words coming out of the mouth.

SAY
Move the extended index finger, palm facing chin and finger pointing left, upward and outward in a small arc from the mouth.
Hint: Shows words coming out of the mouth.

TELL
Bring the extended index finger, palm facing neck, forward in an arc from under the chin.
Hint: Directing words from out of the mouth.

COMMAND, ORDER
Bring the extended index finger, palm left, forward and downward from the chin in a deliberate movement.
Hint: Direct the words from the mouth.

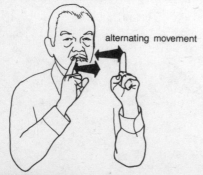

TALK, CONVERSATION
Move the extended index fingers, palms facing each other and fingers pointing up, straight forward and back from either corner of the mouth with an alternating movement the entire forearm.
Hint: The exchange of conversation to and from the mouth.

COMMUNICATE, COMMUNICATION
Move both "c" hands, palms facing each other, forward and back from either corner of the mouth with an alternating movement by moving the entire forearm.
Hint: Initialized sign showing the exchange of conversation to and from the mouth.

BAWL OUT
Place the wrist of the right "s" hand on the wrist of the left "s" hand, right palm facing left and left palm facing right. Repeatedly open the fingers into "5" hands.
Hint: Shows a lot of words coming at a person from all sides.

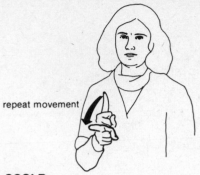

SCOLD
Shake the index finger up and down repeatedly, palm left.
Hint: Mime scolding someone.

DISCUSS
Repeatedly tap the inside of the extended right index finger, palm left and finger pointing forward, across the upturned left palm.
Hint: Presenting your point.

QUARREL, ARGUE
With both extended index fingers pointing in opposite directions toward each other, move them up and down with alternating movements past each other, palms facing body.
Hint: Two people giving opposing views.

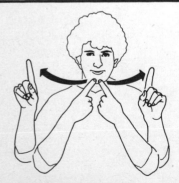

ANNOUNCE, PROCLAIM
Start with both extended index fingers side by side on chin, palms facing in. Twist the wrists to bring the fingers outward to shoulder width, palms facing out.
Hint: Take words and tell them broadly.

LECTURE, PRESENT
Shake the open hand at shoulder level, palm left, forward and back repeatedly by twisting the wrist.
Hint: Gesturing from a lectern.

VOICE, VOCAL

Bring the "v" fingers, palm facing neck, forward in an arc from under the chin.
Hint: Initialized sign showing where the voice comes through the throat.

SPEECHREADING, LIPREADING, ORAL

Make a small counterclockwise circle around the mouth with the fingertips of the crooked "v" hand, palm in.
Hint: Fingers encircle the lips used for speechreading.

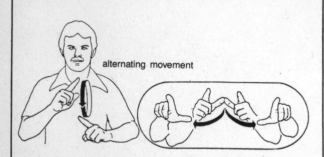

alternating movement

SIGN LANGUAGE

Move both extended index fingers pointing upward, palms facing each other, in alternating circles outward around each other once changing into "l" handshapes. Bring the "l" hands, palms facing down, from together in front of chest outward in an arc to shoulder width.

alternating movement

SIGN

Move both extended index fingers pointing upward, palms facing each other, in alternating circles outward around each other in front of the chest while moving the entire forearms.

FINGERSPELLING, SPELL, ALPHABET

Wiggle the fingers of the "5" hand, palm down and fingers pointing forward, as the hand moves from the middle of the chest outward to the right.
Hint: Mime fingerspelling very quickly.

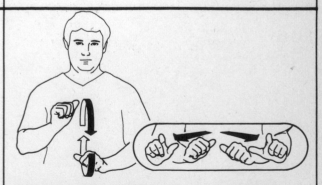

AMESLAN, ASL, AMERICAN SIGN LANGUAGE

Move both "a" hands, palms facing each other and thumbs pointing up, in alternating circles outward around each other changing into "l" handshapes. Bring the "l" hands, palms facing down, from together in front of chest outward to shoulder width.
Hint: Initialized sign formed like "sign language."

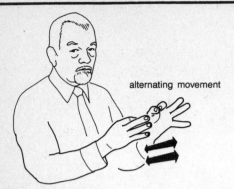

alternating movement

EXPLAIN, DESCRIBE
Move the "f" hands with an alternating movement forward and back, palms facing each other.
Hint: Similar to "decide" only moving the thought forward in explanation to the other person.

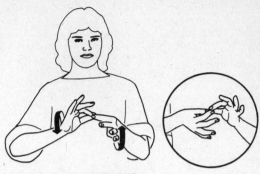

INTERPRET, TRANSLATE
Touch the thumbs and fingers of both "f" hands, palms facing each other. Twist the wrists in opposite directions with alternating movements toward and away from the body.
Hint: Turning one language into another.

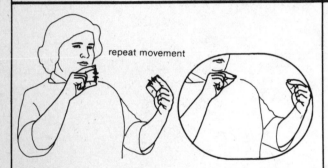

repeat movement

GOSSIP
With both "g" hands facing each other, open and close the thumb and index fingertips repeatedly.
Hint: The hands represent the lips of two people talking back and forth to each other.

repeat movement

WHISPER
Place the thumb side of the right "c" hand at the right side of the mouth. Wiggle the fingers of the curved left hand near the right palm, palms facing each other.
Hint: The sign seems to hide the sign "fingerspelling" to show secrecy.

SCREAM, YELL, CALL
Move both "claw" hands, palms toward face, from near the chin upward and outward.
Hint: Voice coming from the mouth loudly.

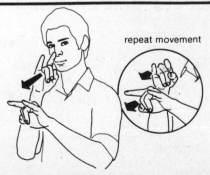

repeat movement

MOCK, SCORN, RIDICULE
With the index and little fingers of both hands extended, place the right index fingertip against the side of the nose, palm left, and the left hand lower and forward, palm down. Move both hands forward with two deliberate movements.
Hint: This is the handshape often used for "ridicule."

COMPLAIN
Tap the fingertips of the "claw" hand against the chest a couple of times, palm facing in.

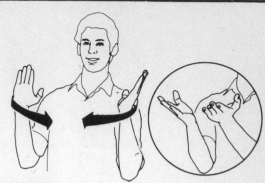

CONVINCE
Move both open hands, palms facing and angled upward, from near the shoulders downward toward each other in a deliberate movement.
Hint: Shoving your opinions forcibly on another person from all sides.

CONFESS, ADMIT
Move both open hands from touching the chest, palms facing inward and fingers pointing toward each other, outward by twisting the wrists, ending with both palms facing up.
Hint: Taking thoughts from the heart.

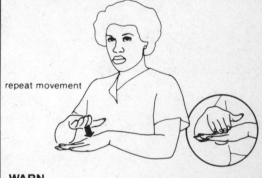

WARN
Slap the back of the downturned open left hand with the fingers of the downturned right hand, with a double movement.
Hint: Tapping the hand to get one's attention.

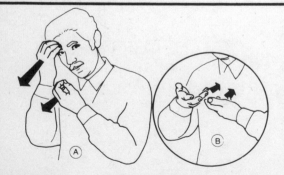

INFORM ME
Begin with the right fingertips of the flat "o" hand touching the forehead and the left flat "o" hand held lower and forward. Move both hands down and toward the chest, ending with both palms up against chest.
Hint: Taking information from the head and giving it to yourself.

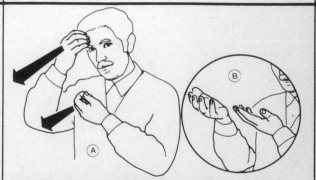

INFORM YOU, INFORMATION, INFORM THEM
Begin with the right fingertips of the flat "o" hand touching the forehead and the left flat "o" hand held lower and forward. Move both hands forward simultaneously, ending with both palms up.
Hint: Taking information from the head and sharing it with others.

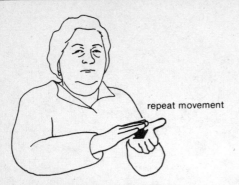

PRAISE, APPLAUD, CLAP, COMMEND
Pat the palm of the downturned right open hand on the palm of the upturned left open hand, twice.
Hint: Mime applauding.

CALL, SUMMON
Slap the back of the downturned open left hand with the fingers of the downturned right hand. Bring the right hand back toward the right shoulder, bringing the fingers up into the palm.
Hint: Tapping the hand to get one's attention.

LISTEN, HEAR
Place the "c" hand, palm forward, with the thumb near the right ear.
Hint: Hand cups the ear so you can hear better.

LETTER
Bring the thumb of the "a" right hand, palm facing left, from the lips downward to the thumbnail of the left "a" hand, held in front of the chest, palm facing right.
Hint: Mime sticking a stamp on a letter.

INSULT
Starting with the extended index finger pointing forward, jab it forward and out by thrusting the wrist forward and down.

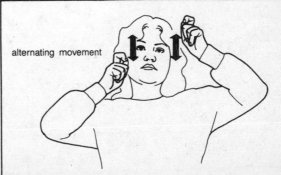

EXPRESSION
With an alternating movement, move both "x" hands up and down at the sides of the face, palms facing each other.
Hint: Showing how the face moves with expression.

selected readings

Baker, C., and Battison, R. (Eds.) *Sign Language and the Deaf Community: Essays in Honor of William C. Stokoe.* Silver Spring, Md.: National Association of the Deaf, 1980.

Baker, C., and Cokely, D. *American Sign Language: A Teacher's Resource Text on Grammar and Culture.* Silver Spring, Md.: T.J. Publishing Co., 1980.

Bender, R. *The Conquest of Deafness.* Cleveland: Case Western Reserve University, 1970.

Benderly, B. *Dancing Without Music.* New York: Doubleday, 1980.

Furth, H. *Deafness and Learning: A Psychosocial Approach.* Belmont, Calif.: Wadsworth Publishing Co., 1973.

Gannon, J. *Deaf Heritage: A Narrative History of Deaf America.* Silver Spring, Md.: National Association of the Deaf, 1981.

Greenberg. J. *In This Sign.* New York: Holt, Rinehart, and Winston, 1970.

Hoemann, H. *Communicating with Deaf People: A Resource Manual for Teachers and Students of American Sign Language.* Baltimore: University Park Press, 1978.

Jacobs, L. *A Deaf Adult Speaks Out* (Rev. ed.). Washington, D.C.: Gallaudet College Press, 1980.

Klima, E., and Bellugi, U. *The Signs of Language.* Cambridge, Mass.: Harvard University Press, 1979.

Mindel, E., and Vernon, M. *They Grow in Silence.* Silver Spring, Md.: National Association of the Deaf, 1971.

Moores, D. *Educating the Deaf: Psychology, Principles, and Practices* (Rev. ed.). Boston: Houghton Mifflin Co., 1982.

O'Rourke, T. (Ed.) *Psycholinguistics and Total Communication: The State of the Art.* Silver Spring, Md.: The American Annals of the Deaf, 1972.

Schlesinger, H., and Meadow, K. *Sound and Sign: Childhood Deafness and Mental Health.* Berkeley, Calif.: University of California Press, 1972.

Spradley, T., and Spradley, J. *Deaf Like Me.* New York: Random House, 1978.

index

about the author   about the artist

Dr. Elaine Costello has been an educator and author associated with the field of deafness for more than twenty years. For ten years a classroom teacher and supervisor in schools for the deaf in Texas and Michigan, she is now the director of the Gallaudet College Press in Washington, D.C.

Although she is a native of Oklahoma, Elaine Costello spent most of her life in Texas. After graduating from Concordia College in Austin, Texas, she received a Bachelor of Science degree from Washington University in St. Louis, and a Master of Science degree from the University of Kansas, both with a major in deaf education. Her doctorate was earned in 1973 from Syracuse University in the area of instructional technology after demonstrating research skills relating to the linguistic structures in sign language most readily understood by young deaf children.

In addition to numerous articles, pamphlets, and booklets, Dr. Costello has authored three successful series of English workbooks, *Structured Tasks for English Practice,* the *Action English Series,* and *Growth in Grammar Series,* a total of sixteen workbooks. In her role as director and editor-in-chief of the Gallaudet College Press, she oversees the acquisition and preparation of manuscripts related to deafness throughout the publication process including all aspects of marketing and sales.

Lois A. Lehman, who has been deaf since birth, is a native of Buffalo Center, Iowa. She is a graduate of the Iowa School for the Deaf in Council Bluffs. She received her Bachelor of Arts degree from Gallaudet College in 1976, where she majored in studio art. Lois has designed and illustrated numerous books and materials and is best known for her skill in drawing the human hand. She was the illustrator for *Intermediate Conversational Sign Language* by Will Madsen which included more than 2,500 sign language illustrations. Presently, Lois Lehman is employed as an illustrator at the Navy Yard in Washington, D.C.